"An enjoyable read, which brough[ ] iting all these sites back in the mid [ ] PAUL FRODSHAM, archaeologist and author of *From Stonehenge to Santa Claus: The Evolution of Christmas*

"An intriguing and often amusing journey through what little we know – and the great deal that we don't – about our Neolithic and Bronze Age ancestry." STEVE ANGLESEY, Editor, *The New European*

"An energetic and informed historical adventure shining a light on Neolithic Cumbria." EMILY ATHERTON, Editor, *Cumberland & Westmorland Herald.*

Praise for *Walking the Line*:
"An endearing love-letter to the Settle to Carlisle Railway. It is an enticing mix of reminiscence, history, characters and practical information that lift it far above the level of a conventional guide book. It is evocative and affecting, with a rich sense of time and place. Written with both style and clarity, it is a must for anyone who wants to walk the route or ride the train." PETER GILLMAN, author and former chair, Outdoor Writers & Photographers Guild

"A compelling journey along the Settle-Carlisle railway, full of detailed research and engaging insights on this treasured line." *Cumberland & Westmorland Herald*

RING OF
STONE
CIRCLES

Exploring Neolithic Cumbria

Stan L Abbott

Saraband 🔘

Published by Saraband
3 Clairmont Gardens
Glasgow, G3 7LW
www.saraband.net

ISBN: 9781913393434

1 2 3 4 5 6 7 8 9 10

Printed and bound in Great Britain by Clays Ltd, Elcograf S.p.A.

MIX
Paper from
responsible sources
FSC® C018072
www.fsc.org

*Please note that the author's description of routes and sites does not imply that
they are either safe to visit and free of hazards along access routes, or legal
rights of way. Please use due caution, as neither the author nor the publisher
can accept liability for any injury or damage.*

Contents

Map and list of principal sites

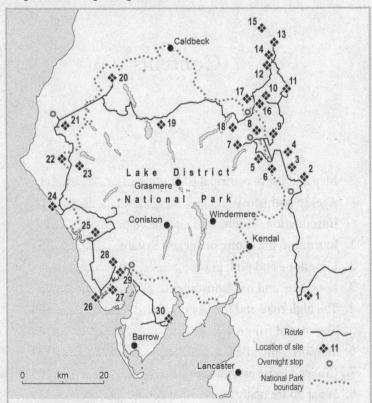

This book is dedicated to the memory of those who made their homes on the fells and in the valleys of Lakeland thousands of years ago, whose legacy of stone structures poses as many questions as it answers.

Ages in prehistory

Academics involved in the study of our prehistory use a variety of terms to describe the various evolutionary periods prior to the arrival of the Romans in Britain, this being the significant moment at which a written record of our history first began (although there is no continuous written record linking the departure of the Romans with our current times).

The sub-title of this book refers to 'Neolithic Cumbria'. I employ this term in a very loose sense, as – while some of our finest Cumbrian prehistoric monuments are for sure Neolithic in origin – many have later, Bronze Age roots, most especially those 'stone circles' that are actually all that remains of ring cairns or other round burial monuments.

The earliest evidence of humans in Britain goes as far back as 950,000 years ago. However, human history was punctuated by successive Ice Ages that rendered 'Britain' uninhabitable, and there is no evidence of human occupation between 180,000 and 60,000 years ago. Neanderthal humans eventually returned via the Doggerland 'bridge' in the North Sea, but continuous human occupation goes back only as far as 12,000 years ago and perhaps not even continuously for that long.

The following are the main terms used in this book.

Paleolithic – technical term for the 'Old Stone Age'. Refers to any possible periods of human occupation, featuring the use of stone, antler, shell and ivory tools and jewellery, prior to the Mesolithic period.

Mesolithic – 9000 to 4300 BC. Development of new stone and wooden tools. Domestication of the dog to assist with hunting. Some of the prevalent hunter-gatherer people make more permanent settlements, such as that excavated at Howick, Northumberland.

Neolithic – 4300 to 2000 BC. Starts with the arrival of a more settled way of life, featuring the rearing of native cattle and pigs, followed by sheep and goats from the European continent. Characterised by the widespread clearance of forest cover using stone axes. The earliest permanent Neolithic settlements in Britain have been thought to be those in Orkney, including Skara Brae. Some Cumbrian remains, at Long Meg, for example, may be of similar age. However, less permanent structures dating from a similar time have been found in locations including Grassington, in the Yorkshire Dales. The later Neolithic is marked by the arrival of grooved ware pottery and then by that of so-called Beaker ware, brought from Europe by the Beaker People, whose DNA would in due course supplant that of the indigenous Neolithic people almost completely.

Chalcolithic Age – 2500 to 2200 BC. A term used to describe the early transition from Neolithic to Bronze Age, typified by the discovery and working of metals, including gold but, more importantly, copper, alongside the arrival of new ceramics and a change in burial rites.

Bronze Age – 2200 to 800 BC. No Neolithic person awoke one day to find they were suddenly living in the Bronze Age: change was gradual, following the discovery that copper could be mixed with small amounts of tin to make the more versatile alloy – bronze – which was far more practical for making agricultural, hunting and other tools. In Britain, tin was found only in Cornwall, but copper was mined in Ireland, Anglesey and North Wales, Cheshire, Shropshire, Galloway and in Cumbria, around Coniston and, very probably, in the northern Lake District, around Skiddaw, Borrowdale and Buttermere. We do not know precisely how bronze was discovered but its use in Europe and Middle East predates its arrival in Britain, so we may imagine that the discovery was accidental and occurred where the two minerals were found close to each other. Around 1600 BC, imported bronze began to replace that made from indigenous sources. We have to infer a significant traffic in bronze both over land and by sea. Society also evolved greatly during the Bronze Age, with more deforestation, more settled farmsteads, the establishment of round houses around 1500 BC, and a radical evolution in burial practices.

Iron Age – 800 BC to AD 43. Begins with the arrival of the more versatile metal from Europe, replacing bronze for the manufacture of tools. Evidence of a pattern of increased conflict in the later Bronze Age is reflected by the appearance of Iron Age hill forts. Farming became more efficient, thanks to better tools and the arrival of the cart and, indeed, the horse to pull it. Chickens were added to the list of animals domesticated for food. The later Iron Age is marked by the emergence of powerful local clans, many of which (in the South of England) would have had increasing contact with the Roman Empire, prior to the invasion in AD 43. Various Brittonic tongues would by this time have replaced the earlier non-Indo-European languages. Beyond the reach of the Roman Empire, Iron Age practices would continue for some time.

BC and AD – the foregoing terms stand for Before Christ and *Anno Domini* (in the year of the Lord). It has become increasingly common for these to be replaced respectively by BCE and CE (Before Common or Current Era, and Common or Current Era) in the interest of religious impartiality. These terms have been in common use since the 18th century, and while BCE and CE are intended to be secular terms, both are still linked to the notional birth date of Jesus Christ. For these reasons, and because BC and AD are still more widely recognised by a general readership, these are the terms employed in this book.

Introduction

Riddles and circular logic

'The past is a different country,' to paraphrase L.P. Hartley in *The Go-Between*, where he noted that 'they do things differently there'. His context may have been quite different, but there's a universal truth to his words, for The Past is our Dark Continent, only parts of which have been thoroughly explored.

In this book, I set out to probe the part of that continent that lies in the Neolithic and Bronze Ages and, specifically, why people back then built so many stone circles. My exploration takes place in Cumbria, where England's tallest mountains are ringed by somewhere close to fifty stone circles and henges, most of them sited on gentler terrain, in the foothills or on outlying plateaux, but some cradled within the majesty of towering surrounding fells .The county is, in terms of absolute numbers and the frequency of its circles, the most important in England. It may even be the location of the oldest stone circles in the British Isles.

This is not, however, a scientific study, nor even an attempt to discover some 'deeper truth' about those who built these structures or why. There'll be no dramatic 'reveal'; no radical new theories. But through my calling in on more than half of all the known circles in Cumbria, I'm hoping that a better understanding may emerge, perhaps to indicate which of these sites tick which particular boxes. I'd like to shed light on which may have had a ritualistic justification; which may have genuinely served an astronomical purpose; which may have been burial sites; which were no more than meeting places.

The context for making this adventure is that we seem almost to know more about the future than we do about so much of our past – we can predict things that are likely to happen with reasonable certainty, based only upon current levels of scientific and societal knowledge and understanding. But we don't have to journey very far back in time to reach huge expanses of that country called The Past about which we know very little. Of the Dark Ages, we can assert little beyond the possibility that there may (or may not) have been a Brittonic King called Arthur.

Of the days of Danelaw, our knowledge is rather more extensive, and yet it feels like it's really only within the last half-century or so that the true extent of the Viking settlement of these isles, and how the people lived then, has been better understood. Of the Roman occupation, we know rather more – even though this is a more distant area of The Past. The thread here is, of course, that the Romans wrote things down. By and large, the Vikings – whose society had oral history at its heart – and Dark Ages Britons did not.

Knowledge abhors a vacuum, and into these unexplored tracts of The Past intrudes speculation. In the furthest reaches of The Past, such speculation becomes increasingly… speculative. What we know about the Neolithic and Bronze Ages in Britain has a firm foundation comprising the various archaeological finds at sites across the length and breadth of the country. While there's no easy way to pin a date upon the action of erecting a tall stone in a shallow foundation, we may well be able to carbon-date tools, fire remains and ornaments with some accuracy. Skeletons may tell us how people died and the diseases they may have contracted, and we can – on those rare occasions when bodies have been preserved in peat – even work out what people were eating thousands of years ago.

But imagine this for a moment: in, say, fifty years' time paper has become obsolete and our entire body of knowledge is encoded and stored in huge data banks. A cataclysmic event occurs and wipes out all that data and any means of recovering it. A thousand years later, archaeologists seek to explore the Data Age, but all they have is skeletons, some fitted with artificial hips or pacemakers, and huge pits filled with plastic debris. They speculate that humans in the Data Age may actually have enjoyed quite an advanced civilisation, in which an artificial compound called plastic and certain precious metals were worshipped, to the extent that society's elders even had pieces of these prized artefacts fitted into their bodies.

These future archaeologists will seek to build an understanding of our times based upon the little that they know for sure. In just the same way, archaeologists today extrapolate from unambiguous foundations of Neolithic, Bronze, and Iron Age 'finds', using the prism of contemporary societal norms to create upon those firm foundations an edifice that represents but one possible interpretation of these ancient times. Such constructs may be more or less fanciful and more or less personal, driven by the pet ideas and theories of individual specialists. And so, we move from an area of The Past that is called 'certainty' into one governed by inference and imagination.

The early history of humans in Britain was not chronicled. Next to nothing appears to have been 'recorded' beyond early rock engravings (at Cresswell Crags, in the East Midlands), more recent 'art' discovered in Kilmartin Glen, and the mysterious Neolithic cup and ring marks on stones found mostly in Northern England and Scotland as well as throughout the Atlantic seaboard of Europe. Quite extraordinarily, similar marks have been witnessed in places from the Americas to Africa, India and Australia. Yet the physical reminders of where and how our Neolithic and Bronze Age ancestors actually lived or practised primitive agriculture here in northern Britain remain scant. By contrast, while people were busy erecting stone circles in Cumbria, the ancient Egyptians had been building pyramids and writing on papyrus for centuries. The Minoan and Mycenaean civilisations in Bronze Age Greece built enduring structures of stone that still stand today. Mycenaean Linear B script was written on both stone and wood and tells us a great deal about how this advanced society functioned.

The enduring permanent legacy of parallel times here in Britain is limited. Relatively little can be understood of how people lived as so few settlements have survived well, the principal exceptions being at Skara Brae, in Orkney, Jarlshof, in Shetland, and the numerous Iron Age brochs scattered across Scotland. In England, archaeologists have excavated a Mesolithic (pre-Neolithic) village on the Northumberland coast, while Amesbury, in Wiltshire, is now believed to be the oldest site of continuous settlement in the country.

Some of the stone circles visited in this book sit in landscapes where other prehistoric evidence includes hut circles or ancient field systems. Fewer of these than you might expect have been excavated, and so they have not perhaps told us all there is to know about how people lived. My aim is not to try to fill in the gaps with idle speculation; rather, to paint a fairly broad-brush picture of why Cumbria seems to be quite special in this regard. Might it conceivably be possible to speculate that the area's defining social characteristics have somehow lasted long beyond Neolithic and Bronze Age times? That may be a rather fanciful idea... but what is not fanciful is the fact that Cumbria remains today rather 'special', with its own enduring customs and traditions. This is my justification for permitting these enduring traditions to provide a more contemporary backdrop to my Neolithic adventure.

My initial thought was to link Neolithic and Bronze Age stone circles with a walking route that would take me from a stone circle near the Cumbrian village of Orton, via other circles on the east side of the mountain massif, to a cluster of three circles at the foot of the Pennines, east of Penrith. From here it would either cross the Pennines towards the Neolithic circles in the Cheviot foothills of Northumberland or swing west to visit other circles that effectively encircle the mountains of the Lake District. The idea of a trans-Pennine route came up because I had been contemplating, in a different context, alternative potential coast-to-coast walking adventures, such as from Furness Abbey to Lindisfarne, or a nuke-to-nuke odyssey from Sellafield to Torness.

Two things nudged me towards an exclusively Cumbrian route, however. Firstly, although there are stone circles in the northern Pennines and near the Hadrian's Wall, these are mostly modest remains and quite far apart from one another. So my journey from Cumbria to Northumberland would have lacked relevant content in its middle section. Secondly, the more I looked for extant stone circles ringing the Lake District, the more of these kept coming to light. Indeed, so profuse did these remains prove to be that I found myself facing a walk of more than two weeks if I was to visit even just the 'best' ones.

This was the point at which I thought about undertaking the journey by mountain bike, an idea that quickly evolved into doing it by electric cycle. I'd first tried one of these in Norway a year or so previously and been bowled over by the possibilities. These machines are not just low-powered mopeds; they are, more correctly, described as power-assisted cycles. The more pedalling you do, the more the machine will top up your efforts from its battery. If you sit on the bike and don't pedal, it won't go. Nor will it offer any relief from saddle-soreness or shelter from the wind and rain; nor will it give you faster speeds. Electric cycles will surpass 25kph only when freewheeling downhill.

And so I flogged my thirty-something-year-old mountain bike and, just as bicycles became the must-have lockdown accessory, managed to get hold of an 18-speed electric hybrid machine from a friend's cycle shop in Carlisle. It had been hiding in a corner while I tried out a more modest machine, but once I spotted it, it proved to be love at the first turn of the pedals. I quickly came to call my newfound pride and joy The Beast, on account of 'his' enthusiastic acceleration and hunger for rough tracks and steep hills. Two weeks and more became, at a stroke, a manageable seven days and six nights, with hopefully enough time to truly appreciate the setting of each circle, learn about its legends, and meet people along the way and exchange stories. For Cumbria surely is, above all else, a land of stories – and those stories may have their roots in otherwise forgotten times.

I thought long and hard about whether it might be possible to identify some threads that might link pre-historic life with the world we know today. Paul Frodsham's book *From Stonehenge To Santa Claus: The Evolution Of Christmas* quickly reassured me that, even without any written records, it might be possible to identify ways in which Neolithic and Bronze Age times have laid the foundations for more modern lifestyles. A book devoted to the history of cheese began its story in Neolithic times, and so I thought about what people might have eaten and how they might have been able to preserve food sourced during times of plenty for consumption later during scarcer months. Although such early times were not his specialism, the food historian Ivan Day suggested some enormously useful insights as we speculated over his kitchen table about the grains, nuts, fruits and meats that the ancients may have eaten.

And then there was the real evidence, on the ground: the routes taken over land and water by early traders, such as those who 'exported' the highly valued stone axes from Langdale, in the heart of the Lake District; or the Beaker People, who brought to our shores the earthenware pots that began to turn up here in ancient graves. This movement of people from Europe's western seaboard threw up further interesting questions: how did Neolithic people converse with each other? Were there any vestiges of their language to be found in our own tongue, or indeed in any early written texts? Might our ancestors have spoken a language that died out completely in these islands but whose continental cousin went on to evolve into the esoteric Basque tongue, of northern Spain and south-west France?

Even before I began my journey around the circles, I was becoming increasingly aware of certain facts about them: not all of them are circles, per se, but are, rather, the remnants of 'ring cairns', or burial mounds. And all circles need to be considered in the context of the landscape in which they sit, whether that be the precise nature of the site itself or the totality of various Neolithic and Bronze Age features in their proximity, such as tumuli, cairns, stone avenues or (rarely in Cumbria) the so-called cup and ring marks carved on boulders and standing stones that so baffle even the best academic minds.

It seemed that the more I got into the subject, the less I knew for sure, but also just how much remained unknown even to specialists.

We talk in broad terms about the Neolithic, Bronze Age, Iron Age and so on, but these are not neatly divided timespans, rather periods that morphed across long stretches of time. Few stone circles have been accurately dated as there is usually no easy (or difficult) way to do this. However, we do know reliably that the mighty Neolithic monuments of Orkney predate Stonehenge, and this is important because the clear inference is that some aspects of Neolithic civilisation spread south across sea and land to the rest of these isles. We also have good evidence that activity around Cumbria's Long Meg stone circle may predate even Orkney. Among other things that we don't know is why cup and ring markings are common in Northumberland and other places east of the Pennines, but rare in Cumbria. Conversely, why does Cumbria have so many stone circles, while these are relatively scarce on the other side of the hills?

We still have no real idea as to the purpose of cup and ring marks: were they directional signs, artworks, doodles, or something quite different? It's not the purpose of this book to even attempt to answer that $64,000 question, though I am personally deeply curious about the apparent lack of what we might call 'art' during the Neolithic and Bronze Age eras, given that paintings on the walls of caves (such as the celebrated examples at Lascaux, in the Dordogne) go back so much further.

There are lots of very clever people who are devoting their lives to the quest for answers to these conundrums. My focus is more on the ways in which these curious monuments continue to fascinate and move us. Why do we find them such spiritual places? Why do they inspire so very many poems, songs, novels, crime dramas? Conversely, why did our more recent forebears, the Victorians in particular, treat them with such seeming disdain?

Inevitably, the COVID pandemic impacted upon my plans, and my 'core journey' and associated research took place later than intended and somewhat against the clock. That said, it did cause me to reflect that the advent of more collective living, stimulated by the arrival of better stone and bronze tools, which facilitated early agriculture, might have brought its own downside in terms of infectious disease.

Like all journeys, my own stirred the pools of my imagination and brought to the surface some fond, and a few less fond, memories. During the pandemic, I had plenty of opportunities to chat with other authors about what we all collectively understood by the not-so-catchy term used to describe books like this: 'narrative non-fiction'. We agreed that the idea of a journey of some sort was a fundamental part of the definition, though this could be not just a literal journey from A to B, but equally a metaphorical journey, or a life journey, as in a biography. The other fundamental, suggested by my good friend Tim Ecott, who has written about places and people I know well, was that the theme should be a truly 'valid' one justified by the author having a genuine passion for it.

Which brings to me to my own interest in stone circles... clearly I can't pretend to be an academic specialist in archaeology, nor a Druid, nor even a member of a local history group. But my interest does go back to my youth when I recall the curious sense of calm I experienced whenever I visited a stone circle. I remember my parents once telling me how they had taken a walk on a Northumberland moor that they hadn't visited previously and which went by the romantic name of Blawearie, evoking a wild, windswept, desolate landscape; and how they had experienced the most curious feeling of awe and mystery. I went there myself and knew precisely what they meant. At that time, we didn't properly appreciate the antiquity of the place where, years later, further excavation would reveal a bit of an archaeological gem, including a cairn circle and grave goods, set within a much wider ancient landscape.

I have since then visited tombs and circles throughout the British Isles, from Jersey and Scilly to the Isle of Man, County Clare, Lewis, Orkney and Shetland. And others in mainland Europe, from Brittany to Sardinia and Corsica. Though the latter stones, lost for centuries in an orchard on this wild Mediterranean island, bear complex representational carvings of faces pretty much unseen elsewhere, there is a rather obvious common thread linking all such structures throughout Europe – it is, of course, their shape.

Why circles? While I have already said that my aim is not to come up with new explanations and theories, I'll say just this: the building of more permanent circular structures seems to have roughly coincided with the beginnings of agricultural cultivation and the exchange of a nomadic lifestyle for a more settled one. Prior to this, nomadic people may have built less durable circular structures, like wigwams. I find myself wondering if the physical properties of the circle – an eternal shape with no beginning and no end – may have had a symbolic link with the notion of an afterlife or spirit world, as some people at least began to live longer lives. Certainly, we can draw parallels with the annual circular nature of life itself: the coming and going of the seasons and the need to predict these as agriculture evolved. In this regard, the extensive studies of Jack Morris-Eyton into the predictive capabilities of some of Cumbria's finest stone circles have felt to me to be perhaps worthy of wider consideration.

On the whole, however, none of these structures appear even remotely ready to yield the truth about the original purpose they may have had. In planning my journey I consciously decided to 'follow the circles', even though some may indeed not represent a stone circle as such, but rather the circular stone structure that once supported an earthen mound atop a burial cist, or 'coffin'.

All are collections of stones, which may or may not be carved or shapen, carefully positioned to form a circle or an ellipse. And I extend this to the incidence of circles within other structures from similar times. The Mycenaean culture in what we now call Greece was, as already remarked, far more advanced than that of our ancestors in the British Isles. But again, I have been struck when visiting Mycenaean remains since beginning this project just how prevalent the circular shape is within such sites. Similarly, at places as far apart as Easter Island and Mount Nemrut, in eastern Turkey, more recent stone monoliths continue to reflect some of the fundamental characteristics of the stone circles, cairns and avenues that are the subject of this adventure.

My journey saw me visit the majority of stone circles, cairn circles and henges that have managed to survive in Cumbria. Some that were known to exist barely a single lifetime ago may already be lost forever, and others proved either too hard to locate (especially when built on limestone!), lost beneath vegetation, or out of bounds beyond barbed wire. It proved also to be a more spiritual 'journey of the mind', during which I found myself encouraged to rethink events in my life and to use my imagination to put myself in the sandals of the ancients. And it was a journey of discovery, as I talked with so many people who had their own Neolithic, Bronze Age or other passions. It was a journey of observation: of places, people, and landscapes, and the stories that lie within all of these, if we only trouble to lift a lid, turn a page, or slip a trowel into the earth.

Chapter 1

Journey to the centre of ancient Britain

The Orkney enlightenment

Like all the best stories, this one begins in a distant land, far away across the sea. In the islands of Orkney, to be precise. To say that Neolithic British 'civilisation' began at the northern edge of Great Britain and then spread south and west from there remains far too categoric a statement to make with any certainty. However, what we can say is that the magnificent stone structures that endure on Orkney date back to around 3000 BC and hence predate Stonehenge and, for that matter, most – though not all – of the stone circles and other ancient sites of Cumbria.

We know as much as we do about Neolithic Orkney in part because of the extraordinary discoveries made in the last two decades at the ongoing excavations on the Ness of Brodgar, which lies between the Neolithic circles of the Ring of Brodgar and the Stones of Stenness on Orkney's Mainland.

Speaking with an excitement married with a variety of certainty unusual in their profession, archaeologists told of the discoveries which effectively shattered the prevailing understanding of our prehistory at the time. Speaking in 2012, Orkney archaeologist Nick Card, who discovered the site at the Ness of Brodgar, said: 'We need to turn the map of Britain upside down when we consider the Neolithic and shrug off our south-centric attitudes.'[1] For what has been unearthed these recent years at the Ness of Brodgar is a quite extraordinary complex of buildings that appears to represent a huge ceremonial centre, comprising large buildings clearly designed to 'make a statement', and smaller dwellings. It appears to have served a central function in the ceremonial life of the wider Orcadian landscape with its nearby monumental stone circles and countless burial chambers, standing stones and other relics scattered throughout the archipelago.

The ongoing excavations at the Ness of Brodgar were featured in a 2016 BBC 2 series, *Britain's Ancient Capital – Secrets of Orkney*. In the course of excavations that summer, charcoal fragments were found and carbon-dated to even earlier: 3512BC, or a whole millennium before Stonehenge. The series' presenter, Neil Oliver, summed it up thus: 'It's beyond speculation that in the Neolithic, Orkney was the centre of something – an idea or a series of ideas, a way of living evolved here and its influence spread the length of the island of Britain.'

Once you accept that Orkney played a crucial role in the evolution of Neolithic culture you also have to accept certain other things as given. Most important among these is that some people in the early days of the new agriculturally-based society moved around a lot and, most importantly, that they must have moved around by boat. Just as Orkney became a hugely important centre in the Viking Age because of its central oceanic location, so must this have also been the case 4,000 and more years previously.

We can say this because all the evidence points to the Neolithic inhabitants of Orkney having arrived from the Scottish mainland with their domestic animals and, although sea levels were most probably rather lower then, they would still have had to cross turbulent open waters. Furthermore, if Orkney was the geographic seat of a strand of Neolithic civilisation, then other seas would have needed to be crossed to enable the 'export' of that civilisation to other parts of the British Isles. Some have dubbed this aspect of Neolithic life the 'cult of the stone circle'. However it is wrong to infer from this that the first stone circles were built on Orkney. Although stone monuments are by their very nature very difficult to date, associated archaeological evidence suggests that Long Meg and Her Daughters may be at least as old.

Of particular importance to the story told in this book is the fact that the numerous spectacular finds made at the ongoing excavations at the Ness of Brodgar include fragments of material originating from the so-called Cumbrian axe factory. Although the total number of stone axes found across Orkney is modest, a single flake of Cumbrian tuff was found at the Ness. Neolithic Cumbrian axes were 'tuff' in origin and tough by nature, hewn from seams of volcanic greenstone tuff high in the Langdale Pikes and around Scafell Pike in the central Lake District fells.

Axes made from Cumbrian tuff were of such exceptional quality that some appear to have been used for ceremonial purposes only, rather than for chopping wood or butchery. They are found all over the British Isles and beyond, and appear to have made up close to a third of total axe production in the British Isles. A great many have been found to the east of the Pennines, in Yorkshire and Lincolnshire, and so a theme that will recur in this book is the idea that our modern trans-Pennine routes – specifically via the passes of Hartside, via Alston; Stainmore (today's A66); the Eden Valley and Wensleydale route; and the Aire Gap (A65) – may well have their origins way back in these times.

So, when the Romans built their road network they would in many cases have simply followed much earlier established trading routes and there is good evidence that some such routes dated back to Neolithic times when they were punctuated by stone monuments that served important cultural roles in the society of the time. Karen Griffiths, Interpretation Officer at the Yorkshire Dales National Park, writes in her blog: 'The concentration and complexity of some of these ritual places tells us that the communities that built them were able to invest a great deal of time and resources in them. The placing of the imposing avenue of standing stones at Shap, at the entrance to the geological routeway through the hills, seems to be no coincidence.'[2]

She continues: 'By the Later Neolithic, long-established lines of exchange were in use. Scarce commodities like salt and polished stone axes had value and were moved long distances. Axe rough-outs from "factories" in Great Langdale, in the Lake District, have been found the length and breadth of the country. The rough-outs were polished up into their final beautiful forms some distance from where they were quarried. Sea routes seem to have been the main way these axes travelled such long distances and rough-outs have been found at the Humber Estuary and along the west coast of Cumbria. There is also a concentration of axe rough-outs around Penrith to the north and in the Aire Valley to the south. It isn't too much of a stretch of the imagination to see the Lune Gap as lying along one of the southerly routes for these sought-after axes and other essentials like salt.'

Griffiths suggests that controlling access to the route or to the items which moved along it would have given communities around Shap status and power. 'Erecting a grand processional avenue would have been a reflection of that status. Power and privilege was reinforced for those who participated in whatever rituals took place along the avenue.'

Moving forward to Roman times, not all Roman roads have been adopted by modern highway-builders: High Street – which runs from Ambleside (not far from the axe factories) to Penrith – traverses a high but relatively gentle ridge and remains popular with walkers. It also passes right through a major site of stone circles and cairns, sitting at an ancient crossroads and offering as clear evidence as you'd wish to find of much earlier traffic. Beyond Penrith, with its mighty henges of Mayburgh and King Arthur's Round Table – as you head towards the old Roman route up Hartside – are other Neolithic remains, including the magnificent Long Meg and Her Daughters, Little Meg and Glassonby, and the cluster of circles in Broomrigg Plantation, near Kirkoswald.

Join the dots between these ancient sites and what begins to emerge is the idea of a network of trading routes over which one of the commodities traded would have been Cumbrian axeheads. So, we can start to imagine that the various collections of Neolithic and Bronze Age remains east of the Cumbrian mountains may have reflected not just the location of early farming settlements but also the routes that connected those settlements.

But what about the early remains that lie to the west of the mountains, on the Cumbrian coastal strip? Although less dramatic or visible than the magnificent circles and henges, which lie mostly (though by no means exclusively) towards the eastern side of the central Lake District massif, the settlement evidence on the western flanks of that massif offers extraordinary insight into how these early agriculturalists may have lived. The remains of settlements can be found at regular intervals, and many are inscribed on the Historic England register of monuments, which notes that the land above the coastal strip comprises 'one of the best recorded upland areas in England', with Tongue How (south of Ennerdale) bestowed with 'prehistoric stone hut circle settlements, field systems, funerary cairns, cemetery and cairnfield, Romano-British farmstead, shieling and lynchets'. Although much of the settlement activity came in the later Bronze Age, there is also evidence of earlier settlement coincident with the start of the axe quarrying in Langdale.[3]

The Neolithic axe 'rough-outs' from Langdale would have passed through these settlement areas on their way to the Cumbrian coast, some for 'finishing' and some to make their way by sea as far as Ireland and Orkney. Excavations at various sites on that coastal strip have yielded artefacts, including axe rough-outs, suggesting that the 'value-added' function in the stone axe industry – the grinding and polishing – may have been concentrated here (and in other lowland locations at the edge of the fells). The *North West Rapid Coastal Zone Assessment* catalogues archaeological finds from the length of the coastline, including a number of key locations at which axe remains have been found. Among these locations is Ehenside Tarn, a small body of water largely drained in the mid-nineteenth century, when it yielded up axes, a grinding stone, dugout canoe and possible paddle. A polished axe and numerous stone tools were found at sites near Askham-in-Furness and Barrow, and there was also evidence of at least another four henges and circles along this strip.[4]

In a paper entitled *Polished axes, Petroglyphs and Pathways: A study of the mobility of Neolithic people in Cumbria*, Peter Style revisits (in an undated dissertation thought to have been written around 2010) the whole subject of Cumbrian axeheads and the movement of people. He identifies concentrations of axe finds around Derwentwater, along the banks of the Eden and the Eamont and on the coast at the Solway Firth, Seascale, Drigg and the previously mentioned sites in Furness. It was to these areas, and to the polishing 'workshop' at Kell Bank, near Seascale, that the rough-outs were transported for finishing.[5] This process of movement and transport was of particular relevance to my visit to meet the Cumbrian axe factory expert, Mark Edmonds, in Orkney.

Of course, it would be one thing to transport some rough-outs by boat in Neolithic times; quite another to transport cattle. Which brings us to the inevitable question: what kind of boats did these people build and sail? Mark Edmonds believes they must have been substantial, but that would not be enough to guarantee the survival of any traces of them across thousands of years. Similarly, where are the wooden axe handles? Where are the wooden roof timbers at the surviving stone hut foundations? Where are the heftier timbers that may have supported roofs above some of the cairn circles? In a paper in the 2013 publication, *The Oxford Handbook of the European Bronze Age*, Benjamin W Roberts does cite one example of a surviving seagoing boat: 'The rare excavation of shipwrecks such as the Dover boat [...] certainly demonstrates that vessels of sufficient size existed when cross-Channel connections were established in the early second Millennium BC.'[6]

While this may have been later than when the first settlers crossed the Pentland Firth to Orkney, Roberts cites Needham 2009 as his source and this original work refers to a re-*emergence* of sea links following a period of relative isolation in the British Isles, during which a distinct 'local' culture appears to have evolved. Given that the Dover Bronze Age boat is claimed to be 'the world's oldest *known* seagoing boat', it seems reasonable to infer that similar seagoing vessels might quite plausibly have existed for hundreds of years prior to the date attributed to the Dover Boat after it was found by construction workers on the A20 in 1992. The boat is now on display in a customised room at the Dover Museum, whose description states: 'The workers, who were working alongside archaeologists from the Canterbury Archaeological Trust, uncovered the remains of a large and well-preserved prehistoric boat. This was a transformative discovery: archaeologists estimate the boat would have been in use around 1500 BC, during the Bronze Age. The archaeologists were aware that past attempts at excavating similar boats in one piece had been unsuccessful. Consequently, a decision was taken to cut the boat into sections and reassemble it afterwards. It was also necessary to leave an unknown part of the boat underground as its burial site stretched out towards buildings and excavating close to these buildings would have been too dangerous. After nearly a month of excavation a 9.5-metre length of the boat was successfully recovered and has since been marvellously preserved.'

The Dover boat is special because it was found substantially intact, but it is by no means unique: *Heritage Daily* says there are nine others found in Britain, though these comprise fragments, rather than whole boats. Remnants of three such boats were found near Hull, thirty years previously. They exhibit a significant degree of complexity in their construction, which comprised oak planks 'sewn' together using withies. The structure was several metres long and was braced by cross-members and the gaps caulked with wax to seal it. *Heritage Daily*[7] says: 'It must be said that the construction techniques used to create these types of boats are astounding and Renfrew and Bahn[8] agree, saying "in perhaps no other area of pre-industrial technology did the world's craftspeople achieve such mastery as in the building of wooden vessels…"'This is the context in which I find myself weighing up Mark Edmonds's wry smile when we talk about the 'Neolithic boat' reconstructed for the BBC series *Britain's Ancient Capital: Secrets of Orkney*. My wife Linda and I meet Edmonds on a perfect Orkney midsummer day, the high sun exaggerating the lush green of the rolling pastoral Orkney landscape, relaxing beneath an unusually windless sky. The world is emerging a little sleepily from lockdown when we meet at the car park at the Ring of Brodgar, Orkney's premier stone circle. My initial thoughts on learning that the world's prime authority on Cumbrian stone axes was a Professor at York was that it should be a pretty 'easy fix'. The visit would be a mere 40 minutes on the train and a bus out to the university. I had, of course, failed to grasp the crucial word 'Emeritus' in his title – otherwise known as an academic licence to roam in semi-retirement. Not that Mark looks particularly like a retired man of leisure: in fact, he is every bit the part of the working archaeologist, clad in denim, high-vis jacket, and with a fine head of straw-grey, curly hair.

We are standing beneath one of the towering Stones of Stenness – where else could a Neolithic expert reasonably choose to be? But just being there does not mean that you necessarily have to swim with the crowd on all matters. We quickly find ourselves discussing the boat recreated especially for the BBC series. Its structure comprised lengths of pliable willow covered in animal hide. It was flimsy and, though the team did manage somehow to row it across the Pentland Firth to the mainland, Mark, for one, struggles to imagine heavy cattle aboard a rather fragile vessel of skins. While this reproduction is viable, there would surely have also been more sturdy vessels: 'There's just a flow of people back and forth between the isles and up and down the Irish Sea: these trips are not to be sneezed at, even now, but we know that they happened because we have a number of stone artefacts in Orkney that came from mainland Scotland, the Western Isles and from other parts of the country. They must have had better boats than this – the fact that we haven't found one is neither here nor there.' Well, why would you find the remains of a five-thousand-year-old boat? Organic matter is the scarce resource that archaeologists yearn to get their hands on so as to put dates upon things that are excavated. The manner in which it has been possible to attach dates to the extensive settlement on the Ness of Brodgar and place Orkney 'civilisation' before that of Stonehenge is the exception rather than the rule; the Dover Boat is exceptional; ancient human corpses dug from peat bogs with stomachs still full of undigested food are exceptional.

What does survive is generally fragmentary, though Mark cites the finding of a large oak plank, buried in the silt of the Bay of Ireland, not far from where we are standing now. It was discovered in 2014 when Dr Scott Timpany, of the University of the Highlands and Islands, was documenting the remnants of a submerged forest of willow and birch carr. The discovery might have raised more than one intriguing possibility: that oak forest may have covered some of the land here; and that it might provide evidence of an early craft of far more substance than the wobbly BBC mock-up. Frustratingly, it turned out that it was most likely not part of a boat at all, though it was a very early piece of rough-hewn timber. Around the time it was being unearthed, a team at the National Maritime Museum Cornwall, led by Professor Robert Van de Noort of Exeter University (now at Reading), was setting sail in a 15-metre 'Bronze Age' boat called Morgawr, after the legendary Cornish sea serpent. The reconstruction was based on the Bronze Age boat fragments found at the mouth of the Humber and similar to the Dover Boat. It had a beam of about two metres and made a number of successful voyages around Falmouth harbour. The team constructed it using a Bronze Age 'toolkit' and the chunky oak planks were sewn together with soaked willow branches. And therein lies the big question: could the task of shaping the two keel members and the sides of the boat have been accomplished hundreds, thousands even, of years earlier using only stone tools? The oak 'worked timber' has been dated to the early fifth millennium BC and, in his book, *Orcadia*, Mark comments: 'It could have been washed in, but trees capable of producing this kind of timber were a part of the regional landscape at that time.'

Mark suggests that the availability of boats would have been fundamental to the survival of Orcadian society back in its 'golden age'. 'There are seventy-three islands, and if you live on one of the small islands and have a small herd of cows, then, after a while, they will start to go a little strange – as will your relatives.' He's unambiguous: those who crossed the water and settled on the Orkney Islands brought domesticated cattle with them, and they were already accomplished seafarers. The missing piece of the jigsaw is precisely how the seagoing boats were built. 'I think people are moving all the time – there was movement before the Neolithic. I don't think it's mass movement, rather dribs and drabs.' And those people would have arrived with both new ideas and new artefacts.

Mark suggests we move on and visit the Unstan Chambered Cairn, a substantial structure a kilometre or so from the Ness. On arrival, we discover that not only is the site yet to awake from its pandemic slumber, but nor is it likely to any time soon – a pair of oystercatchers have built their nest on the path to the large mound. We resume our conversation by the gate and a lady from a nearby cottage thoughtfully brings us coffee and biscuits as our conversation turns to things smaller than either the people or their cattle, who may have arrived in Orkney by boat: those prized Neolithic axe heads from Cumbria.

'There's a fragment of the rock from the Langdales found at the Ness of Brodgar,' resumes Mark. Of the other axes found in Orkney, Mark tells me, some are the finished object, though quite small. 'Perhaps the axe blades had a lot of use and were reworked a lot of times.'

The more we talk about the Ness and wider Neolithic Orkney, the more it becomes apparent that this Neolithic landscape is very different from those of Cumbria, however rich the historic remains of the latter may be. Although the chronology of this book places aspects of Orkney's Neolithic before much of what can be seen in Cumbria – in line with the chronology of the 'cult of stone circles' – I make my visit here having already completed my tour of Cumbria's circles. It is the first time I have been here in more than twenty years and in the couple of days prior to meeting up with Mark, it has felt as though each field is home to another Neolithic, Bronze Age or Iron Age monument. These monuments take a variety of forms: the extraordinary Hobbit-like complex of Skara Brae, with its little stone houses and their stone bunkbeds, hearths and 'dressers'; the countless burial cairns, of which Maeshowe, with its crucial winter solstice alignment, is the grandest; the vast circle that is the Ring of Brodgar and the dramatic angular forms of the Stones of Stenness that gaze up towards it from a few hundred metres away. All are now interpreted through the prism of the extraordinary complex that is the Ness of Brodgar: a Neolithic treasure trove which, until 2003, was thought to be no more than a glacial moraine.

The Ness is a narrow spit of land running down from the gently sloping elevated site of the Ring of Brodgar to the flat, low-lying bowling green of the Stones of Stenness. There are residual signs of a ceremonial avenue of some kind linking the two. When excavation began at the Ness, the initial presumption was that it was an early settlement; its true nature has gradually been revealed since 2006 with each successive summer's digging. Principal features include two huge walls, respectively two and four metres thick, and a succession of buildings, which numbered thirty-eight at the time of writing. Buildings were erected on top of earlier ones in what seems like haphazard fashion. They include very large structures with hearth-places, leading to the supposition that this was less a place to live and more a centre of ritual for the wider Orcadian community.

Mark tells me: 'Everything that we see suggests there were times when hundreds of people were coming into the buildings. It's a bit like thinking about church: the Church deals with seasonal events, but also births, deaths and marriages. With the help of the Church you make sense of your life.' In the same way, the Neolithic monuments helped the ancient people make sense of their lives. 'In Orkney there are alignments built into some of these monuments. Maeshowe has an alignment so the sun shines straight along the passage at midwinter. People were aware of the cycles of the sky and what these cycles meant: farmers are concerned about whether things will start growing again and that endures in our own Harvest Festival and other seasonal celebrations.'

Recent geophysical survey work suggests that there may have been more of these 'central' socio-ritual complexes in the islands. On the Ness of Brodgar, this ritual activity culminated in what appears to have been a single huge event around 2400 BC that now appears to have signalled, for whatever reason, the end of the entire complex, perhaps even a wider collapse of Neolithic ways. As the Ness's own website puts it: 'The end of the Ness complex itself was marked by what appears to have been an incredibly ostentatious feast, which saw the slaughter and consumption of over 400 cattle, whose remains were carefully placed around the last building on site – the monumental Structure Ten.'

Why? What happened next? Well, we can't really say, and, in *Orcadia*, Mark puts it this way: 'Overall, our picture of Neolithic beginnings is patchy and fragmented.' However, we do at least know something about how people lived: residual traces on pottery shards confirm that they ate beef and consumed dairy produce and supplemented their diet with fish, as well as growing crops, including oats and 'primitive' bere barley. Indeed, Barony Mill, in the north of the Mainland, continues a tradition of milling this crop, which can certainly be traced back to Viking times and quite possibly earlier. It's even returned to use in brewing and distilling and I have some at home with which I have been experimenting. Cast your eyes across the landscape of Orkney and you do not see a wild, sub-Arctic island: this is neither Shetland nor the Faroe Islands, to the north. It is a pastoral land with some cereal and mixed farming thrown in. I'm not sure if the island is self-sufficient in such products, but the likes of Orkney butter and cheese are widely available. The islands may have yielded even more bounty back in Neolithic times, though, as Mark Edmonds comments: 'The archipelago was well suited to farming, whatever form it took. A gift of the bedrock, the soils on many islands were patchy but often sandy and well drained.' It was warmer then by a couple of degrees and the long summer days meant the growing season was long. And the close proximity to each other of the many islands of the archipelago was a critical factor in the emergence of the particular Orkney society.

Writes Mark: '… the configuration of the archipelago shaped the social geographies of the time. Composed of 70 or so islands, it provided a frame across which small-scale farmers were able to foster a sharp sense of local identification, at the same time acknowledging their place in wider communities defined by descent, by affiliation and by alliances operating on a regional scale. As it had been for centuries, movement back and forth across the water was fundamental to identification and to politics on these different scales.'

So, we can imagine our Cumbrian axe rough-outs, perhaps honed near Seascale and then making their way, possibly in stages, up the coast and a few of them ultimately ending up in Orkney. What some suggest to have gone in the other direction, however, was of far greater import: a fashion for erecting stone circles that mimicked the earlier ones in Orkney, and for building burial cairns. That there is a predominance of these towards the west of

Scotland and England may reflect the ability of primitive boats to travel that way within relative shelter, though the abundance of recumbent stone circles and other remains in North East Scotland suggests that we shouldn't jump readily to easy conclusions. Although it made for good TV to portray the idea of Orkney driving both a cultural and an architectural revolution throughout the islands of Britain, the reality is almost certainly more nuanced. Rather, I take on board Mark's notion of an exchange of goods and ideas going on over a long period of time.

The iconic marks of Neolithic culture may have travelled south, but Cumbria can boast none of the skilfully built dry stone buildings of almost monumental proportions, which have been found at the Ness of Brodgar and across the islands of Orkney. Mark goes on to stress to me that, in contrast, the totality of Orkney's Neolithic remains provides evidence of high standards of construction in stone. These stone dwellings don't tend to appear in Cumbria until the late Bronze Age or Iron Age, he says. The first settlement evidence in Cumbria, beside Ehenside Tarn, as previously mentioned, exhibits no stone building remains, only traces of stone hearths along the shore. All of which leaves us to wonder whether the inhabitants of Cumbria chose not to use stone; had not learned to use it; or indeed preferred to stick to traditional building methods for their homes, using wood. Perhaps it was the incidence of more frequent gales (even in a more benign Orkney climate than we know today) that encouraged the creation of masonry homes in Orkney.

I find myself comparing the solid nature of the Orkney remains, such as Skara Brae, with those in some of the landscapes I have crossed in Cumbria. In the latter, the largest visible remnants besides the stone circles are somewhat more modestly sized burial mounds, ring cairn fragments and circular piles of stones that may just represent the more solid foundations of wooden huts, perhaps with walls of wattle and daub and thatch of reeds or heather.

The conversation returns to those Cumbrian axeheads, as I'm trying to get a better handle on the extent to which the Langdale 'factories' might have stimulated trade and traffic in and out of the Lake District. Mark dampens possible notions of significant movements, however, saying: 'There are tonnes of waste on the site [in Langdale], yes. The numbers are massive, but people are there quarrying these stones for 1,500 years so there doesn't have to have been a very big "industry" as we might envisage it.'

Has he personally said all there is to say about the axe factories? 'The idea was that it would be nice to go back and do more work on the quarries. I am carrying on doing surveys of the implements around different areas. The impression that I have got over the years is that there are people coming up [to the quarries] from different directions to get stones and make axes.'

In his extensive work on the Neolithic axe factories and on pre-historic tools in general, Mark Edmonds has striven to place these in their societal context. If we are looking for stone tool 'factories', then perhaps we should look more towards the flint 'mines' associated with the Downs and other chalk hills. Here, deep pits were dug to extract the lumps of flint that were the raw material for axes and other tools. As Mark himself observes in his book, *Stone Tools and Society*, just as the causewayed enclosures of the early Neolithic were succeeded by henges and then by stone circles, so flint gave way to other rocks, not just in the world of tool-making, but also in the ceremonial value of the tools thus produced. Causewayed enclosures comprised a peripheral ditch and raised embankment, pierced in places by causeways or 'entrances' to the enclosed central space. In England, they have been found almost exclusively to the south of the River Trent, though there is one near Houghton-le-Spring, near Sunderland, and one in our own Cumbria, close to Ullock, west of the Skiddaw massif.

Of the manner in which causewayed enclosures came to be succeeded, Mark writes: 'These changes appear to be broadly contemporaneous with an apparent expansion in the scale of stone axe dispersal in the second quarter of the third millennium BC and with the end of activity at many of the early flint mines. In addition, recent work [the book was published in 1995] at Great Langdale suggests that the character and perhaps the social context of stone axe production may have changed at around the same time.' What I have not previously appreciated is that the Langdale axes, quarried from precarious seams of tuff high in the mountains, could just as reasonably have been sourced lower down. Mark suggests that the location of quarries in 'dramatic and highly inaccessible locations' may have had less to do with the physical qualities of the rock and more with 'the assignment of a special significance to stone retrieved from isolated and even dangerous places'. At the same time, he observes, more of the production process began to take place high in the mountains, as witnessed by the extensive waste piles. The axe rough-outs leaving Langdale and other nearby sites would have required relatively little work at the coastal and other locations where they traditionally went for finishing.

Increasingly, the trouble taken in sourcing these axes from 'high in the heavens' appears to be directly associated with their acquiring something of a mystique, elevating many above the status of mere tools and attributing to them more special ceremonial and other qualities. Many Langdale axes made the relatively short journey across the Pennines to Yorkshire via the routes described earlier. One particular type of Cumbrian axe has been found in some numbers in Yorkshire and, unlike those of local stone, these are usually given a complete polished finish, rather than just on the cutting edges.

Just as the Neolithic Age was not neatly succeeded by the Bronze Age, so neither did the Cumbrian axes disappear overnight with the arrival of metal tools. In his book, Mark laments the lack of settlement evidence of the 'later history' of axes hewn from tuff. However, he speculates that 'the outcrop of tuff may have seen the slow erosion of its symbolic importance'. 'The imposing peaks of the Langdale Fells may have remained an important point of geographical and historical reference for many generations. But where the quarries had once stood as testaments to the importance of the stone axe, they may now have taken on the patina of an archaic order.'

As if to emphasise the frustrating lack of surviving evidence of Neolithic and Bronze Age homes in Cumbria, when compared with the rich stone legacy in Orkney, Mark's parting advice is to go and take a look at the remains of the Neolithic village of Barnhouse, just a short walk from the Stones of Stenness and standing on the shore at the head of Loch Harray. People lived here around the same time as they did at Skara Brae. Around fifteen dwellings have been found since the site was discovered in 1984 but it appears that the stone walls were destroyed at some point (perhaps deliberately, though possibly simply by agriculture). Might this have been when the Ness of Brodgar itself was abandoned at the time of the 400-cattle slaughter? The village had a ritual hearth similar to the one at the heart of the Stones of Stenness, so some have speculated that this was a sort of elite 'navvie' camp for those who came to oversee the erection of the Stones of Stenness and was therefore dismantled upon their departure. So much we don't know; such temptation to speculate to fill in the gaps. I find myself reflecting that in the world today some societies do still retain that intrinsic connection to the land and to the stones that make up the land. Ambelin Kwaymullina, of the Palyku people in Australia, explains: 'For Aboriginal peoples, country is much more than a place. Rock, tree, river, hill, animal, human – all were formed of the same substance by the Ancestors who continue to live in land, water, sky. Country is filled with relations speaking language and following Law, no matter whether the shape of that relation is human, rock, crow, wattle. Country is loved, needed, and cared for, and country loves, needs, and cares for her peoples in turn. Country is family, culture, identity. Country is self.'[9]Indigenous people feel a profound connection with the land and feel its pain in a very real sense.

As we wander back to the Ring of Brodgar for a final look, I reflect that our ancient peoples may once have shared the gift of connection that endures among indigenous Australians but which we have long since lost. Does the tingle that I myself feel at the heart of a stone circle represent the ephemeral vestiges of some long lost gift? I defy anyone not to feel at least something special at the Ring of Brodgar. I walk its perimeter again, reflecting as I go on the way it relates to the lochs on either side and to the Stones of Stenness beyond the end of the isthmus. My eye catches a single furry caterpillar – a 'woolly bear', or tiger moth, I think. Like me, it is enjoying the sun's warming rays on the bare peat, where visitors have worn a track around the perimeter of the circle. It is a thoroughly pleasant 20°C. We walk up to where the ongoing excavations at the Ness have lain COVID-fallow for more than a year. There isn't a great deal to see: the excavation site is covered in black tarpaulin, held in place by as many old tyres as I've ever seen anywhere other than an unsightly used tyre dump. Well, at least one of the most unpleasant by-products of the motor car is being put to positive use. The digging will resume in some form within a few weeks.

On leaving Orkney, I reflect that these islands are no strangers to inward migration. I find myself on the plane back to Glasgow sitting next to a woman who's moved, mid-pandemic, from the South of England to the isle of Rousay, just to the north of the Mainland. Later, I make some enquiries. I've always understood that Orkney has been acquiring a growing English and lowland Scots diaspora over the past decade or two and this is borne out when I talk to Luke Fraser, at Aspire Orkney, the council's COVID recovery team: 'We have seen net in-migration every year for the last 20 years,' he tells me. 'Our population has grown in that time from just over 19,000 to 22,000, at the same time as Shetland and the Western Isles more especially, have seen their populations drop.' Might Orkney society once again be on the road to something dynamic and influential, which could change the way the rest of us live?

* * *

Travelling on from Glasgow to the Isle of Jura, I haven't anticipated any significant addition to my Neolithic understanding: the island does boast a number of relatively modest burial mounds and standing stones, but seemingly no stone circles. However, our hotel has on a wall a modest wooden display case in which are exhibited several flint and other stone tools found on the shores of the island.

'They're mislabelled and belong in a museum,' a fellow guest tells me bluntly, later. She's one of a group of women who've arrived on the little fast ferry that runs twice daily from the Scottish mainland pretty much direct to the door of the hotel. They are all pals from around Lochgilphead and the village of Kilmartin. Bear in mind that merely to hear the word 'Kilmartin' is calculated to send Neolithic experts into ecstasies – specialists in cup and ring markings especially. Kilmartin Glen is a treasure trove of Neolithic remains – cairns, standing stones, stone circles and the extensive piece of rock art known as Achnabreck. I know something about this because earlier in the year I watched a presentation on cup and ring art, which was part of a series of online presentations by Durham University during lockdown.

What I do not know is that the woman remarking on the flints is none other than Dr Sharon Webb, Curator and Director of the Kilmartin Museum, whose Neolithic artefacts are recognised as among Scotland's most significant historic collections. The fickle finger of coincidence sees us talking about a rare recent find in Kilmartin: figurative rock carvings of stags, with antlers, on the cap stone of a burial cairn. Sharon seems a little bruised by the discovery: by rights, this should perhaps be her discovery, not that of Hamish Fenton, who is a visitor to Kilmartin Glen. And yet this happens so often in this field of work – you could walk past the rock a thousand times without seeing anything there. Sophisticated technology was required to enhance the images to the point of recognition.

Having mused more than once on the fact that most of our figurative prehistoric art in this country dates from well before the Neolithic Age and appears to fall from favour during these times, the discovery is a fascinating one, reconnecting a link with how our ancestors may have expressed themselves artistically.

My visit to Jura was never intended to be part of my Neolithic and Bronze Age discovery but, in the way of these things, it neatly completes a circle that began with reflections on the (limited) evidence of cup and ring markings in Cumbria, and thus opens the door to future discoveries at Kilmartin, once the refurbished museum reopens.

We leave Jura better off by the acquisition of two new friends and one bottle of Lussa gin, crafted by three women from local botanicals, including sea lettuce we have ourselves helped to forage. But I digress…

Chapter 2

Limestone and pink granite

Ancient routes to Shap, Neolithic capital

May 2021 was memorable for mostly the wrong reasons, destined to go down in history as hosting the slowest starting spring in recent memory. I'm not even sure that frosts in May were ever expected, even when I was a kid and climate change was not a term on anyone's lips. By the middle of the month, there was at least a bit of a plus as restrictions invoked to counter the COVID pandemic were further lifted (albeit against a backdrop of 'new variants')… and the threat of frost finally seemed to be receding (though not before it had, for the first time ever, nipped the buds on the vines at my home in Durham). But that did not mean it was either warm or dry. So, when I changed train at Carlisle to witness a hesitant sun – if not actually beating down upon, then at least gently warming the station canopy – I allowed myself a modest note of cautious optimism.

When I got off the train at Dent station and freewheeled, brakes hard on, down the winding road from 'England's highest main line station' to the valley floor, the sun was still giving it its best shot and I felt as though I'd thrown the dice and landed the 20 per cent possibility of no rain that the weather app had promised. Nonetheless, some of the surrounding fells had invited brooding black clouds to their summits and these were hinting at thunder. It was as I coasted onto the cobbled streets of Dent village, 20 minutes later, that I felt the first drops of rain.

Leaving this most idyllic of all Dales villages in my wake, The Beast then bore me effortlessly up the fellside through the village of Gawthrop and on to the lofty summit from which you can expect to gaze down the full length of lonely Barbondale, pretty much all the way to the Irish Sea. Barbon and neighbouring Kingsdale are probably the two least visited dales in the whole of the national park: both are blessed with a wildness tempered by a desire to delight the discerning collector of fine vistas.

But Barbon today is being coy and shielding its more distant delights beneath a mantle of cloud and rain: a storm is fast advancing up the dale towards me. Given that the dale has been gracious enough to afford me such advance warning of the weather it is poised to cast upon me, I pull up and don a full set of waterproofs and then check my map to locate the bridleway I'm planning to take. This should lead me round the back of a hill and direct to the little stone circle, near Casterton, which is the first on my itinerary and the only one I plan to visit today.

Now, when I packed for this trip, I was conscious of the need to keep both weight and bulk within reasonable limits and so I skimped on clothes and toiletries, thereby permitting myself the luxury of bringing my laptop, SLR camera and zoom lens. These all fitted nicely into my two panniers and the new top-bag that sat above them. I also meticulously copied more than thirty individual map sections and organised these in sequence, grouped by day. These would be displayed in turn beneath the little plastic window on the nifty little handlebar bag I'd bought. What I did not do when setting up this system was destruction-testing... I had simply presumed a degree of weather resistance.

I resume my descent of Barbondale; the storm front continues its own advance without pause. Inevitably, rider and storm collide: it's rain, Captain, but not as we know it. It is a sheet of water cascading from the heavens and reinforced with the odd hailstone. I arrive at the point at which I'd intended to head off along the bridleway. Now, the issue with bridleways is that they are, technically, rights of way for people on horseback. Legally speaking, they are also available for use by cyclists and this has been something of a boon in the off-road era. However, such rights of way come with no guarantee that they possess a surface suitable for cycling, be it on an off-road machine or any other. Today, said bridleway is two ruts in the heather, each transporting a vast quantity of water off a bleak expanse of moorland. The Beast and I decide that discretion should step forward and be the better part of valour.

Unfortunately, changing my route now will necessitate reading the map. More specifically, reading the next bit of the map fragment in my handlebar bag. I duly remove it from its now steadily leaking window-pouch: it turns to papier-mâché in my gloved hands and the fragment with the stone circle marked vanishes before my eyes. I have no more than a vague idea where I should be going and have only one arrow remaining in my quiver. I retrieve my phone from its inside pocket and am amazed to see that it is enjoying 4G coverage with several bars of signal. Perhaps there really is a god. I look up Casterton Stone Circle on the *Megalithic Portal* and, hallelujah, a helpful punter has posted detailed directions, right down to the number of fields I'll have to cross.

Sticking now to quiet roads rather than tracks, my task is to locate the second track on the left off Fell Road, which leads from the village of Casterton to a remote farm. I take a punt on the answer to the question 'When is a track not a track?' and the Beast and I go through the double gates marked Bull in Field and set off across country. The Portal says there'll be five fields to cross before we reach the stone circle but it is, quite suddenly, there before us on a raised platform at the top of field number three.

My immediate impression is that there is rather more to this circle than I had come to expect. I suspect this is in part down to the fact that it's a bit hard to locate and not everyone wants to share a stroll to a circle with a bull. But what I find is both reasonably intact and reasonably substantial, suggesting a raised embankment of about 16 metres in diameter, with seventeen stones of up to perhaps half a metre high on the inner edge of this. I guess that it affords a commanding view across the wide plain of the Lune valley, possibly extending as far as Morecambe Bay. Today, however, I'm happy just to see from one side of the circle to the other. Opinion seems divided as to whether this is an embanked stone circle or the remains of a ring cairn, though I personally err towards the former.

I walk the circle a couple of times, post a few pictures on Instagram and toy with pausing a while to soak up the atmosphere. The very damp atmosphere… The torrential rain has taken its foot off the gas and is now no more than a downpour and I, foolishly, decide to top up my phone by means of my portable charger. Foolishly, because my phone starts to complain that it's detected water in its vitals. I encase it in a sandwich bag and bury it as far from the weather as possible before setting off back towards the Bull in Field gate.

An electric cycle is quite a heavy machine: the more so when laden with kit. These two characteristics increase the likelihood that the machine may topple when ridden at a slow speed on uneven ground. Sure enough, I catch a pedal on a protruding stone and have the first fall of my journey. Not too much damage, though I'll discover later that I've knocked the front dérailleur a little out of place. Sadly, it will take a bigger and far 'better' fall to really learn my lesson.

* * *

Casterton Stone Circle lies about half a mile to the north of extensive ancient remains, including a large cairn field and settlement remnants. On the day of my May visit, I had thought better of making a closer examination as the rain was still purposeful and time was getting tight.

However, I made a point of returning, minus The Beast, a few weeks later. It was a beautiful sunny day and I was happy to note that the view from the road near the circle was indeed commanding, although it did not extend all the way to the sea. I further noted that the Bull in Field was not just one of those virtual bulls so fondly cited by farmers as a deterrent: the field really did contain a large and rather impressive bull... and his harem. Discretion triumphed over valour once more.

On this return, my suspicion that any public access to the area of cairns and settlement relics was strictly limited was confirmed. However, a gate from the lane further up the hill did open onto a track which led some distance towards this area. As with the location of the stone circle itself, this sloping pasture was replete with piles of stones, some of which might have been no more than the product of agricultural clearance. By this point in time, I had visited more than thirty stone circles in Cumbria and more in Orkney, so I was increasingly of a frame of mind in which even quite random collections of stones might acquire the look and feel of a stone circle. The temptation to see collections of rocks in this way was, I found, heightened by the knowledge that many stones in 'real' circles have, over the centuries, collapsed and become partially buried. To further complicate things, in limestone country the bedrock is never far below the vegetation and so chunks of limestone do protrude at random in fields. And yet, here I was, standing on a level platform on a spur where the fell began to drop into a shallow valley and finding myself surrounded by a clearly visible ring of about a dozen stones, partly submerged, but standing on top of a slight embankment. It looked more like a stone circle than some of the 'real circles' I have seen on the limestone fells.

I was unable to find any reference to there having been a circle in the specific location I was exploring and so all I will say is that the protruding stones I spotted did indeed present a roughly shaped circle. I resolved to post my observations on the *Megalithic Portal* and await comment… or ridicule. As I write, such comment remains awaited. My aspiration is to return with someone who may be able to pass more expert judgement. In the meantime, I also share my photographs with Paul Frodsham, who comments that they 'look quite convincing', while also cautioning me always to make clear what is proven and what is speculation. 'That way, you can't be wrong!'

* * *

On leaving Casterton, I calculate that I should be able to arrive at my overnight stop, at Tebay, on time for a planned rendezvous with the artist who has been making her own tour of some of the Cumbrian circles in preparation for creating the little linocut illustrations that mark the start of each chapter of this book.

However, this is the first day that The Beast and I have journeyed significantly together while the latter is fully laden. I judge that my notional 50 or so miles range is going to turn out to be closer to 30, tops. It is still raining steadily and the last thing I can look forward to with relish is an unscheduled halt for lack of electric support. I decide on a return to the Barbon Inn, where I last stayed the previous October, on the eve of increasing lockdown restrictions.

Today, the rain is actually easing as I arrive and I make myself at home by the welcoming open fire. It is a lovely village pub and I can vouch for its food offer too on the basis of my previous visit. Today, I'm the only customer and the benevolent bartender indulges me with an hour's top-up to my battery, while I indulge him with the purchase of two coffees and a reasonable tip for his trouble. I later do a bit of research and conclude that my top-up probably added about 5p to the pub's electricity bill.

The rain has resumed as The Beast and I get back on the road and I elect not to stop and search for various historic mileposts and other landmarks as I head north along the old Roman road of Wicker Street – I reckon I'm now running half an hour late for my intended meeting at Tebay. Progress, though, is both swift and efficient on a broadly level, well-surfaced road, skirting the western edge of the Howgill Fells and ultimately entering the Lune Gorge, where A-road, motorway, West Coast railway and Roman road are all threaded through the narrow gap gouged by the river.

Just ahead of this conjunction, the road dips to cross the Lune on the historic Salterwath Bridge, whose name suggests this was once a place where salt dealers may have traded their wares. I had hoped to follow a track partially following the line of the old Roman road, on the east side of the gorge here, but the first stretch of this is little more than a footpath and I'll have to complete my final three kilometres or so on the A685.

Salt, of course, was for centuries a valuable commodity, essential to the preservation of foodstuffs. There was a significant salt production industry on Morecambe Bay as far back as Roman times and it's not hard to imagine these salt traders travelling inland to the point at which such routes intersected with the cross-country pathways taken by drovers and others who may well, in turn, have followed tracks first forged by Neolithic traders in Cumbrian axes and other goods. While we can't assert that salt passed this way in Neolithic times, we can say that salt was being produced on the Atlantic seaboard of France in the fourth and third millennia BC. Perhaps of even more relevance is the recent discovery of evidence of salt production on the Yorkshire coast, near Skinningrove. A recent paper[1] published in the journal, *Antiquity*, details the finding of a Neolithic saltern, or salt production site and a brine storage pit at a long-term archaeological dig at Street House, near Loftus. It dates the site to between 3800 and 3700 BC. The seawater would have been concentrated by evaporation at a sheltered spot close to the sea and the process completed at the higher site. Who is to say that similar salt production did not take place here on the west coast and very possibly on Morecambe Bay, where salt production certainly was practised in later years?

I note on my left the visible remains of the Roman fort of Borrowbridge and ponder briefly if an associated civilian settlement, or *vicus*, may have witnessed such trade 1,800 or more years ago. It was only quite recently that a lidar (ground laser radar) survey confirmed that the Roman road struck off eastward from here, crossing Crosby Ravensworth Fell and ultimately bisecting another Roman artery at Kirkby Thore, then to scale the Pennines to Whitley Castle, where excavation at a pre-Roman Bronze Age burial site recently yielded the only known examples of Beaker pottery in the North Pennines, not to mention gold jewellery.

For no better reason than not having rechecked the map, I take a right turn before the road dips beneath the railway and motorway. It turns out to be a cul-de-sac serving only a railway maintenance yard, which matters only because it has sliced a crucial 500 metres off my battery range. This proves critical as The Beast suddenly and without warning transfers to Low Power mode just as I recross the Lune and start the climb up the long ribbon that is Tebay's main street. It is with relief that I reach The Cross Keys Inn with that tiny flicker of residual energy still easing my progress.

Tebay is not a village that shoulders easily the descriptor of 'pretty'. It's not that it's ugly or without interesting buildings: the Cross Keys for one is an old coaching inn boasting 500 years of history and a ghost with an alleged taste for stealing make-up. More recently it's had a bit of a chequered past, having been acquired out of liquidation a few years ago, only for the new owners to find themselves having to deal with all the implications of a pandemic.

'Straggling' seems to be the most oft applied adjective when writing about Tebay and, when you count in Old Tebay to the north with its motte and bailey castle, it is an apt one. But, to be fair, if you had mountains to your east and west wouldn't you end up straggling north to south? My lodgings at the Cross Keys are a new room in the attractively managed gardens to the rear of the pub and, having bounced him down the steps to the rear of the pub, I'm invited to permit The Beast to share my bedroom, which has a pleasant enough little balcony to the front. I quickly fill every inch of its wooden railings with wet clothing in the hope that the evening sun may work its wonders before dipping down behind the fells that rise above the motorway on the opposite side of the gorge.

Tebay, whose population could previously have been counted on the fingers of two hands, certainly prospered from the arrival of the railways and was once a modestly important junction, with the trans-Pennine line from Darlington joining it deep in the gorge below the hotel. Deprived of its station back in the 60s, the village nonetheless still boasts a Railway Club, reflecting the days when railway maintenance was still carried out in-house, before the creation of the ill-fated Railtrack. Four private sector rail workers died near Tebay in 2004 when they were struck by a runaway maintenance truck at night. The owner of the maintenance company and his crane operator were both convicted of manslaughter and health and safety breaches.

If the railway is all but invisible and unheard from the Cross Keys, the same, unfortunately, cannot be said of the M6, which projects an uninterrupted drone day and night from its lofty position on the opposite hillside. It is the only blight upon this otherwise thoroughly pleasant country inn. I reflect that railway noise is generally quite easy to tolerate because it comes and goes, whereas motorways pump out constant noise pollution.

I continue my endeavours to dry out my various pieces of kit, including my phone, which I leave for a few minutes propped on a pillow in the full blast of the hair dryer on its Death Valley setting. When I return from having now soaked another pair of socks by walking minus shoes on the artificial turf on my balcony, it is to find that the 'water detected' message on the screen has been replaced by a jet black display and a picture of a throbbing red thermometer, warning me that the gadget has overheated and that I'll now have to wait for it to cool down. Honestly, I think, there's just no pleasing some people!

A few minutes after my own arrival comes that of my artist colleague and her husband in their newly furbished camper van. It is our first opportunity to meet face to face and talk about which of

Cumbria's many stone circles may merit her attention. Alex turns out to have an Allen key that fits the adjuster on my slightly bent dérailleur, my own set annoyingly being without this particular size.

I'm fed well outdoors at the Cross Keys and, inside, find myself chatting to a chap called Nod, who's a stonemason's assistant who also buys and sells 'hippy stuff' at music festivals. Neither of us can easily remember right now when such activity was last permitted. Nod boasts a goatee beard and ponytail and his girlfriend is the daughter of a Nigerian diplomat, he tells me, to illustrate his contention that Tebay is actually quite a cosmopolitan and outward-looking place. I wonder out loud if many Romani would pass this way, bound for the annual horse fair at Appleby, and Nod says he recalls how, as a kid, his parents' house was a popular rendezvous for travelling people of all kinds.

Sharing a couple of tales with Nod of various nomadic people I've known myself, I reflect that putting down roots may or may not be hard-wired into the human psyche. While some of us may be content merely to make an annual journey of discovery to new places, others feel constrained by the demands of living within four walls. Inevitably, those ancient Beaker People spring to mind and I can but marvel at their bravery in setting off with their goods across unmapped lands and uncharted seas to arrive, here, in the northern half of an island off the continent of Europe. Indeed, it appears that these people came in some numbers and settled as far north as northern Scotland though not, it seems, in Orkney.

As Nod and I immerse ourselves in ever more random topics, I'm curious to know whether local folk here still regard themselves as Westmorlanders or if they'll settle these days for being Cumbrians. Westmorland, of course, was once a proud county in its own right, with Appleby its ceremonial county town, though Kendal was its administrative centre. In 1974, people a long way from the North of England created a new local government map with but scant regard for local sensibilities. In these parts, this meant the absorption of Westmorland into the new county of Cumbria, which also took in the Furness area of Lancashire (including the southern Lake District) and a big chunk of the old West Riding of Yorkshire, including Dentdale and Sedbergh.

Prior to this, the Yorkshire Dales National Park had been designated entirely within the bounds of that old county, so from 1974 parts of the Yorkshire Dales suddenly found themselves in Cumbria. Then, in 2016, the Yorkshire Dales and Lake District parks were both extended by some 188 square miles, almost up to either side of the M6. This means now that much of what was Westmorland, including Barbondale and the limestone plateaux north of Tebay, is now in the Yorkshire Dales National Park, prompting this body to reinvent the moniker 'The Westmorland Dales' on its signage.

'Oh yes, we're Westmorland, all right,' Nod says. 'Very much. We look towards Appleby.' He goes on to tell me how Westmorland itself had its divisions and cites how the weather can change abruptly at a place called Bents Corner. 'The temperature can drop five degrees,' he says. I make the error of failing to elicit from him precisely where said corner is, assuming it be a point in the Lune valley beyond which the sea air does not readily penetrate. Subsequently, I seek guidance from readers of *The Cumberland and Westmorland Herald* and learn that he is referring to Bents farm, near Newbiggin-on-Lune, over towards Kirkby Stephen. I'm slightly surprised that this topographically inauspicious dot on the map should be such a determinant of the local micro-climate and conclude it must be all tied up with the flow hither and thither of air across the Pennines: the same conjunction of sometimes very different types of air mass as is responsible for the local Helm wind.

Such is the stuff of bar-room craic and it's been a real treat to indulge in inconsequential talk in a manner reminiscent of pre-pandemic days. I retire to my room feeling the warm glow of interaction with random strangers once more. I tumble into sleep to the tuneless lullaby of lorries on the M6 across the valley.

* * *

The Gamelands Stone Circle is just a few kilometres from Tebay, not far from the pretty village of Orton, with its craft chocolate factory. Unusually among the circles on my itinerary, it has been the subject of archaeological investigation recently, as part of a project by the Westmorland Dales Landscape Partnership, supported by the Heritage Lottery Fund. I'm looking forward to seeing Gamelands 'in the flesh': the online presentation I saw, for sure, would not have been able to do it justice.

The consensus is that Gamelands should be pronounced Gamm-ee-lands, after the twelfth-century landowner, Gamel de Pennington. It sits beneath the limestone escarpment at the southern edge of Crosby Ravensworth Fell, very possibly on an old watercourse, just below the surface. It comprises forty substantial boulders in a rough circle, one of them of local limestone and the others mostly of the distinctive pink speckled Shap granite. The latter are a common feature of the landscape round about, having been strewn widely as the ice sheet that once covered Shap Fell retreated at the end of the last Ice Age. None of the boulders, then, would have needed to be dragged too far. The recent survey has revealed that some of the 'granite' boulders may in fact be sandstone.

Today this is what's known as a recumbent circle, or one in which the stones are lying flat rather than upright. They may at one time have stood upright and I'm reminded of the words of Mark Edmonds, in Orkney, when he proclaimed that these circles were, by and large, intended to be essentially temporary structures.

Gamelands, unlike Casterton yesterday, is not blessed with a prominent position in the landscape: it is substantially lower than the fell that rises to the north, and no higher than the flat fields to the south. All the more reason, then, to infer that the nearby spring line and water not far below ground may have been factors in its siting. However, some archaeologists have argued that these circles were sited with great care in a way that enabled them almost to reflect the features of the surrounding landscape, with Long Meg and Her Daughters, near Penrith, and Castlerigg, near Keswick, particular cases in point. The prominence of Great Asby Scar, to the north of Gamelands and the more distant fells, have tempted speculation that this may have also been the case here. I clamber onto one of the boulders, with more difficulty than I've anticipated, to get a better impression of the circle and its setting, still holding their own above the unmown pasture.

Another potential factor of which I am acutely aware is that it may well have been sited on an ancient trading route, leading from the Cumbrian axe factory via Shap Fell and on eastward to the upper Eden Valley, where early traffic may well have taken the route traversing Mallerstang Edge into Wensleydale and on down to the Vale of York. The Mallerstang route was later adopted to become 'Lady Anne Clifford's Way' – an early coach route used by the said Lady Anne when visiting the various castles she inherited after a long legal battle.

Of course, I'm not suggesting that the trade in Cumbrian axes would ever have been so vast as to demand the construction of its own road network – merely that we can say with some certainty that these axes were transported across the Pennines by this and indeed other routes. Who knows what other goods might have been traded this way? We know that salt was an important commodity as early as Roman times, but we know that its properties as a preservative were known long before that, so who is to say that salted fish and meat, the latter perhaps hunted in the large areas of uncleared forest that remained in the mountains, was not traded throughout the area. Later, Beaker pottery and other household artefacts may have made a trans-Pennine journey in the opposite direction.

What is not too clear is what that trans-Pennine traffic may have looked like... Just as no Neolithic boat remains have ever been found, so neither do we have clear evidence as to whether those working the fields may have used cattle as beasts of burden, perhaps dragging roughly-made sleds, it being almost certain that they did not enjoy the use of anything even vaguely resembling a wheel. It seems more than likely that, by the time the Beaker People began to arrive with their cargo of pots, they would have domesticated ponies to help them. Indeed, research into horse remains found at various sites, including one on the northern edge of Morecambe Bay, leads Laura Kaagan, of University College, London, to suggest that the horse was reintroduced to Britain in the late-Neolithic Beaker period.[2]

Cumbrian fell ponies still lead a semi-feral life on the fells, particularly around Tebay, and the breed most likely dates back to Roman times. It might be a stretch to talk of earlier origins, but equally the kind of animal that might have served these Beaker traders over long distances would perhaps have been not too dissimilar. Indeed, equally, we can infer that substantial wooden boats must have existed simply because we know that the sea journeys were made and that a lighter structure would not have sustained the kind of loads required, and so we must also infer that the Beaker traders must surely have made use of something a bit more substantial than a backpack. It would be quite a big leap to suggest that rough sleds would have been suitable for long distance carriage of goods; more reasonable to think of smaller, lighter boats, which could have been carried around rapids and shallows on otherwise navigable rivers, such as the Eden.

Another suggestion that I find intriguing is that 'traders' did not necessarily transport their wares over long distances. Rather, goods, such as salt and stone axe rough-outs, may have made their journeys via series of relatively short stages, perhaps being swapped and bartered at locations where paths may have crossed. Kate Sharpe, of Durham University, in her 2015 paper, *Connecting the dots – Cupules and communication in the English Lake District*, shows how the intersection of ancient routes appears to coincide with the presence of cup and ring markings. If I permit my imagination to roam a little: might trading 'porters' have set out with instructions to carry their axe rough-outs, Pony Express-style, to a specific marked location at which they might be either passed on or traded with a porter walking the subsequent stage of the route.

The Gamelands boulders themselves would almost certainly have been dragged on crude sleds from where they had been dumped, as glacial erratics, at the end of the last Ice Age. The one other boulder is of equally accessible limestone and a few stones are missing, though one contributor to the *Megalithic Portal* suggests some may have been used to support a barn a kilometre or so away. Tom Clare, in his comprehensive work, *Prehistoric Monuments of the Lake District*, suggests that ploughing at some point led to the loss of two or three stones from the circle.

Recent survey work coordinated by the Yorkshire Dales National Park as part of the Westmorland Dales Landscape Partnership project employed a variety of modern techniques to reaffirm the earlier suggestions that the stones of the circle did indeed originally sit on an embankment, around two metres wide, but which is no longer easily visible.

The thing about Gamelands is that it speaks not through its dramatic location – for this it has not – but through its undeniable substance: that it has remained largely undisturbed for a few thousand years is down to the sheer bulk of its boulders, whose quartz fragments today twinkle in the morning sun.

I had considered heading north from Gamelands onto the limestone plateau of Great Asby Scar, where there are the remains of numerous burial cairns. The remains of ancient settlements dot both the limestone and the lusher valleys that nibble into it, reinforcing the conclusion that the substance of Gamelands is no more than a reflection of the importance of the surrounding landscape. Today, the rough track remains extremely wet and the going is not going to be easy. My decision to instead continue to strike on westward is tinged with doubt and some regret.

In another project under the auspices of the Westmorland Dales Landscape Partnership, Hannah Kingsbury, Community Heritage Officer at the Yorkshire Dales National Park, led a three-week survey of Great Asby Scar, which revealed the existence of some three hundred potential 'new' archaeological sites, many of which would, for sure, have been linked in some way with Gamelands.

The Beast and I make swift progress to Orton, and on across the open fell for a couple of kilometres to where the road is crossed by my old friend, Wicker Street, the Roman highway north from Tebay to Kirkby Thore and Whitley Castle. The 'road' here is little more than a grassy pathway through the heather, but it's easy riding and I'm soon at the highest point of Crosby Ravensworth Fell. I do love Westmorland's limestone landscape, which has a different look and feel to that of the hillier Yorkshire Dales, to the south. Both limestone landscapes bear evidence of ancient human activity, though this is not to say that humans were more active in these relatively inhospitable lands. Rather, it may be more a reflection of the fact that, unwelcoming as they are to agricultural activity other than rough grazing, they have been left relatively undisturbed. On the Westmorland limestone fells, successive eras of human occupation came and went, with

Iron Age and Roman remains as evident as earlier Neolithic and Bronze Age. Indeed, as I follow Wicker Street, I reflect that only a few miles to the east was the location of the discovery of the Crosby Garrett Roman Helmet, among the most intact such pieces of headwear ever found on these shores (Tullie House museum, in Carlisle, lost out in a bidding war when the helmet sold for £2.3 million in 2010, though it subsequently negotiated the right to exhibit the piece from time to time).

On the high heather moor, the tracks divide near a hut that's obviously to do with grouse moor management, but my attention is better captured by lapwing and curlew and the occasional skylark as the sun teases me in the still unseasonably tepid air. As I take stock of my precise location against the map, one thing is immediately apparent: the moor is crisscrossed by far more numerous tracks than the measly two-plus-Wicker-Street that have made it onto the large scale OS map. I am trying to locate a small stone circle above the headwaters of Crosby Gill and close to a limestone scar I can see ahead of me. I choose the route that best corresponds to the direction I need to take and cycle towards the limestone. As I proceed, I notice a field of large boulders below me to my right and suspect this may be my intended 'quarry', if you'll pardon the possible pun. I skirt the edge of the limestone to the right and drop down towards the boulder field, only to find that it is just that and no more: a field strewn with large glacial erratics. I return to the limestone and search all around it for the missing stone circle, also known as White Hag, but to no avail. It feels like searching for a needle in a haystack or, as I shall come to adapt the proverb for my own circumstances, like searching for a stone circle on a limestone pavement.

Eventually, after a great deal more searching and lugging The Beast through and around the limestone I come upon a substantial limestone enclosure, which may or may not be the nearby White

Hag Cairn. In principle, it should be easy to find the eleven-stone circle from here, but I am unable to do so. In my defence I quote the oracle, Tom Clare: 'Unlike Wicker Street the White Hag stone circle is easily missed.' Frustrated and annoyed I may be, but I am conscious that I have much ground yet to cover today, starting with the riches of Shap. Once again, as I begin the gentle, greasy ride down off the fell, evidence of early settlement is all around – field patterns and more cairns, begging the question as to precisely what activity took place here. Can we infer, for example, that the areas around the limestone scars may have been cleared of woodland for summer grazing? It feels like a huge empty canvass upon which the artist has done no more than pencil in a few key features while the completed whole is nowhere other than inside his or her head.

The Oddendale Bronze Age circles are the first of a number I plan to visit in and around the village of Shap itself, all of them seemingly dicing with death as massive quarries encroach from all sides. Most of these quarries are for limestone, with the most visible of these being the Tata quarry, near Hardendale, and its associated works just to the south of Shap itself. Also in the more central area is Armstrong's quarry, where the archetypal pink granite is sourced to be used for building or (the poorer quality stone) aggregate.

The Oddendale circles should be easy to find, standing as they do close to a junction of two tracks. So my heart sinks when I see no clear indication as to precisely where to look for them. Applying intuition, I park The Beast and follow a rough track through the heather till, lo and behold, not one, not two, not three, but four circles! Two of these are concentric and comprise the principal monument, but there is also a smaller, rougher double circle, just to the north of the main enterprise and this is surely the feature also described by Tom Clare. The outer main circle is more than 26 metres in diameter and comprises thirty-four distinctive boulders of Shap granite. The inner circle is a quarter of the size and made up of twenty-three smaller granite boulders which may have formed a cairn, at which older records suggest burning may have taken place. This inner circle appears to have stood upon a raised platform. Visitors to the *Megalithic Portal* have also noted outlying stones to north and south, which are certainly visible, and I speculate that these might have been signposts or pointers to what was surely a significant site of communal activity. I walk up to highest, western-most, point of the complex and climb onto a recumbent stone, the better to take everything in. I imagine returning in August, when the heather will be a riot of whites and purples. My sunken heart has risen again and come alive, throbbing with the realisation that I have hitherto scarcely shared in the riches that are Cumbria's ancient landscapes. My pulse quickens in anticipation of so much more to come. The stone circles are believed to have replaced earlier timber structures. This is surely my best circle visit yet.

Substantially buoyed by both having located Oddendale *and* found it to be good, I head north through the road system created explicitly for the extraction of stone: that same stone unto which our ancestors were in such thrall. It's barely two kilometres to my next location: a cairn at Iron Hill, above Hardendale. I pass the vast lake left behind by the older upper workings of Hardendale Quarry and take a grassy drove road up the hill. Clare notes various nineteenth-century references to three, perhaps even four separate stone circles. Most of the stones are, however, within a substantial 'modern' walled enclosure, making it difficult to determine precisely what is there. Clare also notes an early reference to the finding of a bronze dagger nearby, though there is no information as to where it may eventually have turned up. All that said, the stones represent another substantial monument.

I reflect that the huge quarry lake below the site possesses a kind of easy tranquillity. It is a depression where once there was a hill. We do not know precisely what other remnants of Neolithic and Bronze Age Shap may have vanished with the hill but we do know that there was a timber circle beneath a ring cairn, which was excavated in 1997 prior to the extension of the quarry. There may also have been a crouched skeleton. My final circle before reaching Shap itself is at Castlehowe Scar and turns out to be a little bit of an anti-climax. On private farmland, but nonetheless accessible, it comprises of two small arcs, suggestive of a burial cairn, each of five stones, and an eleventh stone, set slightly apart. Clare suggests that some of the stones are no longer in their original locations. I am just a little underwhelmed.

I descend into Shap at its north end: Shap is the archetypal ribbon settlement, extending for a couple of kilometres along the old A6. In days gone by, drivers would seek shelter here if the weather worsened over the Shap summit, but these days it is bypassed by the M6, and West Coast Main Line trains thunder through without stopping, as has been the case since the station was a relatively late Dr Beeching closure in 1968. So today the village is still in some ways looking for its contemporary purpose in life: some of its buildings are grand old Westmorland; others are more recent and a bit down at heal, though a global pandemic never helps. Its most incongruous shop is the New Balance sports footwear factory outlet, which perhaps draws its trade from people who decide it's just too much to drive further up the M6 to the outlet shopping at Gretna. I did once stay in Shap overnight at a modest bed and breakfast while walking a long-distance route I had planned from Pateley Bridge to Wastwater. That trip did rather sow the seeds for my later fascination with walking routes that cross the grain of the country, rather than following its more natural north-south orientations. My most recent such walking adventure was to walk from Settle to Carlisle, roughly following the route of the iconic railway. More recently, however, that interest has evolved into covering distance faster and more efficiently in the company of The Beast…

My plan on reaching Shap had been to head west of the village to where a number of standing stones can be seen on the map. At this point I had yet to fully research what might perhaps be seen as the crowning glory of Shap's Neolithic and Bronze Age landscape: the location of a once monumental stone avenue to rival that of Avebury. The very name of the village actually comes from *hjáp*, 'a pile of stones' in Old Norse, which is, presumably, precisely what the Vikings found upon their arrival. Today I quickly establish that the rights of way to the various standing stones are not accessible by The Beast but make a note to make a return visit on foot.

Instead, I return to the village's main drag in search of refreshment and find The Crown, just down the road from the aforementioned New Balance outlet. There are just two customers as I enter and these seem to be on close terms with the landlord and landlady, who happily permit me to plug in my battery for a good recharge. I enjoy an excellent homemade tomato and basil soup and take a peripheral interest in the conversation. My fellow guests are a couple of motorcyclists of early middle age who, prompted by the strange circumstances of a global pandemic, have recently decided to tie the knot after some years.

On this subject, the landlord suddenly proclaims that a local lad had died in an accident on the A6, 'just a few weeks sin' … he were, not to put too fine a point on it, decapitated.'

I'm wondering what this might have to do with the price of fish or the prevalence of COVID, when he adds: 'And you know what, because he'd had a positive test less than a month before, they recorded him as having died of COVID…' I say something like 'no kidding' while organising this in my brain into a drawer marked Apocryphal Stories. Given that any fatal road accident will trigger an inquest, it seems deeply unlikely that such a death could conceivably be categorised as COVID-related. Only when I come to write up the conversation and check the procedures online does it appear that this might actually have been possible. Indeed, it seems that the Government shortened the time after a positive test during which a death might still be recorded as COVID-related to 28 days precisely because random unrelated deaths, like road accidents, were getting scooped into the broader gross figure. Shortening the post-COVID period, then, may have been no more than attempt to compensate for the unfortunate inclusion in the figures of the likes of young motorists who have been unfortunately decapitated.

I make another unsuccessful attempt after lunch to locate features towards the southern end of the former ceremonial avenue before heading south down the A6 towards what remains of Kemp Howe, once a large stone circle marking the terminus of said avenue. Curiously the OS map *appears* to show Kemp Howe as standing to the west of the A6, while the railway is to the east.[3] Given that it is widely known that the stone circle was largely obliterated by the arrival of the railway, this feels impossible.

Indeed, I locate the remains of Kemp Howe – an arc of half a dozen substantial granite boulders at the foot of the railway embankment – in a field beside said line. I guess we have to look at what happened here in the context of the times. The Victorian Age is symbolised by a firm belief not only in the greatness of Britain but in the ability of British people to triumph over nature in the pursuit of a greater future. In such times, lines of rough stones – however carefully and lovingly they may have been arranged – represented the past and not the brave, new and exciting world.

* * *

I make my promised return to Shap a few weeks later and begin with a return to Kemp Howe, where I discover a large pebble tucked down the side of one of the boulders. It has been painted deep red and has a pattern of wavy leg-like symbols around its perimeter and a curly, three-legged, swastika-style motif in pink at the centre. Remember that the swastika has a long history of positive symbolic associations predating its appropriation by the Nazis as a symbol of the 'Arian race'. I tuck it back in where I found it.

I go back up the road to the village, taking note along the way of the large number of huge boulders that have found their way into garden walls. A mum with a pushchair detects I'm unsure exactly where I want to go and directs me up a lane, which leads in due course to the impressive Goggleby Stone, a standing stone, around two metres high, in the middle of a field, whose shape is somewhat reminiscent of a flint axe head. It is set in concrete, having been re-erected in the 1970s after it had fallen. Tom Clare pictures the process in his *Prehistoric Monuments of the Lake District*, noting that he had excavated the foundations himself. Historic England notes that 'a flint scraper, one piece of chert and one chert flake were found amongst rubble used for packing around the stone's base'.

It's worth quoting the Historic England listing in a little more length: 'Shap stone alignment survives well and is a rare example of this class of monument in Cumbria. It is exceptionally long and lies close to other prehistoric monuments – notably Skellaw Hill bowl barrow and Shap stone circle. It thus indicates the importance of this area in prehistoric times and the diversity of monument classes to be found here. The monument will contribute to the study of the ceremonial function and date of stone alignments and other spatially associated monuments.' My observation here is the rather obvious one that if the Shap avenue 'survives well', I'd hate to imagine what a less successful survivor might look like.

Another toppled stone is embedded in the boundary wall a couple of fields further north and is adorned with what appear to be cup and ring marks. I take a walled lane to reach Skellaw

Hill burial mound, towards the northern end of the 2.4-kilometre avenue. The first part of the lane is easy walking as it is used by a farmer to move cattle. The latter part is heavily overgrown and soaking wet, and I regret not having bothered to don waterproofs.

Clare sees Skellaw Hill as a central feature of the wider landscape, suggesting that it was the focus for more than one line of stones. Back in the seventeenth century there was a great deal more to be seen – Lady Lowther even produced in 1776 a sketch of the avenue, which survives. Clare quotes one William Stukeley's account of what he found in the early eighteenth century, including an avenue '70ft broad, composed of very large stones, set at equal intervals'. He continues: 'It seems to be closed at this [the south] end, which is on an eminence and near a long flattish barrow, with stone works upon it; hence it proceeds northward to the village which intercepts the continuation of it… Though its journey be northward, yet it makes a very large curve, or arc of a circle, as those at Abury [sic], and passes over a brook too.'

He suggests that the stones on either side of the avenue were spaced at intervals of '35ft, half the breadth of the avenue'. He notes a variety of other circles and ovals of smaller stones and remarks that the avenue appears to have narrowed towards the stone circle at the southern end, Kemp Howe.

The Historic England listing notes a variety of boulders now within garden and other walls and places the northern end of it all at the Small and the Large Thunder Stones. I content myself with standing beneath Skellaw Hill and following the line of sight south towards Kemp Howe, all the while saddened that, contrary to Historic England's assertion, so little of this hugely significant landscape survives, leaving us only to surmise its true purpose.

A comprehensive local Shap website includes an interesting reference to the work of the antiquarian, Rev J Simpson, who was the Vicar of Shap in the middle of the nineteenth century.

'He described the avenue and gave an intriguing account, writing that from tradition there was a stone circle 130 metres in diameter with a large stone at the centre.'[4] This was presumably Kemp Howe, before its near obliteration. 'It's said that this huge centre stone was cut into seven pairs of "Yat Stoops" or gateposts. The Reverend Simpson was also something of a pioneer in the field of prehistoric rock art and was the first person to describe and draw the cup and ring marking on the Goggleby and Asper's Field stones.' It goes on to say that Aubrey Burl (one of the leading authorities on Neolithic monuments) describes these stones as 'mistakenly claimed to be cup marked', but goes on to say that this is 'an opinion which is not shared by Stan Beckensall who describes them thus "the symbols on the Goggleby Stone are a shallow wide cup mark with a smaller one beneath it on the vertical face of the stone".' Most archaeologists in the North would defer without question to the opinions of Dr Beckensall on matters cup and ring…

On Kemp Howe, the website suggests that the railway embankment was simply laid on top of the pre-existing stone circle. So, much of the circle may actually still be there, albeit beneath tonnes of railway ballast. Later, when the quarry sidings were installed to the east of the track, the remaining eastern perimeter of the circle was lost forever.

* * *

From Kemp Howe I strike west, the eastern valleys of the Lakeland massif luring me towards their shadowy presence. We tend to think of the western Lake District as 'the quiet side', but that is to quite forget the lonely valleys on this eastern fringe, exemplified by Wet Sleddale, four-square in my sights as I leave the A6. Technically, these valleys lie within the rain shadow cast by the central Lakeland fells. All things are relative, however, and Wet Sleddale most likely 'does what it says on the tin', as they say, hence the construction of a reservoir here in the 1960s to supplement supplies to Manchester from nearby Haweswater.

Wet Sleddale is, however, rather better known as the location for the cult film *Withnail and I* than for the supply of water to a thirsty city. The very wet location for the 1987 film by Bruce Robinson is Sleddale Hall, which, despite its unforeseen fame through film, began to fall into ruin across thirty-odd years. The film was, of course, inspired by Robinson's own experience as a hard-up actor in North London, which is mirrored by that of the characters Withnail and Marwood. Grant earned an Oscar nomination for his portrayal of Withnail and had been out of work himself for nine months when the role came along.

It long seemed a shame that the hall's rise to fame as Crow Crag, a key 'character' in the film about an 'accidental holiday', hadn't resulted in it being lent a new lease of life. This did eventually happen in 2011 when, after much to-ing and fro-ing, it was ultimately bought by Tim Ellis, an architect from Canterbury, who was able to secure the necessary permit from the national park authority confirming that the building still remained 'a house' after years of dereliction. Having renovated the property at the head of the valley, he now permits fans of the film to participate in *Withnail and I* events, including occasional outdoor screenings.

If you are not among the fortunate few able to get tickets for such shebangs, you can still take a pleasant walk around the reservoir, passing the hall, or up onto the lonely fells. Today, however, I am leaving the road to Crow Crag behind, and turning right onto the United Utilities concrete highway, which sweeps round the foot of the dale and neighbouring Swindale all the way to Haweswater, broadly following the line of the underground aqueducts that transport water to Manchester.

A sign warns me not to use the road because of 'subsidence' but I figure I should be able to halt The Beast before we plummet down any hidden gaps. Indeed, I meet enough cars travelling in both directions to suggest that any subsidence is nominal at most. I'm looking back across towards Skellaw Hill and the Shap Avenue, with the ruins of Shap Abbey, on the banks of the River Lowther, in my foreground. The map tells me I should also see earthworks between me and the abbey, but these are too indistinct to recognise easily.

The way ahead may be no Yellow Brick Road, but the off-white concrete ribbon contours gracefully and comfortingly towards my destination. Such is the volume of water passing from Haweswater that the aqueducts beneath me do not need always to flow downhill, Manchester's water being effectively syphoned up and down on its journey south. It sweeps gracefully into the foot of Swindale, where a single farmhouse is carefully positioned to create a perfect sunlit valley vista beneath the backdrop of dark fells.

The road rises gently to a crossroads at a modest summit where a conventional public road sign directs me to the right. A few minutes later I arrive at The Crown and Mitre, a sturdy traditional pub opposite the tree-lined churchyard at Bampton Grange. Finding no one at home, I secrete most of my luggage beneath a bench in the back garden and head off towards Four Stones Hill.

My destination here is not listed as a stone circle, though the name rather suggests that there were once more than the two stones now extant. 'Four stones' might well suggest that there was indeed once a more complete ring but, in any event, what seduces me is the promised view from the site, which those who have seen it describe as among the finest in the eastern Lakes, with its panoramic vista across Haweswater and towards the lofty fells at the head of the valley.

I retrace my tyre tracks for a short distance before striking off right on a quiet road, which inexorably climbs up the foothills of this northern shoulder overlooking Haweswater. The map shows the metalled road expiring at Windy Hill, just short of a farm called Drybarrows, whence it becomes a track of some sort. There's a public right of way comprising the third side of a triangle, but this is not cyclable and I decide to take a chance on the farm track. This proves to be a metalled road leading directly towards the farm and its large yard of cracked concrete. Dogs bark, but there's no sign of human life beyond the sign, which states firmly that there is no right of way through the yard. I take my chances, cycle through, and emerge onto the open fell.

Here I face a choice: to take the steep and stony route directly up the shoulder of the fell, or a gentler way to the left. I try the latter before commencing a more thorough reconciliation on the OS map on my phone. It's clear that the steeper, more direct route is the correct one and so I backtrack. Any anxiety that The Beast might not be up to such a steep and rough ascent is quickly dispelled as he makes short work of the initial climb onto a gently graded plateau. The track weaves through peat hags and puddles until it meets a slow-flowing beck at right angles. The ducks swimming at the fording point should have given me a clue but I nonetheless ride straight into the water, aiming for the exit perhaps three metres further on. As the water rises, I lift my feet from the pedals and stretch my legs out to either side. It must be more than half a metre deep at one point and I find myself hoping that The Beast's motor casing is more than merely splash-proof.

I add 'if ducks can swim it's too deep to ford' to my list of new proverbs and keep my fingers firmly crossed as I continue my ascent, now up a steady, if quite steep, grassy slope. I am firmly committed to the lower gear ratio but the machine copes well. The map implies I should veer left as I near the summit and so I make a short descent to an area that proves to be mostly sphagnum moss: no place for any self-respecting cyclist. I abandon The Beast and strike off on foot. Then, rounding a modest summit, I find myself gazing at two standing stones, the left one slightly toppled. Together they frame an almost perfect vista of Haweswater far below, beneath a near cloudless azure sky.

The pure magnificence of the location, in near-perfect weather, soon overwhelms my incredulity at not having had to search interminably for the stones. I quickly observe that the stones stand at the westernmost lip of a level plateau, all but perfectly round and standing slightly higher than its surroundings. I walk its perimeter but observe no signs of the two 'missing' stones nor any evidence of the past presence of any other monoliths. By the time I complete my journey around Cumbria's ring of stone circles I shall remain open-minded as to the true identity of Four Stones Hill. On the one hand, as I have said, the location shares many of the attributes of smaller stone circles, in particular, its circular symmetry and slightly raised elevation. On the other, the appearance of the two remaining stones – although they are smaller than many other monolith pairs I shall encounter along the way – has powerful echoes of standing stones that mark the entrance to a Neolithic or Bronze Age landscape. Indeed, as I begin my descent to the east, I pass two disturbed burial cairns, one of them quite extensive. Later research reveals that there may also be evidence of a small enclosure lower down the hill to the west with the remains of cairns within its arc.

Before leaving the spot, however, I have to sit awhile simply to absorb the view: I place my feet before me, between the standing stones and close to a small pool of water, and take a picture for Instagram. I'm wearing my red football shoes and the toes of these intrude into the foot of my picture, provoking subsequent comments about a Wicked Witch. The tiny pool in the foreground of the shot shines blue, with fluffy clouds reflected in it, making a curious juxtaposition with the pure blue lake below. I find my mind cast back to my first ever visit to Haweswater, back in my 20s, on the same long-distance walk that had seen me staying overnight in Shap. Specifically, I recall taking a picture with a tarn shining blue in the foreground and a seemingly similarly-sized Haweswater 300 metres below. I think the tarn in question must have been Small Water, if only because there appears to be no route marked on the map to get you up the steep crag that lies behind Blea Tarn onto the Racecourse Hill summit on the High Street ridge, by means of which I was bound for Ambleside via the Kirkstone Inn.

However beautiful Haweswater was back then and, in its unchanging way, however beautiful it is today, it's impossible to talk about this 'lake' without bringing in the story of the lost settlements of Measand and Mardale Green. Back then, the lake was only about 4km long and was all but divided into two parts – High Water and Low Water – by a peninsula at Measand. Work on damming the valley began after a controversial Act of Parliament was passed in 1929, and was completed six years later. Its purpose was, as we've previously noted, to secure water supplies for Manchester and it still sates about a quarter of that city's thirst today.

Although, technically, the dam only added about 60 per cent to the length of the lake, it increased its depth by some 29 metres and, if statistics are our thing, it can hold up to 84 billion litres of water. Prior to flooding, both villages were demolished for military practice. Stone and windows from the church were used in the construction of the water take-off tower and bodies in the graveyard were exhumed and taken for reburial at Shap. The late Alfred Wainwright described the loss of Mardale as an act of rape.

Inevitably, as with other drowned communities, stories abound of people hearing the church bells still chiming eerily and the abandoned communities provide popular settings for fiction. From time to time drought raises Mardale Green back to our consciousness and I recall not many years ago wandering the village's abandoned streets and crossing the little bridge between tumbled walls. Last summer city kids camped on the exposed reservoir bed during the summer COVID break, blissfully unaware that they themselves might suffer the fate of the lost villages and disappear beneath the rising waters.

Destroying communities by flooding remains de rigueur across the world, not least in China and Amazonia, though I think Kielder was the last such major event on these shores. The decline of thirsty industries like textiles and chemicals means we need less water and the water companies have, by and large, got rather better at managing wastage, so plans to flood lovely Farndale on the North York Moors, back in my youth, came to nought. It could be argued that Kielder has added to the landscape in a way that the damming of Mardale has not but, for all that, it remains a beautiful and otherwise unspoiled corner of the Lakes. The art deco Haweswater Hotel is hardly a like-for-like replacement of the Dun Bull at Mardale Green, but it does command fine views across the 'lake', while the 'new' road the length of the valley side leads to a parking spot from which you can walk up to any of the many subsidiary ridges that lead ultimately to High Street.

I recall one particularly fine day's walking when *The Guardian*'s 'man in the North', Martin Wainwright, invited a group of us to share in the launch of his book about Alfred Wainwright's (no relation) Coast to Coast walk, taking in Kidsty Pike, after which we toasted the book in the Mardale Inn at Bampton, now closed, possibly permanently, though its ghost lives on online.

On another occasion, Linda and I walked from the head of the 'lake' to see Cumbria's lone golden eagle. Eagles had lived in the valley on and off since the 1950s and had raised sixteen chicks between 1970 and 1996. This particular one arrived with his mate in 2001, but she died three years later. Her mate went on to keep lonely vigil until his own disappearance, presumed dead, in 2016. I recall walking to the viewing location at Riggindale, not far along the eastern shoreline from where I am sitting now. You could just about glimpse the eagle on his perch using an RSPB telescope. I have recently heard it suggested that the RSPB maintained this public vigil so as to protect a breeding pair elsewhere in the area from prying human eyes. I've also heard it suggested that the Lake District is insufficiently fauna-rich to support eagles, which I find a little surprising. Perhaps we don't have the same numbers of mountain hares as may be found in Scotland, but of smaller mammals, I struggle to imagine a shortage. We did use to take our cats to the Lake District sometimes: we have now banned them as they tend to embark on a mad killing spree, suggesting an abundance of small mammals.

Walking down from Four Stones Hill, I quickly realise that one track actually leads directly down to Drybarrows; I could have cycled all the way up to the standing stones. Back in the saddle, I choose a more judicious route to cross the beck at the duck ford but there is no easy way to avoid passing back through the farmyard. So my advice to anyone who seeks to visit Four Stones Hill has to be to stick to the right of way. Sadly that will most likely require you to leave your own 'beast' behind or to see if you can lug it over the stiles on the footpath.

I'm back in Bampton Grange in a trice and so decide to steal a bit of the evening to complete my first task of the following day. I race right past the Crown and Mitre, turning left to follow the road along the foot of Knipe Scar. I pass a notice telling me I am now on Lowther Estate land and reflect that this must be among the largest landholdings in all Cumbria, as I know that it extends northward for some miles.

My evening destination is intended to be a small stone circle on the limestone atop Knipe Scar, though I know from online accounts that it is a tricky one to find. I pass a well-mown pathway that rises directly up the face of the scar towards a nick in its lip. It is not marked on the map and I also judge it too steep to cycle, so I head instead through the farm at High Knipe and take the farm track up the fell. Halfway and several gates up, I meet the farmer coming the other way on his quad bike. He informs me that there is no right of way, to which I plead innocence. He's happy for me to proceed, providing I close the gates behind me but tells me a sorry story of being abused by a gang of youths who left all his gates open for his stock to wander. There's been a lot of it about during the pandemic. He warns me that the stone circle can be hard to spot.

Ascending the scar by this route requires me to back-track to where I think the circle should be, not far from where the mown path reaches the top. After quartering the limestone plateau fruit-lessly for 45 minutes or so, I feel I have no alternative but to admit defeat and return to the Crown and Mitre. Here, the landlady tells me she and her husband are selling up and I have visions of this, the only remaining pub in the valley, closing. 'Try running one for fifteen years,' she harrumphs.

So, the pub is really only ticking over as I stay, the bar open only to residents of whom I comprise 50 per cent. The other 50 per cent is an elderly chap from Hexham, a regular guest who's enjoyed a walk to Shap Abbey today. I'm delighted to confirm that the food is excellent, notwithstanding the clock ticking towards the departure of mine hosts. The landlady's husband is a friendly ex-Army chap and he tells me how they thought they had achieved a sale and had gone so far as to organise shipping some of their belongings to Normandie, where they plan to run a business with horses.

Only at the eleventh hour, when much money and effort had been expended, did it emerge that the would-be 'cash' buyers were not such at all and hadn't even begun to look for finance. 'I ask you, who on earth did they think was going to lend them money to buy a pub in the middle of a pandemic?' he sighs, exasperation written across his face. 'I had the devil's own job getting back into the UK when I drove home, as Brexit had happened between times and nobody had the foggiest what rules they were supposed to be applying.'

* * *

I make another attempt to locate the Knipe Scar circle after my return, a few weeks later, to the Shap Avenue. Once again, I find myself quartering the limestone plateau atop the ridge. I am about to accept defeat for a second time when I elect to take a look at the observations of other visitors on the *Megalithic Portal*. One person has posted a picture suggesting that the location of the circle is marked by a single wooden post: a potential indicator that is not made of stone. But it's a big landscape and this discovery need not of itself solve the problem. A few minutes later and I am, once again, feeling a sense that Knipe Scar Stone Circle has done a runner. I climb to the highest vantage on the edge of the limestone pavement. And then, just as I am about to give up hope, my eye falls upon a single wooden post, just about visible above the bracken, about 75 metres away. I pick my way across the clints and grykes of the limestone and then, there it is, an unassuming stone circle, with a raised perimeter of limestone fragments and larger slabs. The tall bracken does not assist in appraising the remains, but there is no question that this is indeed the right place. A single limestone block is at the centre of the 'circle' – I use the inverted commas as the area within the metre-high embankment is actually about 15 metres across in one direction, but only about 11 in the other.

It is a struggle to work out exactly why this construction is where it is: it is set well back from the edge of the scar and hence does not enjoy significant views. However, Clare offers the explanation that the rising, wooded land to the east 'must have looked like a giant long barrow when seen from afar'. This explanation, however, presumes that the 'barrow' was not wooded in ancient times, which feels like a rather bold presumption. As I pick my way back across the limestone, my eye falls upon a magnificently colourful moth: it is a tiger moth, no less, the flying metamorphosis of the caterpillar seen a month previously at the Ring of Brodgar. I do wonder who's bright idea it was to call these magnificent insects tiger moths. It has a bright red head, black thorax and orange tail. Its front wings are white with dark brown shapes, something like a cross between a zebra's markings and those of a cheetah. Its rear wings are orange with big, black spots. Have you ever seen a tiger matching that description?

To some extent the elusive circle at Knipe Scar is part of a broader historic landscape: the remains of a subsequent Iron Age hill fort are on Clare's 'giant barrow', while there's a tumulus on the east-facing slope of the hill. Clare also refers to 'lost circles' at Shapbeck, a couple of kilometres to the south-east, which may have been excavated by the aforementioned Rev Simpson in the nineteenth century.

Historic England's research records state: 'A previously unrecorded stone circle discovered during field walking in 1985 and subsequently excavated. The circle comprises the plough-damaged remains of three concentric rings of stones, surviving up to 0.90m above present ground level. The outer ring has twenty-eight surviving stones and a diameter of c20-50m; eighteen form the second and seven the innermost. A small cairn, possibly added at a later date, overlies the second ring of stones at its south-west limit: no funerary evidence was found with it.' The location of the circles appears to tally with Simpson's previously lost examples. They are but one more element in the giant mysterious jigsaw that is the prehistoric landscape of Shap and its surroundings.

* * *

Day breaks with promise and The Beast and I make rapid progress towards the point at which the Knipe Scar ridge fizzles out around Rosgill. Here we strike out along a so-called BOAT or Byway Open to All Traffic. These are sometimes controversial trackways upon which any vehicle is legally entitled to travel. The status is a legal legacy of other times and often has the contemporary consequence of permitting convoys of Chelsea tractors and other four-by-fours to pass through, often causing immense damage. Excluding such traffic is always a long and complex legal process. But no such issues today as we swish our way through the residual puddles, on towards the thumping and clanging of the huge Sweetholme limestone quarry. We slip across the railway sidings, south along the A6 towards Shap and then over the northbound M6 carriageway, under the southbound, then first track on the left, through a field of stock.

Our destination is Gunnerwell Farm, to meet Geoff and Judith Robinson, proud owners of Gunnerkeld Stone Circle. Geoff used to work at Kirkby Thore gypsum mine and I've been put in contact with the couple by a friend who lives up that way. Most farmers are at best ambivalent about stone circles on their land: note the Bull in Field at Casterton. But Geoff and Judith appear to feel positively blessed at their good fortune.

The farmhouse and yard are classic Westmorland and, despite their quite lofty elevation, they're surrounded by a small woodland, which conjures up the feel of a lowland location rather than a high fell farm. I begin by apologising for my 'back door' approach through the field of stock but am reassured that's no problem by Judith, who comes to the door in a T-shirt that has surely seen better days.

I suggest it might be nice to record a short interview, at which she summons Geoff to keep me company before undertaking her cake deliveries for her. I know from our mutual friend that Judith is big in the WI cake world. I am soon the proud possessor of a sumptuous slice of chocolate sponge and millionaire's shortbread as I'm joined in the cosy cottage garden by Geoff.

The couple are owners of the farm, this having been their ambition on Geoff's retirement, but sheep farming is never an easy or prosperous life. And it's about to get a whole lot harder, says Geoff. In his sights is an impending UK trade deal with Australia and the likelihood of the arrival of cheap Ozzy lamb on our shores. The only way it can be so cheap after it's travelled halfway round the world is if corners are cut on welfare standards, says Geoff, as we begin to dissect the intellectual qualities of the UK Cabinet one by one, only to conclude that there are none. Geoff bemoans that so many of his farming colleagues were seemingly seduced into supporting a Brexit that was never likely to benefit them. For my part, I'm always happy to engage with anyone in any walk of life who does not match the stereotype.

Geoff and Judith would like to diversify a little: specifically, they'd like to provide a parking space, interpretation and public access to their stone circle. They say they've approached English Heritage but encountered little interest. Given that upland farmers have been encouraged to diversify into tourism for years I'd like to think that this need not be the end of the story. I also can't help but wonder if they'd have received the same answer had they been down south somewhere: the disinterest in their ideas feels like just one more insult to add to the systematic destruction through quarrying and the construction of railways, roads and houses that has seen Shap's extensive Neolithic landscape trashed across the last two centuries.

Changing the subject, I ask Geoff if he knows Katy Cropper, the quite famous sheep dog handler. I first knew Katy when I lived at Hawes, in upper Wensleydale, when she was the protegée of Richard Fawcett, a friend and top sheepdog trainer. She was a bit of a wild young woman and a huge character, who claimed male judges always marked her down in sheepdog trials. Years later, in 2014, she featured on Channel 4's *Come Dine With Me* and then, in 2019, on the same channel's match-making show, *Love in the Countryside*, in which the object is to find a mate for lonely farmers. By this time Katy was farming on land near the M6, to the south of Geoff and Judith's. She has a huge sign by the north-bound carriageway, advertising her business. The slightly bizarre thing about this particular episode of *Love in the Countryside* was that one of Katy's suitors turned out to be our decorator, from Newcastle. John could be quite dapper when he swapped his overalls for a suit and tie, even if that may not go down so well in a farmyard. He was often a film extra when not painting or wallpapering. We were disappointed for him when Katy chose instead a chap who'd struck us as a bit of a wide boy, who was unlikely to enjoy farm life. 'That didn't last long,' says Geoff, 'but she's found a new fella since then and she often comes to help out here.'

This new topic of conversation is interrupted by a glamorous new arrival. Judith now sports a smart top, pretty scarf, fresh lippy and carefully coiffed hair. She guides me enthusiastically through the woodland and across the slight depression beside the stone circle. More or less equidistant on the other side of this double circle is the M6. Motorists thundering south who chance to glance left at just right moment will be familiar with Gunnerkeld. Should

I applaud those engineers who at least managed to avoid the circle itself? After all, they could so easily have just used the stones for hard core and blasted right on through it, as did their Victorian predecessors at Kemp Howe.

Nonetheless, I find myself wondering if Gunnerkeld can still exude that feeling of calm serenity so many of us sense when standing within a stone circle and Judith's observations do not disappoint. 'It is strange to imagine with the traffic, but about ten years ago, not long after we first came here, it was a very frosty morning and we were over at the stones. It was very calm, a winter morning, and I just got this feeling… it was almost like there was an aura. It was the strangest feeling but we were looking back towards the farmhouse and it just had this amazing feeling of calm. It was lovely.'

Gunnerkeld is a late Neolithic circle, its outer elliptical ring of nineteen large granite boulders around a raised inner platform, surrounded by a ring of smaller stones. It is not huge – about thirty metres north to south and twenty-four across, while the central platform is about eighteen metres across.

Two large stones to the north side of the outer 'circle' appear to comprise a 'gateway' opening up, for me at least, the intriguing possibility that there may once have been an avenue leading in a more northeasterly direction from Shap towards the Eden Valley stone circles and on up the Pennines at Hartside. I find myself dreaming of a somehow restored Shap landscape enjoying the reputation it surely deserves, as enthusiastic visitors drop in at Gunnerwell farm, there to enjoy Judith's delicious home-made cakes.

Chapter 3

Long Meg and her landscape

Across Eden Vale

I exit Gunnerwell Farm by the 'front door' and begin the descent
from the upland fringe of Shap Fell towards the more gentle pas-
turelands of the Eden Valley. I reach Bedlandsgate Farm and note
the wide gates on the left of the road and the large 'farm buildings'
on the right. A limp orange windsock tells its own story: this is a
small private airfield. I have a soft spot for small airfields and have
flown in and out of many, in both small and very small aircraft,
from microlights to private planes to gyrocopters.

I check the location out online later. It's most likely that this is an unlicensed private airfield, basically for the private use of the owner, though not closed to other traffic. An aerial photograph shows that it possesses two short, mown 'runways', though both are broadly orientated north to south. A little more research tells me that it was the scene of an accident in 2017, when a two-seater Jodel – a French aeroplane similar to the one in which I enjoyed my first light air-craft excursion, in eastern France, aged fourteen – hit turbulence and struck the ground nose-first. The Air Accident Investigation Branch notes that the sixty-seven-year-old pilot turned all the switches off and exited via the canopy and a hole in the fuselage. He was unhurt and, more surprisingly, the aircraft lived to fly again.

All of which is rather by the by... I'm sticking to B-roads here, rather than trying to contrive a route using bridleways or BOATS, and I'm quickly in the village of Newby. I thought I had discovered every pretty Eden Valley village while walking the route of the Settle & Carlisle Railway a year previously, but here is yet another perfect composition of red sandstone and whitewashed cottages, their gardens afire with spring blooms, that would happily grace any picture postcard. I continue through Morland and Cliburn, my sights firmly set on the wooded hill in front of me that is the location of the Center Parcs holiday village, built once again, as it happens, on Lowther Estate land.

My hope is that I'll be able to reach a small cairn circle situated on private land not far from the old Appleby to Penrith railway line. One option might be to take the railway 3km all the way from the road to this circle, called Leacet Hill. However, I find that the railway is clearly marked 'private' as I cross the old line and start the climb up the hill. My next hope is a track marked on the map as heading off to the left, which then intersects with a right of way, which passes within half a kilometre of my target. This, however, turns out to be an active forestry track and there are all manner of vehicles churning it up in a way that would make it impossible to cycle.

Slightly further on, I find a footpath heading off into the woods at the very edge of the Center Parcs village. It's a permissive route granted by said village and is just about wide enough to cycle. Cycling on footpaths is not really allowed but on permissive paths? Of that, I am not sure, but opt to take my chances and swing left to cut back onto the path, the end of which I have already passed. Too late do I spot the stump of a felled tree just protruding from the long grass. I know what is coming, but have no time to prepare myself. My pedal catches the tree stump and I am flung forwards and sideways down the slope, where I land with a thump on my knees, hands and chest.

My first thought is relief that the day has been cold enough for me to wear gloves for that has saved my hands from the fate my knees have quite obviously suffered. I've also taken quite a blow to my chest and, while I most likely won't have broken a rib, I know from experience that bruising one is no laughing matter (quite literally) either. It takes me a minute or two to feel competent to actually lift myself from the ground. When I finally do, shakily, it is with relief that I find that The Beast, bless him, has come out of this rather better than I have. In addition to my sore chest, I am leaking blood from both knees, one rather faster than the other.

In these circumstances, it's always best to get promptly 'back in the saddle' and so I do. The route is for sure a footpath, not a cycleway, but initially – in the absence of any walkers – I can make decent progress. Such progress ends abruptly when the path becomes sandwiched between a collapsing dry stone wall on my left and a tall wire fence on my right. Enthusiastic brambles don't help either. The fence is presumably there to prevent guests from escaping from Center Parcs. I do recall after the resort first opened back in the '90s that you'd sometimes see guests on the main road trying to hitch a lift to Penrith because they found the food too expensive. To be fair, I have to say that I enjoyed my only visit to Center Parcs. We went to the one in Sherwood Forest in the middle of winter and loved it. Nor did we find the food outlets especially pricy.

Back in Cumbria, I shove The Beast the final 50 metres or so to the point at which the wall and security fence part company, and then coast down the winding path to the edge of the forest. It's just a short distance to the riding school, from which a footpath descends through Leacet Plantation. I reckon it should take me near enough to the cairn circle for me to walk the final stretch along the field edge.

I chain The Beast and set off. The plantation is in production and heavy-duty machinery has carved deep ruts with intermittent deep puddles. The path has been pretty much obliterated by the activity, so I make my way warily down the steep hillside to where a gate gives access to a large field, lying between the forest and the old railway line, mentioned earlier. Bright young barley shoots paint the field green, and the sky is now a deceptive blue, suggesting the day is warmer than it is. The odd gull and crow flutter beneath optimistic fair-weather cumulus clouds.

I stick to the very edge of the field and head towards where the circle is marked on the map. Suddenly it looms into view: despite its modest size, it's far more impressive than I'd expected, its chunky perimeter boulders rising from a russet ring of dead bracken. As I get closer, a roe deer leaps dramatically from the centre of the circle, or what's left of it... Forestry has been to Leacet Hill cairn circle as the Lancaster and Carlisle Railway was to Kemp Howe.

Cairn circles are understood to be the remains of burial structures that were likely covered in earth following construction.

This covering then washes away through the centuries, leaving the boulders upstanding. My slight unease at this explanation is that the earth covering appears to have been washed away irrespective of whether or not there is a nearby watercourse. To cut to the chase, what's happened to all that earth?

In the case of Leacet Hill, it does sit slightly higher than the surrounding land, so that may provide the answer. The sun is shining directly upon the circle and the boulders and bracken make this a sheltered and peaceful spot. Four or more thousand or so years on it's difficult to work out why this circle is where it is, but it is of course possible that there were other landscape features now buried beneath forestry and agriculture. Though the circle is strictly 'out of bounds', someone has installed a simple stile at the edge of the plantation and there's a reasonable track along the bottom edge of the forestry, so there's no good reason for anyone not to visit.

Reunited with The Beast, I explore the possibility of completing a partial circumnavigation of Center Parcs, aiming to avoid having to retrace my tyre tracks. Notwithstanding what appears on the map, I encounter only a dead-end and return to the track leading to the stables. A woman and a young girl appear, driving a Romani-style caravan and wearing faces that suggest relief at the partial easing of lockdown: horses are expensive machines to keep running when there's no income coming in.

I return via a winding path through the woodland, thereby avoiding the constricted course between the wall and the Center Parcs defences. For the first time, I see real live holidaymakers beyond the fence and then soon find myself back at my accident ground-zero. Back on Tarmac, I head up and over the modest rise that is Salter Hill, passing beneath the A66 and taking a left along the old Roman road immediately to the north, shortly to enter the driveway to Winderwath Gardens.

Most people looking for a garden to visit in these parts will head for the National Trust's Acorn Bank, with its flower borders and vegetable gardens lovingly tended by an army of volunteers. Once the home of the Yorkshire dialect writer, Dorothy Una Ratcliffe, it's certainly worth a visit. Far fewer folk will trouble to visit Winderwath and, today, I must count myself among that number, my purpose being to seek out the supposed remains of a once substantial stone circle.

The driveway is long and straight and I locate one of the stones about two thirds of the way down to Winderwath House. It's a substantial boulder, whose size may have deterred vandals from lobbing it into the River Eden along with the now missing stones that completed the circle. There's no record as to when, or indeed even if, this destruction may have taken place, but oral memory is, on the whole, quite reliable and so I've no reason to doubt its existence. A second large boulder lies at the edge of the field beyond the substantial hedge that borders the lane.

Later in summer, when time is less pressing, my wife and I return to Winderwath and park up in its cobbled courtyard. This is bordered by barns, stables and what looks like a small gin gang, in which barley may once have been ground by a horse tethered to a pole that rotated around the millstone at the centre of the structure. Finding no one around, we pop some cash in the honesty box and begin to explore the elegant and neatly manicured gardens surrounding the substantial house.

It and the gardens belong to Jane Pollock, third of three daughters of one Hugh Wykeham David Pollock, a former High Sheriff of Westmorland. Jane Pollock was in her seventies at the time of writing and the elder of her sisters was still living in Warwickshire. I would have liked to have met her to acquire a taste of the passion that must underlie the creation and main-tenance of such wonderful gardens, which she is quite happy to share in return for only the most modest 'fee'. In the curious way of these things, while talking matters gardening with the food historian Ivan Day in his remarkable old kitchen at Shap, some weeks later, he mentions Jane Pollock, praising her gardening and conservation interests and mentioning how she had, while on a cruise, formed an unlikely friendship with a very brash woman from Texas, whose drawl sounded like a different tongue alongside Ms Pollock's received pronunciation.

The gently sloping lawns are guarded by a stand of tall trees, including Wellingtonia and Japanese maple, and conclude on the shores of an old mill pond, its surface covered in water lilies. A notice tells you that you're very welcome to picnic in this serene spot. The walls of the house itself are fringed by extensive beds of creeping juniper and I wonder if perhaps Ms Pollock is the owner of a hidden gin still secreted somewhere in the woodland. At the edge of the lawn, a little pavilion appears designed to suggest that the croquet team left in a hurry long ago and won't be returning any time soon.

You have to admire the manner by which William the Conqueror did his conquering… the Romans came, saw and conquered by installing their own overlords and administrators, who were ready to work with local Britonnic tribes, like the Brigantes, when mutually beneficial. William, on the other hand, systematically replaced the old Saxon aristocracy with his own people, bringing into the country an entirely new echelon of society that spoke its own language.

The extraordinary thing about this movement of people is that it is the descendants of these original Norman settlers who still yield much influence here a thousand years later. Winderwath is but the most modest manifestation of this Norman legacy, but Cumbria as a whole boasts many substantial country houses and some quite vast estates, of which more later.

The Normans never wiped out the Anglo-Saxons: they merely subjugated them, squeezed taxes out of them and drafted them into service in kitchens, in which the natives learned that sheep meat was now *mouton*, boar became *porc*, cow meat was *boeuf* and all were washed down not with ale or mead, but *bierre* or *cidre*. Again, one thousand years later, our Germanic language contains more words brought to us by the Normans than by the Angles or the Saxons. And the former still to this day make up the more learned, metaphorical stratum of our language, while the shorter no-nonsense and often cruder alternatives are those of everyday, less refined, speech. Many would go on to argue that the aristocracy looks different from the rest of us, even after all this time. They certainly dress that way and amuse themselves in different ways to us commoners.

This slightly abstract diversion is not without relevance: in the late Neolithic period, as early agricultural societies edged gradually via the Chalcolithic towards the Bronze Age, there appears to have been a wholesale replacement of the population. As with everything that happened in these unrecorded years, the evidence is more sparse than anyone would wish in seeking to be categorical. Such evidence as there is tells us that new groups of people began to arrive on these shores from Europe, bringing with them a new style of grooved pots, which earned them the name Beaker People.

That said, earlier interpretations that the Beaker People wiped out the local Neolithic farmers appear to have been losing favour, and contemporary thinking is more along the lines that theirs was a gradual replacement, leading ultimately to the decline of Neolithic genes to around ten per cent of the succeeding people. That said, if the Beaker People were the only folk building substantial burial cairns and putting beakers in them, then it is inevitable that there will be a significant Beaker legacy for us to investigate today. Perhaps the Neolithic natives, on the other hand, may simply have ceased enshrining their people upon death.

So, can the Normans can be seen as offering us a parable for the much earlier arrival of the Beaker People? Coming here as they did with their fancy new-fangled pots and throwing their weight about in a kind of passive-aggressive process of conquest? From this process may have emerged a pre-Brittonic people who would have spoken in tongues of which we know as near to nothing as makes no difference. The Brittonic peoples comprised the Celtic tribes living here when the Romans arrived – the word 'Celtic', here, not to be confused with the more modern usage, which refers primarily to Irish and Gaelic peoples.

These Brittonic folk, including the Cumbric speakers in what is now 'greater Cumbria', appear to have been the first people to bequeath to us any kind of discernible linguistic legacy, in place names like Penrith (red hill); Blencathra (bare hill top chair), the Cumbrian village of Blennerhasset (a highbred of the Brittonic word for 'top' and a Norse suffix meaning 'the shieling'); Pen-y-Ghent (hill of the winds), in Yorkshire; or Caerlaverock (a *castle*, perhaps belonging to a chap called Laverock, over the present-day border in Dumfries and Galloway). And in the traditional northern uplands method of counting sheep, passed down from the old Cumbric tongue – *yan, tan, tethera, methera, pimp, sethera* and so on through the chuckle-provoking *tethera-dick* (thirteen), *bumfit* (fifteen) and upwards to *gigot* (twenty). These numbers are not a million miles away from those of modern Welsh, Cornish or Breton. The fact that people in Cumbria are still counting sheep in 'the old tongue' can only point to the strength of the link between the language and the way of life of the people in pre-Roman Britain.

The emergence of a common family of Brittonic languages seems to coincide with the start of the Iron Age, around 1200 BC, while also overlapping the later phases of the Bronze Age. But no one can put their head on the block and assert that these tongues somehow evolved from how your average Neolithic farmer might have exchanged the time of day with a passing Beaker aficionado. Indeed, it seems far more likely that that Neolithic hearth chat all but vanished with the stone tools that Neolithic people used to till the land or skin the deer.

The equivalent of Brittonic in Scotland is presumed by some to have been Pictish, though the Picts are another group whose tangible legacy is sparse. It's thought that they were gradually subsumed into the culture of the Irish, or Gaels, who arrived in numbers between the fifth and seventh centuries AD. But whether, prior to this, they spoke some form of Brittonic or something quite different is rather an open question.

Dr Philip Shaw, Professor in English and Old English at the University of Leicester, tells me: 'Intriguingly, there are some Pictish stones with Ogham inscriptions that are difficult to decipher, suggesting the possibility that there was a non-Celtic (indeed probably non-Indo-European) Pictish language. So I think the likelihood is that some non-Indo-European language or languages, of which no obvious traces remain, was or were spoken in Neolithic Cumbria, and that during the Bronze Age this or these were replaced by Brittonic.' By inference, then, the Pictish tongue too would have predated Cumbric and its Brittonic cousins. Ogham was an old form of script of uncertain origin, sometimes also known as the Celtic tree alphabet. 'My guess,' says Phil, 'is that it originated as a way for representing a Celtic language, in the same way that the Roman alphabet originated as a way of representing Latin but it's been repurposed to represent English, Irish, Welsh and so on.' When a language is repurposed, says Phil, there are often telltale signs: Latin-based languages don't for example have the soft 'th' sound (as in *thing*) that we have in English and Nordic tongues, nor its hard cousin, as in *the*. So new letters were created: þ and ð, which survive in Icelandic and to some extent in Faroese but have died out in English, leaving us with the two-letter substitute. This kind of written gymnastics can give clues that the script (in this case Ogham) has been adapted to represent a different and, very possibly, earlier spoken language. A more modern example might be Turkish, which was first represented, unsuitably, in written form by Arabic script and latterly by Roman, though with the addition of quite a few modifying accents.

Then there is what linguists call 'language shift', whereby philologists (language historians) can identify linguistic evolutions that might be difficult for mere mortals like us to discern. Without going into too much detail, an example is the English word 'two' and the Armenian word *erku*, both of which descend from a common early Indo-European root, *dwóh*. Taken in the round, what this all means is that specialists can detect traces of 'ancestral' languages in later tongues that would be 'invisible' to the rest of us – but only if they actually exist. In reality, the arrival of a new language can see the complete eclipse of what came before. Referring to the supplanting of Gaelic by English, Phil says: 'It's surprising just how little trace it leaves.' So we can't reasonably expect whatever tongue our Neolithic ancestors spoke to have left any imprint whatsoever on our own language: it was, after all, five or six thousand years ago.

* * *

I leave Winderwath and take the road towards Culgaith, entering the village via the 'back entrance' at the top of the steep bluff above the Eden, having crossed over the Settle & Carlisle Railway at a point at which it is buried in a tunnel. I take the old drove road that I last travelled ten months previously, on foot, when researching my book, *Walking the Line*. After hitting a pothole so hard that my pannier bags fall off, I realise that I am approaching the junction of two of my copied map sheets. However, I'm quite confident I know where I'm going… turn right onto the A686 towards Melmerby, then cut across to the Glassonby Stone Circle and on down to Long Meg, via Little Meg.

Were I to check on the next sheet, I'd realise that there's an extra left before the right onto the A686. So, mistaking an unassuming B-road (confusingly signposted Melmerby) for the A686, I set off at speed – in the wrong direction. This only becomes wholly apparent as I enter another pretty, though unscheduled village some three kilometres further on. Realising I have taken a five or six kilometre penalty, I arrive back at the A686 where a sign labelled 'Druid's Circle' tempts me to opt to take the most direct route to Long Meg and visit the other circles afterwards.

I begin my visit to Long Meg in the traditional manner, by counting all her daughters. So many stone circles have acquired their own legends over the years, and Long Meg's is that the petrified 'daughters' will come back to life if anyone should count them and reach the same total more than once. Other versions, however, suggest that the daughters will only return to life if someone can correctly count the total and that the counter him or herself will be petrified should he or she reach the same (incorrect) total twice.

Setting aside such details there are various iterations of the legend of Long Meg: the following rather elaborate version comes from an anonymous (barring an unattributed Hotmail address) collection of Cumbrian folklore spotted behind the bar of a Lakeland pub. The story goes that there was once a great sorceress called Megaine, much sought after by the people of the area for her magic, wisdom and even her hand in marriage, for she was tall and beautiful and thereby acquired the nickname of Long Meg. Her 'daughters' were her pupils, with whom she shared her magic secrets, she being unwilling to pass these on to men.

A short distance away there lived another magician – a sorcerer called Michael Scot, who was everything that Long Meg wasn't, being boastful, greedy and spitefully jealous of Long Meg. Envious of Long Meg's friendship with Cole Hen, the ruler of Salkeld, he came to believe that the sound of the wind rustling the leaves was the voice of Long Meg, taunting him, just as he thought the rain was her spitting at him. He arrived in Salkeld for the 'Halloween' festival of Samhain, disguised as a beggar.

When Long Meg and her 'daughters' began the traditional fire dance, Michael Scot summoned all his powers to harness the force of the very rocks to overcome his adversary. Long Meg retaliated by calling forth the powers of the earth, trees and waters, but to no avail: in a flash of blinding light Long Meg and her daughters were turned to stone, though Long Meg's own power proved sufficient to turn Michael Scot into a tree. Other magicians managed to save just one 'stone' outside the ring of daughters: she proved to be the daughter of Long Meg and Coel Hen, who called upon the spirit of winter to kill the tree that was Michael Scot, finishing off the job with his sword. The power and influence of Salkeld shrank away with the loss of Long Meg till, today, it is but *Little* Salkeld.

A somewhat more prosaic description of the upstanding red sandstone monolith that is Long Meg, and of her seventy or so porphyritic daughters, positioned in a rough eclipse, 25 metres to the north-east, is given by Aubrey Burl in his authoritative *Stone Circles of Britain, Ireland and Brittany*. He describes a slightly flattened northern arc and taller boulders marking the east and west points. 'Two further slabs at the south-west define an entrance, outside which two extra stones stand as external portals. From the ring's centre, the two western portals stand in line with the tapering outlier [Long Meg] whose south-east face has several carvings of rings and spirals on it.' He continuous, crucially: 'The stone stands in line with the midwinter sunset and the carvings may reflect this. The sun's shadow casts clockwise spirals on its northward journey towards midsummer, anticlockwise as it moves back towards midwinter. The spiral on Long Meg is an anticlockwise one.' Thus, this is one of the circles in Cumbria with a definitive astronomical alignment and it continues to attract midwinter visitors to share the spectacle.

William Wordsworth is just one of many to have felt a sense of awe in visiting the circle across the years and commented: 'Though it will not bear a comparison with Stonehenge, I must say, I have not seen any other relique of those dark ages which can pretend to rival it in singularity and dignity of appearance.' Thus, he felt inspired to write in 1822 a verse entitled *The monument commonly called Long Meg*, which goes like this:

A weight of Awe not easy to be borne
Fell suddenly upon my spirit, cast
From the dread bosom of the unknown past,
When first I saw that family forlorn;
Speak Thou, whose massy strength and stature scorn
The power of years – pre-eminent, and placed
Apart, to overlook the circle vast.
Speak Giant-mother! tell it to the Morn,
While she dispels the cumbrous shades of night;
Let the Moon hear, emerging from a cloud,
At whose behest uprose on British ground
That Sisterhood in hieroglyphic round
Forth-shadowing, some have deemed the infinite
The inviolable God that tames the proud.[1]

Many more writers have felt inspired by this place across the centuries. The Cumbrian crime writer M W Craven has made Long Meg, Castlerigg and some of the lesser circles the locations for a series of murders in his book, *The Puppet Show*, which earned him a Golden Dagger award from the Crime Writers Association. I too set scenes of my own novel, *The Episode*, at Long Meg, Castlerigg and Sunkenkirk (as well as Stonehenge, the Orkney circles and Calanais) for the purpose of creating intersections between the two separate timelines of the book's interwoven stories. At Long Meg, the heroes of the book's two narratives have a chance meeting and set out to count the stones while circumnavigating them in opposite directions. After three attempts each, they have totals of between fifty-seven and sixty-three. Today I count sixty-five stones, which means either that a) I can't count, b) the legend is true, or c) the total cited in the *Megalithic Portal* is incorrect. This source says that there are fifty-nine stones, of which twenty-seven remain upright.

I refer to Tom Clare's *Prehistoric Monuments of the Lake District*, which contains a sketch by Stan Beckensall, that oracle of things Neolithic. This indicates sixty-four stones of varying sizes, some offset slightly from the main circumference. I feel somewhat vindicated: to be one stone out seems consistent with the idea of a slightly fluctuating total, as per the legend. And then I notice a table in the book, suggesting there are actually sixty-eight stones, plus another twenty 'fallen'... Noting Burl's earlier assertion of seventy stones, it seems no one is capable of coming to a consensus on the number of stones.

However many daughters there are or were, what cannot be disputed is that Long Meg and Her Daughters comprise a stone circle of truly epic proportions, it being a slightly squashed oval, measuring about 100 metres at its widest and a few metres less the other way. Some sources even claim incorrectly that it is the largest circle in the UK. In fact, Avebury is bigger by a factor of three, and Stanton Drew and the Ring of Brodgar are fractionally larger, though Stonehenge is slightly smaller.

Take nothing away from Long Meg and Her Daughters, however: with Mayburgh Henge and the Shap Avenue and its associated landscape, they form one third of what Paul Frodsham calls 'the three megasites' of Cumbria 'in terms of the time involved in building them'.

If I were today to rise in a hot air balloon into the clear blue sky that implies a warmer late spring day than the thermometer asserts, I would see that the reason for the slightly squashed northern edge of the daughters' circle is that there was once another, larger, pear-shaped enclosure on this side. It completely surrounds the farm buildings that are accessed via a road that traverses the stone circle. Paul Frodsham is just one of a number of northern-based archaeologists who believes that the entire site is under-investigated and that, had the sorceress and her pupils stood on the South Downs or Salisbury Plain, we might know far more about the entire complex. He led a community archaeology project with the North Pennines Area of Outstanding Natural Beauty, called Altogether Archaeology. The project's aims included investigation of a number of sites in and around the AONB, including Long Meg.

In his report of 2015, he writes: 'Throughout the twentieth century there were occasional references to Long Meg in books and academic papers but nothing of great importance through until the 1980s, when a large earthwork enclosure immediately north of the stone circle was recognised from air photographs. This is now ploughed flat, with its ditch backfilled, so that virtually no trace of it is visible on the ground surface.'

Earlier work by the Altogether Archaeology employing a variety of techniques suggested a number of hitherto unknown or uncertain features, including the possibility that the 'daughters' were originally positioned atop a bank (possibly highlighted with a smearing of local gypsum), though it would require excavation to demonstrate this for sure. Paul Frodsham and Gill Hey write in their introduction to *New Light on the Neolithic of Northern England*: 'By the early Neolithic, Long Meg was integrated into wider networks, as demonstrated by finds of Langdale tuff, Arran pitchstone and Yorkshire flint.' They note that the site sits at a key nodal point from which overland routes to Yorkshire and the North East lead from the navigable River Eden. They observe that the excavations also revealed, remarkably, that the 'very large ditched enclosure adjacent to and conjoining the stone circle predates it by several centuries, seemingly being early Neolithic in date (3950–3790 BC)'. Indeed, material from the socket of one of the stones in the circle yielded a date towards the end of the fourth millennium.'

New excavations in 2015 set out to discover more about the relationship between that enclosure and the stone circle we see today. Frodsham notes in a paper summarising these recent excavations by Altogether Archaeology – contained in *New Light on the Neolithic of Northern England* – that drone flights over both the circle and the enclosure failed to identify the location of an apparently 'lost' stone circle first observed in the 18th century by William Stukeley, an early chronicler of ancient sites.

He speculates that this circle, if it ever existed, may lie beneath the 19th century farmhouse now clearly visible to the north of the Daughters and accessed via the farm road that bisects today's stone circle.

The 'lost circle' would in all likelihood have stood very close to the key midwinter sunset alignment at Long Meg itself, so that the winter sun would have appeared to set into it at the solstice. The excavation trenches in the enclosure revealed material dating from the very early Neolithic period and even earlier, in the Mesolithic.

Frodsham draws clear parallels between Long Meg and other great Neolithic complexes, such as Stonehenge. These parallels include the pre-existence (in the enclosure) of what may have been a spiritual meeting place, where people gathered at key dates, centuries before the stone circle (or circles) were constructed. The complex's location on natural routes by land and water would also have been crucial, while the discovery of artefacts, including Langdale axe fragments, Arran pitchstone and Yorkshire flint, again ties in with the idea of a relatively small number of sites up and down the country that were of 'national' significance.

'Long Meg meets the criteria for these great Neolithic complexes,' says Frodsham. ...'the site lay at the heart of Neolithic Britain, though the extent to which Neolithic people were aware of this, or were concerned about it, cannot be known. It must have been regarded during the later Neolithic (and perhaps earlier) as one of the most important places in the central zone of the British Isles.'

There may well have been strong linkages with the Thornborough complex, in North Yorkshire, discussed in more detail later in this book, which shares with Long Meg the importance of its winter solstice alignment. Such a linkage potentially adds new importance to recent archaeological 'finds' in the Pennines between the two, including henges at Garrigill, near Alston, and Allendale, as well as a possible one, identified by lidar, at Cotherstone, in Teesdale.

While there remains, says Frodsham, 'huge potential' for further research at Long Meg, the idea strikes me that there may be a real possibility that Cumbria's premier Neolithic site actually sits at the centre of a seesaw with Stonehenge and Avebury at one end and Neolithic Orkney at the other. In short, that Long Meg's importance may have been such that we should be thinking of ideas and culture spreading out north and south from here, rather than merely south from Orkney.

Long Meg herself differs from the circle she oversees by being of red Cumbrian sandstone: she may well have been hewn from cliffs on the banks of the River Eden and dragged from there. She bears markings often described as Cup and Ring, though Paul Frodsham says this is incorrect: they are more akin to markings found on prehistoric monuments in Ireland, such as New Grange. He tells me: 'Long Meg bears Irish passage grave art, like that at New Grange.' The basic cup and ring mark has a cup mark with one or more lines around it and a gap or channel running from the inside to the outside.

He continues: 'There are a few cup and ring marks in Cumbria, mostly in and around the Eden Valley.' By contrast, the North East has many cup and ring marks but very few stone circles. 'The North East and the North West were in some ways very different from each other in the Neolithic but we still don't really know what date these carvings are: my aim, for the rest of my career, is to find the answer!' That said, he believes the biggest circles – Long Meg, Castlerigg, Swinside, or Sunkenkirk – are the oldest and most likely date from the 'middle to late Neolithic' or around 3000BC. These larger structures he likens to the 'cathedrals of their time'. The smaller ones, he suggests, 'are a good bit later and it's almost as though they were copying at a local level to create "village churches" or "family chapels" of the time.' Axe trade evidence, he says, can be found across Long Meg and other sites but it is a sobering and relevant fact that the axe factories were almost certainly 'much older' than the stone circles.

It is shocking to learn that, but for the intervention of the weather (or supernatural forces), the whole Long Meg edifice could have been blown to smithereens in the nineteenth century. The story goes that a local farmer instructed a team of men to dynamite the boulders, but just as they were about to start work there was a clap of thunder and a bolt of lightning. Well aware of the legends surrounding the stones, the men downed tools and refused to carry out the demolition instruction.

I chat with a woman called, I think, Tanka, who's visiting with her husband and two young children. They've recently moved down from Scotland and the circle has been a favourite destination for them throughout lockdown. 'What I really like is the sense of peace and calm and it's something very ancient,' she says. 'It's that sense of deep meaning but also mystery, and connection to nature and also to humans and some sort of spirituality.'

I am reassured whenever I hear words like this as it tells me it's not just me. Many others feel a curious sense of calm when surrounded by the stones of a circle or cairn ring. I vow that my next visit to Long Meg shall be for the winter solstice. I sit for a while on one of the boulders, watching the clouds scud above the tip of Long Meg's head. 'Could this really have been the epicentre, not just of the Neolithic North, but of the whole of Britain?' I wonder. I move to the middle of the circle, the better to appreciate its sheer size and to feel its power. Something disturbs what may be a parliament of rooks in the trees by the farm and I set out once again to count the stones: I can reach only sixty-four – I shall survive another day as flesh and blood.

* * *

I leave Long Meg and Her Daughters, bound for Glassonby. The stone circle is on the far (northern) side of another four or five-star Cumbrian village, through a couple of gates and into a field of sheep. In any other location this would be a circle worthy of note, but sitting so close to Long Meg, and on private land, it is all too easily overlooked. It can be said with near certainty that Glassonby was originally built as a burial cairn. Its soil covering was removed when it was excavated in 1900 by a chap called

William Gershom Collingwood, who found therein cremated bones, a collared urn, now residing in Tullie House, Carlisle, and a marked stone. What now remains is a raised mound with an oval of thirty tightly packed stones sitting atop it. It's close to round and the tallest stone is a little shy of a metre. I rather like it.

Collingwood was an interesting fellow: he was a pupil of the aesthete, John Ruskin, at Oxford University, and moved to Windermere upon marriage, having been introduced to the Lake District by his father as a boy. William Morris shared with him his interest in Nordic culture, prompting him to write a book about pre-Norman crosses in the North of England. Morris, of course, was a frequent visitor to Ruskin's home at Brantside, on Coniston Water. He also travelled to Iceland, where he recorded a travel diary marvelling at the ability of the Icelanders to survive in so hostile an environment. I too have a deep interest in Nordic culture and language and once enjoyed an honorary Readership at Lancaster University to aid my research at the time. Morris's diaries make fascinating reading as he made the journey in some despair, his wife Janey having started a relationship with Morris's pal, the artist Dante Gabriel Rossetti. At times it seems like the landscape and climate will overwhelm Morris, but he returns inspired and goes on to create the furniture and decorative arts business whose legacy we so enjoy today.

Collingwood, for his part, was also an accomplished artist and founder of the Lake Artists Society – as well as a climber, walker and musician. He also learned Icelandic for good measure and wrote a seminal text, *The Lake Counties*, published in 1902 and republished in 1988. He went on to write novels, his best being *Thorstein of the Mere, A Saga of the Northmen in Lakeland*, which just happened to be the favourite childhood book of Arthur Ransome, of *Swallows and Amazons* fame. Curiously, he chanced to meet Ransome on the Old Man of Coniston and the pair became friends.

In Orkney, there's good evidence that Neolithic sites went on to be occupied by subsequent peoples in the Bronze and Iron Ages and then by Viking settlers. So this is a moment for me to wonder to what extent the ancient sites were similarly employed when the Vikings settled the Lakeland valleys and Yorkshire Dales. Evidence in these parts is somewhat less categoric, though it certainly exists in the ancient settlement and field patterns on the western flanks of the mountains. I reflect that there's an entire library's worth of PhDs to be written, were some miracle to provide the resources to satisfy the proven desire and will to excavate more of Cumbria's ancient sites.

A rather more contemporary preoccupation is the state of my battery, given my earlier unscheduled detour. The gauge says I still have 15km 'in the tank', but as I ride back up the hill through the village, this tumbles to 10 and then plummets to 0. My nearest prospect of a recharge is all the way to Langwathby, 6km distant. Fortuitously, it is downhill almost all the way.

I stop to visit Little Meg, known also as Maughanby, which sits at the edge of a field part-way back to its bigger namesake. It comprises a collection of eleven large boulders, some of which may at some point have been shunted to the edge of the field by an over-enthusiastic farmer. At least he didn't blow them up! One of them is extensively decorated with similar markings (though far more extensive) to those found on Long Meg herself. This is such a rare spectacle here in Cumbria that I can't help but be impressed. The site is, according to Paul Frodsham, something of an enigma – 'a very curious monument'. It lies about 600 metres as the rook flies east-north-east of Long Meg.

It shares with Long Meg and Glassonby the distinction of being marked, in this case with concentric circles. While one may presume it to be part of the broader Long Meg landscape, it is not aligned with any of the principal axes of its superior namesake. It was, according to both Clare and Burl, once a modest long barrow containing between seven and eleven upright stones and an oval cist, found to contain burnt bones and charcoal in a crude pot. Prior to the removal of the soil covering it stood about 1.3 metres tall. The present arrangement of the stones, many of which have at some stage been relocated from the adjacent farmed field, cannot be considered to be at or even close to their original positions but I deem it having been worth the short detour for the rock art alone.

From Little Meg, I coast all the way down past Long Meg, through Little Salkeld and on past the old watermill, beyond which I encounter my first uphill challenge while relieved of battery support. It's pretty tough coaxing The Beast and its human and non-human cargo up the incline, but once I have accomplished this, the road levels and I arrive in Langwathby not too much the worse for wear. My last visit to the Shepherds Inn was during my *Walking the Line* research, just as the country was emerging form its first lockdown, and I'm pleased to see the place back in business once again. I'm invited to plug in indoors while I sit in the sun on the green and take a rather late lunch.

On the basis of my accumulated knowledge and experience, I calculate that I have enough charge now to complete the day's journey, and take the A686 towards Penrith, diverting via the quieter road through Edenhall. Although sitting no more than a couple of kilometres off the main road, it has consistently avoided my previous attention. Apparently, it's what's called a 'cluster settlement', having initially evolved around a 'cluster' of family farms. The road through the village makes a hard right about halfway through and, straight ahead, there's a grand formal gateway and estate beyond. The Lords of the original manor were the Musgrave family. Musgrave is, of course, an old Border Reiver name, indicating that the family were cattle smugglers in the lawless borderlands, rather than necessarily descendants of William the Conqueror's mates. By the seventeenth century though, Richard Musgrave had been made Baronet for services to the Crown. These 'services' may be presumed to have been raising and leading armies for assorted military campaigns. Well, old habits die hard.

The original estate home was Hartley Castle, but this was demolished in the early eighteenth century to provide materials for the extension of Eden Hall, which had at least a couple of reincarnations, most recently as an Italianate mansion in the 1860s. The death of the Eighth Baronet in 1861 was marked by the erection of the clock tower in Penrith and the Musgraves maintained their political prominence until they fell on (relatively) hard times in the early twentieth century after a run of deaths in quick succession racked up large death duties. With the family removed to London, the house was eventually demolished in the 1930s and may or may not have been shipped, London Bridge-style, to America.

The Church of St Cuthbert actually predates the Norman conquest and sits on the estate, some distance from the village. Cumbria boasts a great many St Cuthbert's, reflecting the saint's posthumous journey back and forth here in a coffin on the shoulders of his acolytes. Nearby was the 'sacred' St Cuthbert's Well, which is associated with an intriguing legend. The so-called Luck of Edenhall was an ornate glass drinking cup allegedly stolen by the Edenhall butler from a group of fairies when he went to fetch water from the well. The fairies were not best pleased and are said to have composed this verse to mark their displeasure:

Whene'er this cup shall break or fall,
Farewell the luck of Eden Hall.[2]

The glass is of Syrian manufacture and was almost certainly bounty brought back from the Crusades, about 600 years ago, by a pugilistic Musgrave. Most likely thanks to a protective leather pouch, it has survived across the centuries, though the fairies, for their part, clearly ceased to deliver good luck a century back, whereafter the glass was first loaned to the Victoria and Albert Museum, in London, and later acquired 'for the nation' in 1958. Or, to put it another way, appropriated for exhibition in the South of England, albeit in more legitimate circumstances than its original appropriation as loot. It is prized as among the finest exhibits in the V&A glass collection.

I rejoin the A686 and am soon at the edge of Penrith, making swifter work of the notorious roundabout on the edge of town than would be possible in a car. A short distance on the A6 and I'm at King Arthur's Round Table. The site has nothing to do with King Arthur, who may or may not have existed after the Romans left these shores, though King Charles's Scottish army very possibly camped here in the seventeenth century. The marks left by their tent pegs were supposedly still visible come 1725 when archaeologists became interested.

The Round Table is a henge, part of the Mayburgh Henge complex, the latter lauded previously by Paul Frodsham. Henges comprise a raised circular, or near-circular, mound, typically of earth or small stones and often with an external ditch. They may or may not have supported wooden posts that in turn may sometimes have supported a roof. Stonehenge is, therefore, either an anomaly or a contradiction in terms, although the original structure may have been a henge, rather than a stone circle with lintels. But then the people who built it wouldn't have known the meaning of henge, would they?

What is most impressive about the Round Table when visiting today is the fact that it is so neatly manicured, as if it were some kind of Neolithic bowling green. It comprises a level central platform surrounded by a ditch and then a raised mound constructed of river gravel. The ditch was apparently cleared out around 1800 to create a 'tea garden' and it has managed to retain its neatness for the subsequent two centuries, despite having a corner lopped off by the building of the B5320. Though, to be fair, it may well have been the Romans who were responsible for this, as the Roman High Street most likely lies beneath.

Apparently, there used to be another nearby henge, the Little Round Table, about two kilometres west, on the other side of the River Eamont. Of this, there appears to be little trace remaining, though aerial photography suggests it was actually about the same size as the 'larger' Round Table.

Other extant features of what once was an extensive and important complex landscape include a number of cairns and standing stones, only some of which have found their way onto the Ordnance Survey map. Among these is one tucked in beside Penrith's other horror roundabout, where the A66 crosses the M6 and where a stone circle was once rumoured. No trace remains of this or of a possible stone row to the west. There are more tumuli to the south, and an ancient settlement and an Iron Age hill fort, in Yanwath Wood, which might have succeeded an earlier structure.

And so to the crowning glory of this landscape: Mayburgh Henge. The first time I visited the site I was struck by two things. Firstly, there was the sheer immensity of the structure. Secondly, there was the narrow escape it somehow secured from the advancing construction of the M6. The motorway could easily have been built across open land further to the west, but we already know from the example of Gunnerkeld that motorway designers care little more for such niceties than their Victorian forebears.

Unlike the Round Table, Mayburgh was built of substantial stones, perhaps dredged from the Eamont or 'rearranged' from a glacial mound. It now comprises a substantially raised, near-circular embankment, with an entrance to the east, aligned with sunrise at the equinoxes. There may once have been four standing stones close to two metres in height at the centre of the henge in the manner of the kind of four-poster monument more common in Scotland. And another four at the eastern entry point. Earlier speculation about an additional outer circle of stones is probably not supported by good evidence, though – if it did exist – much of it would most likely lie beneath the M6. The standing stones were reportedly destroyed in the early eighteenth century and a single central monolith now remains. The whole can be interpreted as lying close to the intersection of the High Street and 'A66' routes into the central lake District mountains with the probably navigable rivers Eden and Eamont and the possible land route over the Pennines at Hartside.

Remember, this is another of Paul Frodsham's mega-sites. Indeed, the first time I saw Mayburgh Henge I was amazed: it's just so big… On its west side, from which the visitor approaches, it presents a daunting embankment that's actually taller than other parts of the perimeter, as the structure was built in such a way that the top of the embankment must have formed a near-level circle. It measures some 117 metres across, but no photograph can ever hope to do it justice as its steep embankments simply lose their drama once rendered on page or screen. These days you enter it by clambering seven metres up the west-facing outer embankment, rather than being welcomed through the monumental east-facing gateway. Aubrey Burl recognises in it traditions more usually associated with Irish henges: there is no perimeter ditch and the internal 'plateau' is scraped up from the edges to create an upturned saucer shape. Both a Cumbrian stone axe and later Bronze Age one have been recovered from the site (the former in the nineteenth and the latter in the eighteenth century) which is thought to be of similar age to the large stone circles in the area.

Aubrey Burl notes that William Stukeley, the eighteenth-century recorder of sites Neolithic, chronicles a cautionary tale regarding the fate of the Mayburgh monoliths, noting that the central stones had by 1725 been blown up using gunpowder so as to enable cultivation of the central plateau. Not content with reducing these towering pieces to shorter fragments, the workmen had another go. 'These small stones were blasted and removed ... one of the men involved in the work having hanged himself, and another turning lunatic, has given a fair opening to vulgar superstition, to impute these misfortunes to their sacrilege in defacing what they suppose was formally a place of eminent sanctity.' Blast, then, at your peril!

Most casual descriptions suggest the material with which the henge was built was dredged by hand from the River Eamont. However, this feels somewhat less likely than the possibility that it all came from a repurposed glacial moraine, given that to have removed that volume of stone from the riverbed would surely have left behind a footprint that would remain visible even 5,000-odd years later? The henge manifests no significant alignment with its King Arthur's neighbour but, perhaps in search of some alignment, any alignment, Tom Clare notes that the only significant landscape feature visible from inside the henge is the distinctive saddleback summit of Blencathra, above which the sun would have set at either equinox. So, you never know...

Today has already been quite long and I'm still a little shaken from being thrown from the saddle, so, having made a number of previous visits, I don't have the appetite to linger here too long as evening approaches. I park The Beast and climb the ramparts, casting once more my admiring gaze and noting that this is indeed a mighty fine edifice, even after so many centuries.

I ride back past King Arthur's Round Table. There's a right of way through Lowther Park, home of John Lowther, First Viscount Lonsdale. This estate is everything that Edenhall may once have wished to be: it is both huge, extending as already remarked some considerable distance southward down the eastern flanks of the Lake District mountains, and it is also diverse.

Lowther Castle itself was once a fine Gothic mansion and the Lowther family seat – a dramatic slice of Transylvania in the heart of Cumbria – but it fell into disrepair between the Wars, having been first requisitioned and then, in the '50s, partially demolished and then abandoned. These days it's been consolidated and hosts a large adventure playground, café and other attractions. Like the Musgrave family, over at Edenhall, the Lowthers supplied establishment MPs to the Commons in the nineteenth century but, unlike the Musgraves, did not fall on hard times. The estate lands and gardens surrounding the old castle these days are also geared to generating money from tourism. Askham Hall – just beyond the estate wall, across the river in the lively village of Askham – having initially succeeded Lowther Castle as the family seat, is now a boutique hotel with spa. Indeed, I shall be staying tonight at another Lowther property, the Queen's Head, one of two pubs in the village and relatively recently acquired and refurbished by the Lowther Estate.

My route through the estate, to Askham, takes me not just past, but right through Lowther Park holiday village, with its chalets and caravans. So far as I can work out, there's full public access to the cycle route, though there may be times at which the entry barrier is staffed as it is not today, on an advancing evening as pandemic restrictions are only just beginning to ease. And so I breeze through the holiday park and, mingling carefully with the many walkers and joggers enjoying the pleasant woodland way, I soon find myself passing Lowther Castle, in the mid-distance, and crossing the little stone bridge at the foot of the lively village of Askham, to cycle up past the first of its two greens to the Queen's Head.

* * *

The helpful staff at the Queen's Head are working hard to catch up on many weeks without so much as a dead kipper for a customer. I make the most of this my most luxurious night stop, eagerly awaiting the arrival of both my wife, Linda, and my more solid walking shoes to replace the red, Wicked Witch footwear, which has attracted too much ridicule on social media.

While awaiting a dinner of near-Michelin qualities, I enjoy at least some of a marvellous Zoom presentation by Peter and Leni Gillman, the then Chair-Secretary team of the Outdoor Writers & Photographers Guild. I shall go on to succeed Peter as Chair. They have produced a fascinating book from the Royal Geographical Society's collection of original photographs from early attempts on Everest. I am reminded that my now impending challenge of High Street, even in incessant rain, is of a wholly different order: a very much smaller one!

Chapter 4

The high road and the heavy rains

In the Cockpit and Castlerigg

When I was planning my tour, I considered whether I should visit a collection of stone circles in Broomrigg Plantation, near Ainstable. To have included this site in my journey would have required something of a detour to the north and it was far from clear that sufficient evidence remained to be seen there. Clare describes excavations by a local archaeologist before and after the Second World War, including three separate circle locations including cremation sites, in one of which he found an urn, thirteen jet beads and a V-bored button. Burl says this was 'a fascinating complex of stone circles, cairn- and kerb- circles and a henge'. Note the employment of the word 'was' – he goes on to note: 'It is now more akin to a Transylvanian forest.'

Broomrigg has been nagging me: it's a scheduled ancient monument boasting several important features. Members of *Megalithic Portal* have been going there. I fear I have made an error in not including it on my route; one that I should address. I duly drive to the location and park at the wide gateway from which *Megalithic Portal* members have entered the plantation and followed a track leading pretty much direct to the various circles. However, the gate is now firmly padlocked and its top is adorned with brand new barbed wire. Entry is going to be tricky and is clearly being deterred. I decide to be creative and drive round to a farm road that leads to a point a couple of fields from the side of the forest where the circles are located. I walk briskly up the field and note the substantial number of boulders: but for the likelihood that they comprise nothing more than field clearance evidence, I think I might be marching up a ceremonial avenue.

I locate a climbable gate and drop into the tall vegetation on the other side – for Transylvanian, read Amazonian… A summer's worth of bracken is chest high and wet; it conceals the irregular forest floor and I'm soon stumbling haphazardly towards where I think the circles should be. This is not the seeking-a-stone-circle-on-a-limestone-plateau challenge of Crosby Garrett Fell, but it is, if anything, harder. After half a fruitless hour, I give up and retreat to the field. I hope that the farmer on his quad bike isn't going to worry about my incursion and attempt to drop beneath his horizon by following the course of the stream at the field's edge. No such luck: he pulls up just above me and invites an explanation for my trespass.

'The gate's on the other side of the plantation,' he tells me.

'But it's padlocked and wired,' I respond.

'Aye, 'tis that. They got sick of it being turned into the biggest dog's toilet in the county through lockdown...'

'So, can I get in to see the circles?'

'Tha's'll 'ave ter go see t' Watsons at Croglin Low Hall. They don't 'ave a phone and they don't do email, so tha' s'all 'ave ter knock on t'door. Mind... it'll be a struggle any road ter find 'em at this time of year...'

And that is how and why I have failed to visit a once significant Neolithic complex, which might otherwise have found a place on the Grand Tour.

* * *

I first enjoyed the pleasure of meeting Ivan Day at the World Marmalade Awards a few years ago. I have, in the course of writing this book, twice visited his farmhouse home on the edge of Shap, where he is a mine of information, not merely on his specialist subject of the history of food, but on myriad other matters, ranging from who's who in Cumberland and Westmorland to highly pertinent questions about who began eating what, and when. He has a large, old, wood-beamed farmhouse kitchen, bedecked with all manner of contraptions employed in times long gone for processing various foodstuffs. On my most recent visit, he had been making oat breads and cakes and showed me a variety of rollers and presses, designed to shape the cakes without the gooey oaty mixture adhering too firmly. I imagine the early Neolithic and Bronze Age farmers attempting to achieve a similar result with no more than textured rock and well-heated stones to aid them.

Prominent in Ivan's Cumbrian Who's Who are the current occupants of Dalemain, a grand pile a few kilometres to the north-west of Askham. Baron Musgrave, late of Hartley Castle and Eden Hall, has already demonstrated how it's a tough old world for today's aristocrats, bequeathed as they have been with huge country mansions, but not necessarily with adequate means to maintain them. The Hasell-McCosh family is descended from a former secretary to one of Cumbria's most famous daughters – Lady Anne Clifford. It was Lady Anne who, having fought a long battle to secure her rightful inheritance, set about restoring her Cumbrian castles and doing good works throughout the North. Lady Anne's diaries provide a fascinating insight into the life of a seventeenth-century aristocrat and the final volumes of her work, part of a bequest to Edward Hasell upon Lady Anne's death, remain in the custody of the Hasell-McCosh family today.

Dusty old diaries don't butter no parsnips, however. Nor put jam on the bread. So, the family seat of Dalemain, on the Ullswater road from Penrith, has for some years opened its doors and the gates of its gardens to visitors. And for a decade of a half, Dalemain has illuminated the dull days of winter with an event to draw the crowds, even in February.

It was Jane Hasell-McCosh, the 'lady of the manor', who had the idea that making marmalade might be a metaphor for community and caring: she wanted to do her bit to help a local charity, Hospice at Home, which provides palliative care at home for people near the end of their lives. And so, in 2005, were born the world's first Marmalade Awards. From small beginnings, the Marmalade Awards have grown astonishingly, with more than two or three thousand jars of marmalade – from amateur and artisan producers all over the world – arriving for judgement each year.

Alongside Paddington Bear movies, Dalemain has delivered a shot in the arm to previously moribund sales of this most British of preserves, thanks to the ursine Peruvian's liking for marmalade sandwiches. Ivan Day is just one of many people who've become part of the vast infrastructure that delivers the awards each year and he told me back on my first attendance at this gathering of the county set: 'The thing that appeals to me is that it's total madness – two days of total lunacy!'

I was inclined to agree as, a few years ago, we trudged through the mud in a blizzard from the temporary car park at Dalemain, home to eleven generations of Hasells. Dalemain's impressive Georgian frontage conceals an older medieval heritage and the rustic cobbled courtyard to the rear of the house was replete with stalls selling country goods that seemed to have more in common with a point-to-point than a jammy jamboree.

With Fortnum and Mason, Aga, Laithwaite's and the Worshipful Company of Fruiterers among sponsors and supporters (not to mention Mackays, the marmalade people), I might have been forgiven for wondering if marmalade-making was the preserve of the entitled, especially when Baron Henley, a Tory peer whose family seat is at Scaleby Castle, near Carlisle, was announced as the winner of the event's 'Political Award.'

But the spoons on evidence that day were far from silver: rather, little plastic ones by the thousand, at the ready for 3,000 visitors to sample some of the jars of lovingly made marmalade, which filled just about every flat space in the medieval hall and a marquee.

The air hung heavy with the bitter-sweet of the preserves and the piles of Seville oranges awaiting their sticky afterlife – and with a palpable sense of warmth and joie de vivre. Jane and her marmalady works for charity are clearly the stuff of legend, and her personal warmth seemed to seep down through the army of green wellie-clad helpers who ensure each year that, amid the lunacy, a jam-packed schedule of talks and demonstrations runs like clockwork.

'Jane is the warmest-hearted person you could ever meet,' Ivan told me. 'It was a stroke of genius to come up with a theme that suited the bleak days of January and February. The first run was a very small event and none of us could remember it very well and then the idea came through to repeat it.'

But Jane didn't feel she was qualified to judge the qualities of the growing number of entries that began to come not just from enthusiastic amateurs, but also from artisan producers for whom a prize might spell commercial success. Step forward the redoubtable ladies of Penrith Women's Institute, Doreen Cameron and Eileen Wilson, who tirelessly award points to every single entry and produce neatly completed score sheets that are posted out to provide feedback from the experts. The artisan entries are judged by a panel comprising big names in food writing, TV and hospitality.

The focus at the event is very much on the Seville orange – renowned for its 'just right' bitterness and chunky peel, but in season for just a few weeks each winter – and its citrus cousins. But Ivan's food historian pedigree encourages a more catholic view as to what makes a marmalade and he shared the sticky story in a fascinating lecture and a marquee display that included quince pastes and a large, knobbly, sweet citrus fruit called citron, but which is NOT a lemon.

With a sacrilegious assertion that set me reeling, he said: 'For me, it doesn't need to have any citrus fruit in it at all and we even have two recipes from the Roman occupation, made with English fruits. I'm very interested in the history of food in general but in particular confectionary, or anything to do with sugar. Originally "marmalade" could be made from a combination of various fruits and the first ones were made from quince, which is *marmelo* in Portuguese.'

Suddenly struggling to establish clear blue water between jam and marmalade, I found my thoughts wandering to picture an early Bronze Age family in a hut near the fruitful valleys of the Furness area of Cumbria. The ceremonial copper crucible, containing the bubbling mixture of honey, sloe and crab apple, plucked from nearby bushes, is carried in great reverence from the hearth in the simple heather-thatched hut to its place at the centre of the small circle of stones. The family give thanks to the gods for bestowing this bounteous luxury upon them as they gaze out to the wide ocean, whence, one day shall arrive sugar, spice and all things nice, Seville oranges included.

'We started making it with oranges in the eighteenth and nineteenth century and Britain became synonymous with preserves,' continued Ivan, jolting me from my reverie. 'So the name "marmalade" found its way into English and it was made with a fruit we couldn't grow here, and sugar from cane grown in the Caribbean. Just like we got tea from China and turned it into the British institution of teatime.'

Marmalade, of course, is more of a breakfast institution than a teatime one, except for one famous bear from darkest Peru. I asked the awards' inscrutable PR, Lou Lou Graham, who it was inside the giant Paddington bear costume patrolling the event. 'Well, Paddington, of course!' she replied without a hint of irony. Lou Lou described how the care that people take with packing and presenting their entries reflects the charitable aims of the event. 'The entries sometimes arrive with the sweetest things, such as family histories – people are very proud of their recipes. But the awards are about community: bringing people together and bringing people to this part of the world and supporting local people.'

Indeed, not only do the entries arrive from all over the world but so do the guests, as evidenced by transatlantic accents and a young man from Anjou, France, who told me about his jam making. Indeed, come 2020, as Dalemain began work on a COVID-safe virtual event for 2021, a new group of marmalade makers would even emerge in Senegal.

I took my plastic spoons and tucked into some of the professional and amateur offerings. 'Mmmm, lime with vodka and tonic! Chocolate orange! Champagne! Christmas pud! Bathtub gin!' Four of the Gold homemade winners hail from Scotland, two from Japan, one from New York and seven from England.

Some weeks ahead of the event, I had ransacked my shelves for a jar of marmalade that might fit into one of the fifteen amateur categories at the 'Marmalade Oscars'. I settled in the end for a sweet orange marmalade with rhubarb and ginger, which I had made the previous summer to try and deplete my garden's 'rhubarb mountain'.

As my entry was simply taken off the shelf, rather than honed to the exacting competition requirements, I expected little. So, imagine my delight when I found that Jar 1,987 had earned a Certificate of Merit and was just one point short of a Bronze Award. I scored two out of two for appearance, three out of five for colour, four out of six for consistency texture and quality, and five out of seven for flavour and aroma, making fourteen out of a possible twenty. 'An interesting marmalade,' said the judges.

'I'll be back,' I drawled, Schwarzenegger-style, returning with two specially-crafted confections the following year. Last Days of the Raj was a liberally spiced preserve, rounded off with Calvados, while Thor's breakfast included hedgerow fruits, angelica and hazelnuts from Cumbria, and an aquavit finish. Once again the judges enjoyed the fruits of my labours but with the supreme Gold prize eluding me, I elected to curb culinary ambitions for a while.

My return to the fray in 2021 is designed to coincide with my Neolithic Cumbrian journey and, with the timing of the awards front of mind, I create a Valentine's Day marmalade, featuring (in addition to sweet oranges), passion fruit, peaches, rosehips and raspberries, with a finish of Shrubb, a sweet-tasting rum-based liqueur, from Guadeloupe.

My concoction proves good enough to secure a Bronze award in the 'Marmalade for a Friend' category. But it should have been a Silver. I say this not peevishly but as a simple statement of fact. Had I made a better job of securing the lid of my jar and then wrapping my parcel, the former would not have come off, costing me three points for presentation and another for the jar not being full enough…

I have reflected with Ivan Day on the possibility, however remote, that our Neolithic ancestors might have had any kind of preserve in their culinary compendium, sugar being – with salt, fresh air and alcohol – one of a quadrumvirate of most popular ways of preserving food for later consumption.

I have pictured our extended Neolithic family sitting round their hearth, an earthenware pot of surplus crab apples bubbling away on the perpetual fire. Ivan's sobering words to me concern the general scarcity of sugar-bearing fruits in ancient Cumbria. There would have been crab apples for sure, though – as we shall be reminded later – these are not renowned for their sweetness. Nor are sloes or bullace. Nor rosehips: rosehip syrup is sweet, despite rather than because of its eponymous ingredient, the sugar being added mechanically after the juice and vitamin C have been wrung out of the hard berries.

'Gooseberries?' I venture to Ivan during one of our chats in his farmhouse kitchen.

'Introduced by the French in the sixteenth century,' he replies.

'Damsons?'

'Came back from Syria during the Crusades.'

Given that the best source of sugar was probably wild honey, and given that such honey might well have been considered a luxury, I suspect that any notions of Neolithic or Bronze Age sugar-based food preservation may have been misplaced.

* * *

The forecast for the day as I leave The Queen's Head is as unambiguous as it possibly could be. The rain and cold shall arrive at midday, whereafter only fools and horses with wellies should consider venturing out. Well, I think, at least my feet should stay dry, thanks to the arrival of my sturdy shoes…Famous last words.

Askham is a deceptively large and well-appointed village: besides its two pubs and hotel, it also boasts a village shop and an outdoor swimming pool, which will not be enjoying my custom or that of any sane person today. It's one of a chain of attractive villages tucked beneath the Eastern Fells and extending all the way from Tirril, between Pooley Bridge and Penrith, in the north, right down to the previously enjoyed Bampton Grange, not far from Shap.

Askham's relationship with the fells is intimate: it does not stand in defiance of them, but rather blends almost imperceptibly into them. The road to the top of the village passes through one moderately sized green, then a smaller one before entering a wide sloping common, decaying as it does so from Tarmacked way to stony and, finally, grassy track.

I've a fondness for Askham born directly of its easy access to the wide-open spaces: more than once did Linda and I visit houses in the village during our long quest to find the right place for ourselves. One of these was almost the last house before the fells: a rambling old Cumbrian farmhouse with gardens that needed, like the building itself, no more than an injection of love… and cash. It might have just been 'the one', were it not for its backing directly onto a large milking parlour: the thought of fifty-odd milking machines clunking away a couple of metres from the back wall sealed its fate. Today, though, I note that someone else has opted to inject love, cash and perhaps a deaf ear as the house is looking pretty pleased with itself.

The grassy track climbs steadily up the fell. I am on High Street, the Roman road that runs from near Penrith, in the north, all the way down to Roman fort at Ambleside, where it joins another Roman route, which most likely began at Lancaster and led all the way to Ravenglass at the southern (unwalled) end of Emperor Hadrian's frontier, on the Cumbrian coast.

The consensus is that there was a thoroughfare here long before the arrival of the Romans and, indeed, this most likely also applies to a second track, which crosses High Street almost at right angles on the broad semi-plateau that extends maybe two kilometres in either direction and roughly corresponds with the edge of the unenclosed land at the north-east end of the fell. Other tracks crisscross the area, some marked on the map and others not, the combined effect of which makes it difficult to determine one's precise location.

The Ordnance Survey map indicates that the plateau is liberally decorated with ancient remains: settlements, mounds, cairns, standing stones, cairn circles, stone circles. Chief among them all is The Cockpit, but there are other, smaller circles and groups of stones scattered over a wide area. Those who have taken the time to catalogue the entire area have counted up to eight circles or ring cairns, all loosely umbrella-ed as Moor Divock (I to VIII). Many of these are on or near to the track that descends towards the village of Helton and so I take a left at the crossroads to explore these. I do not find eight, but I do locate several cairns and burial mounds and conclude that I am now at the heart of another extensive Neolithic or Bronze Age landscape. Shap it may not be, but Tom Clare's book does note speculation that there may even have been a ceremonial avenue, with a single standing stone, known as the Cop Stone, signalling its south-easternmost end. Indeed, it is perhaps not too much of a leap to speculate that this avenue, if it did exist, may have been aligned with the rising sun at the winter solstice. Clare suggests precisely this, noting that the midsummer sun sets over the notched summit of Blencathra when the 'avenue' is projected to the north-west.

Regaining High Street, I head on to the south-west, where the map again indicates numerous remains, prosaically marked simply 'pile of stones', raising speculation that the Vikings may possibly have dubbed this location 'shap', just like the village to the south. And then, suddenly, I am confronted by The Cockpit – a far finer stone circle than it seems reasonable to expect from any of the descriptions I have read. I permit The Beast to pose at the centre of the circle, which measures about 27 metres across.

Around its perimeter is a raised embankment with concentric rings of about twenty-seven stones. What is most striking, however, is the texture of the grass within the circle: it is a relatively lush green, while the surrounding rough fell is of tussock grass, giving rise to the impression of white. It's as though the whole edifice was once a bowling green and Clare again speculates that there may be a paved area beneath the central 'ring'.

Let me turn now to the name… We can safely surmise that 'cockpit' does not relate to what the circle may have been known as in Neolithic or Bronze Age times, but that does not mean that the name bears no relation to its subsequent usage. I would hazard a guess that the circle may conceivably have been a venue for illegal cockfighting after the 'sport' was outlawed in 1835. Located as it is at a crossroads, and affording a vantage from which to easily see any approaching law enforcers, it would also have been an ideal spot for spectators to find and then congregate at.

These days it does attract the occasional Druid and those seeking a quiet spot in which to meditate on life, the universe and everything. Another Ivan anecdote tells of his coming across a woman sitting cross-legged at the centre of The Cockpit, eyes shut and apparently in deep meditation… only to take an orange from her bag and lazily toss the peel over her shoulder. 'I coughed gently, and she quickly picked it up!'

Burl does not appear to find this upland complex worthy of note, though Clare affords it a decent innings, noting that The Cockpit itself most likely comprised a double circle in its youth. David Watson's little book, *A Guide to the Stone Circles of the Lake District*, is more complimentary, describing it all as 'perhaps the largest concentration of Bronze Age remains in the Lake District'. Unofficial excavation of various monuments over the decades has surely eroded its value.

Before I leave The Cockpit I sit awhile, scouring the horizon and reflecting that the aforementioned Dalemain Estate manages the land that is home to one of the largest herds of red deer in England, a little to the south of me, on the fells around Martindale, above the eastern shores of Ullswater. I recall on a visit to Exmoor once having to correct a national park ranger who asserted that Exmoor was the only place you could find red deer in the wild outside Scotland. In fact, besides Martindale and Exmoor, there are also modest-sized herds in the New Forest and Thetford Forest, in Norfolk and Suffolk. The Lake District herd is said to have been around for about 300 years and so must be from reintroduced stock: red deer are the larger of our two native species, with roe deer the smaller. They are magnificent animals, though I have to admit that my own attempts to track them down in Martindale have never succeeded. Apparently, the best plan is to head up as the day fades, during the rutting season and listen for the roar of the stags.

The Woodland Trust estimates that red deer populations are at their highest in a thousand years and this is not without its issues. The natural predators of the red deer are wolves, lynx and brown bears. As we have none of these, it comes down to humans to ensure populations are at a stable and manageable level, but shooting deer conflicts with modern sensibilities. Some people see the reintroduction of large carnivores as the answer, but farmers are naturally more than a little apprehensive about even lynx roaming free, never mind wolves and bears, both of which have been known to attack humans too. There's a romantic idealism to the idea of getting back to the days when nature regulated itself, but that does seem to be to deny that times have changed and reintroduction is best done within the context of where we are now. For what it's worth, I feel there's a powerful momentum behind the idea of bringing back the lynx, perhaps in Kielder Forest, in Northumberland, but maybe this should then be followed by a pause. Indeed, after a first rejection of reintroduction plans by the then Environment Secretary Michael Gove in 2018, the Lynx Trust says it is now confident it has addressed the various objections and hopes to be releasing six animals in a five-year monitored programme. Let's watch this space.

In a Cumbrian context, any thoughts of bringing back the lynx would have to be habitat-led and the most suitable location would seem to be remote and forested Ennerdale. However, the Lynx Trust ruled the Ennerdale habitat out as 'too small' in 2016, having previously been enthusiastic. In any event, Ennerdale is a long way from Martindale, so the herd here has to be culled so as to contain numbers and maintain the health of the animals. I dare say that all this begs the question as to which predators would have roamed these fells before the Neolithic and Bronze Age people decided that forest was just so passé and began to jump on the farming bandwagon. I cast a final eye all around the circumference of The Cockpit and reflect that, once upon a time, this would have been a clearing in a forest – and what would that have done for equinoxial sightlines?

As the uncertain sky gains weight, I realise that pondering on lynx and red deer ain't going to butter no parsnips either: it is after

11 o'clock and I know only too well what is on the way. I negotiate the steep but rideable track down the fell and, arriving in Pooley Bridge, I manage to secure both a table and a battery top-up at the Bridge Café, and tuck into a toasted teacake and coffee. I am hoping to be able to push my battery back towards full and then emerge again from the café while the rain is still holding off. It proves a vain hope.

Pooley Bridge, of course, used to have an elegant stone bridge, which crossed the River Eamont as it exited northward from Ullswater. Few will forget Storm Desmond, however. I was in the Lake District that fateful December weekend, in 2015. We watched in awe as Newlands Beck, usually no more than a foot or two deep, climbed the banks of the three-metre ravine that normally contained it comfortably, and began to lap over into our garden. The wind howled and trees bowed: it felt apocalyptic, as two of us collected turves and built a barricade across the lowest of the door thresholds. And then, even as the wind still howled and rain crashed down, the level inched down again.

The next day dawned to reveal Keswick and Cockermouth under water and our friends' car also 'flooded'. We drove them home to Carlisle but the city was now a large lake. My brother-in-law's house had flooded to head height, significantly up from the previous inundation a decade previously. Storm Desmond was an intense, slow-moving storm centred over the River Eden catchment. High tide prevented the waters from leaving the Solway Firth and Carlisle's flood defences once again proved inadequate. But the local flooding was also dramatic. Coledale Beck at Braithwaite rose and took out the decorative footbridges that used to link a terrace of houses with their gardens on the other side of the beck. The debris lodged beneath the village bridge and dammed the flow, creating a new watercourse through the village itself. Everywhere huge piles of silt and gravel had blocked roads. I sensed all the old mine workings deep within the fells had filled and then spouted out across their surroundings. Springs and becks flowed where none had been seen before.

We do now know that weather movements at a global level have been slowing as temperature differentials between the Poles and lower latitudes have decreased, and so a storm of Desmond's endurance and ferocity can be linked with climate change, it being just another extreme event. Back here on Ullswater, the old stone bridge – swept away by Desmond as it also took out the Ullswater steamer landings – was first quickly replaced by a temporary Bailey Bridge and then by a reasonably elegant structure of bowed steel. It can't be said to have the character of the original, though...

As I cross the bridge today, I know that this is no Storm Desmond: it will pass through. But nor is it the Lake District rain of my childhood. I well remember 'Summer' days at Watendlath, high above Borrowdale, when my sister and I would stare through the rain-striped window and wonder if it would ever stop, the heavy, black-beamed farmhouse ceiling behind us seeming to tell us not to even think about trying to escape our confinement. But that was classic 'Lake District rain': it would fall steadily, but rarely furiously. It was guaranteed to get you wet, but never soaked to the skin, and there'd be no hurricane-force wind to drive the wet down your collar and up your cuffs.

Today, the rain is altogether more focussed in its purpose: as I turn down the lake from the bridge, it ratchets up its intent by several notches. It's now savage, but I know it shall indeed pass, though not any time too soon. As I pass beneath Dunmallard Iron Age Hill Fort, which guarded land and water routes at the narrow exit from Ullswater, I care not to so much as raise my eyes. Now a squally gust of wind pirouettes down the lake and lashes my face with icy lumps of rain. It's getting close to sleet; it's cold; the contorted valley that's home to England's second-largest lake is doing what it's renowned for: taking a straight wind and plaiting it into countless unseen shapes.

My plan is to turn off the main road and climb up first to Wreay and then to Dockray, from near where the Old Coach Road heads a tad north of west, across the shoulder of Matterdale Common and Clough Head, before dropping down towards Threlkeld via an old settlement, marked on the map. It's an unclassified road, or Byway Open to all Traffic, and is recognised as an off-road classic, though not for the touring bikes. But the weather has taken another turn for the worse as I approach Wreay and doubts are creeping in. I picture again the bridleway-turned-twin-rivers in Barbondale and, as the contorted eddies think better of creating a spiralling waterspout on the lake behind me, I decide that discretion is going to be the better part of valour.

The old coach road may once have been just that, though there is little evidence abounding that coaches ever did travel this way. Even the Romans thought better of using this route – which climbs more than 300 metres in its nine kilometres or so, while nevertheless hugging the foot of the highest fells – and chose the line subsequently taken by the A66 to connect their fort at Maryport with Penrith. Some even suggest the route was never more than a collection of local routes joined end to end. This I doubt: it is far too purposeful for that. I prefer the idea that, by climbing the fells, it was possible to avoid the river crossings that a low-level route would have made inevitable. The presence of an Iron Age settlement at its western end gives just a hint that this too may have been a very early through route, though I can find no real evidence to support this idea. Just for the record, the Old Coach Road was badly rutted by Storm Desmond and its repair was in part thanks to close cooperation between local people and users, trail bikers among them, though I have to admit my ambivalence about trail bikers being on Lakeland tracks.

Enough of the road I am now pledged to avoid: I am going to commit cycling hari-kari and join the A66. The only trouble is that my carefully trimmed maplets are without context, designed as they are to show my intended route and precious little besides. I'm going to need both a phone signal and shelter to find the best way to the trunk road. Eventually, I chance upon a large yellow bin filled with salt and grit. I may or may not be at the tiny settlement of Sparket or, possibly, Sparket Mill. I lift the lid of the bin and stick my upper body inside, with my phone. I have a signal! I'm soon on the A66 and making quite astonishing progress. A wind that had seemed anything but easterly in the confines of the Ullswater valley must indeed be easterly as I am tanking westward at a steady 25kph-plus. As The Beast is limited to 25, it can only be wind or a descending road that's sending me along faster.

At times, there's a cycle lane for me; at others it's a case of keeping within the marked white margin of the trunk road, clunking across the drains but hoping that this will deliver a wider space between me and the heavy lorries and buses rattling past. It's among the least pleasant rides I've ever made, its only saving grace being the speed at which I am now approaching Keswick. I now have a decision to make, however. Do I detour via Castlerigg Stone Circle, purely as a box-ticking exercise, or do I settle for having been there many times before and head straight for Keswick? I decide that 'the rules' of the trip cannot permit me to pass on any circle and turn off for Castlerigg. On arrival, I park The Beast, snatch my phone from its triple-layer of waterproof wrappings, and dash to the stones, where I take a single wet and windy selfie before the elements can get the better of my phone again.

My visit to Castlerigg has been so unpleasant that I feel compelled to fill my mind instead with my very first visit a quarter of a century ago to this supremely magical circle. It was on a bright winter's day and followed a drive over Whinlatter Pass, between banks of snow-dusted conifers. Descending towards the marshy scrubland that divides Derwentwater from Bassenthaite, I could see beyond the road that climbs out of Keswick, before dropping down into St John's in the Vale. I hadn't set out to visit Castlerigg: I'm not even sure I had heard of it but a brown sign lured me in and I was greeted by the quite serene spectacle of the circle, sitting on its mountain bluff and guarded by the northern fells of Skiddaw and Blencathra. Each stone was set in the snow like walnuts on an iced cake. The snow softened all sound, rendering it all the more mystical. I think that's most likely the day my interest was really first kindled.

* * *

Returning to Castlerigg in more temperate times, I spot a Lycra-clad middle-aged couple admiring the stones, their cycles parked nearby. They're Sandie and Richard, from Thornton, Leicestershire, and they're in the area visiting their daughter, in Kendal. Castlerigg is by a country mile the most visited stone circle in Cumbria. This is thanks not just to its dramatic setting, cradled by fells on all sides, but also to the very obvious fact that it is only a spit from Keswick, one of the national park's honeypots. Not everyone who comes here has made big plans for the visit, and Richard proves no exception: 'We saw an ice cream van and so we stopped and then we saw Castlerigg was next to it. We've visited the Ring of Brodgar, which is massive in comparison, but they all have their own features. I have no idea what it's all about but it must have meant something to somebody sometime.'

Sandie chips in: 'It's interesting to see how people lived and where they lived in bygone civilisations.' I tell her there are getting on for fifty stone circles in Cumbria which prompts a 'wow' and a raised eyebrow or two: 'We don't realise these things, do we, in our busy worlds? We need to make time; go and have a look: I feel kind of in awe of the people who built them with no equipment except their hands and tools they manufactured out of antlers and wood, I suppose. You realise how much more it must have meant to the people who built it because it must taken so much more effort.'

Given that Castlerigg is so popular, it remains something of an enigma, its purpose uncertain and the context of related archaeology in its immediate vicinity apparently absent. Some have proferred the idea that it was some kind of celestial observatory and others that it was constructed in such a way as to somehow reflect or complement the surrounding topography. Of the first theory, Burl dismisses the various quoted celestial alignments as mere coincidence; of the second, Clare says: 'There appears to be no close correspondence here between the height and shapes of stones and the distant summits.' Indeed, he says, Skiddaw, which is dominant to the north, doesn't even possess a stone of its own. That said, I can easily see why people have clutched at this particular straw... the idea of stone 'art' echoing landscape is a recurrent theme and I do see some features that actually may correspond – the undulating ridgeline of Low Rigg and High Rigg, to the south-east, for example. However, on balance, I think there's a need to be sceptical here: these 16-tonne Ice Age erratics of Skiddaw slate were dragged to this summit (unless they had already been deposited there by the retreating ice, which may be possible in some cases) and then erected unhewn, unmodified. It feels like a stretch to imagine that there was some great plan by which each boulder was then matched up with a landscape feature and allocated a specific spot in the circle.

So what do we actually know about Castlerigg? Well, the summit is big enough for it to have accommodated another feature, such as a palisade, but there's no actual evidence of this. It has an internal skewed rectangular structure of uncertain date but in which some remains were found. Three Langdale stone axes were found in nineteenth-century excavations and one of these can be seen in Keswick Museum. It stands on land that is furrowed and appears to have been farmed over an extended period some considerable time after the circle's heyday. It has 'officially' forty perimeter stones and has suffered no major demolition, though one potential outlier seen on early drawings appears to reside beside a dry stone wall near the stile in the western boundary wall: plough marks on its surface provide good evidence that it hasn't always been where it is now. Spiral marks were once found on one stone but were most probably an inventive later addition. Indeed a 2004 Durham University survey using laser technology could find only graffiti. The circle itself is suggested by some, but without real evidence, to date from around 3200 BC.[1]

Like many circles, Castlerigg, formerly known as Carles, suffered the encroachment of agriculture in Medieval times and it was long presumed that signs of an embankment around its perimeter were attributable to ploughing at that time. A recent large-scale survey of the earthworks was supported by the University of York and carried out by Al Oswald and Constance Durgeat, who concluded that the embankment may well have been constructed some time before the stone circle, lending weight to the idea that this is indeed a very old site[2]. At the same time, some of the internal burial structures may have been added as recently as the Middle Ages.

I shall leave you with your own thoughts on a more mysterious note, as recorded by various sources: the unexplained 'light balls' of Castlerigg. This account is to be found on the website *Mysterious Britain and Ireland*: 'On a more mysterious level the circle has been the focus of one well-recorded sighting of strange light phenomena. In 1919 a man called T. Singleton and his friend watched as white light-balls moved slowly over the stones. Strange lights seem to be a recurring theme at ancient sites throughout the world; they may have been one of the reasons ancient people built monuments at specific sites. There has been a lot of speculation as to their nature; it is most probable they are part of some natural phenomena related to fault lines.'[3]

* * *

The rain actually begins to ease a little as I coast down the hill into Keswick, passing the 'rest a while on your way to the stones' bench as I go. I drop down the 'slip road' onto the newly rebuilt (post-Storm Desmond) railway path just to try it out, only to find it closed and having to retrace my tyre tracks.

I find a chippy in Keswick that's happy for me to put The Beast under cover while I dine and recharge, and order fish, chips and mushy peas. My appetite has curiously deserted me and I spend an hour pushing my fish around my plate, watching the steam rise from my cagoule, slung over the back of a chair. My walking shoes are every bit as wet by now as my red 'witch's shoes' had been on Day One. I find a second plug and treat my phone to a top-up and note there's been a message from my forthcoming Airbnb hostess. Seeing the weather and the forecast, she's made an open-ended offer to pick me up and fetch me to her place if it all gets too much. I thank her but don't envisage even contemplating breaking the cycle-all-the-way rule.

My plan from here is to cut across to Portinscale, then through the little settlements at the foot of Whinlatter Pass: Braithwaite, Thornthwaite and Powter How, and then cut through the gap in the fells towards the north end of Bassenthwaite Lake, at Wythop Woods, and on to the village of Embleton. From here, it's just a short ascent to a modest stone circle, at Elva Plain.

All goes fine until I reach the point at which I need to begin to look out for the forest bridleway at Beck Wythop. And then I do something inexplicable: I can only blame the weather for relentlessly washing all the common sense out of my brain. I see a sign on my left, marked '71' – this is the number of the coast-to-coast cycleway, passing exactly the way I want to go. What I am unaware of is that the national cycle network comprises several alternative routes for any given section. So, I ignore the fact that this track is now taking me south, rather than west and is also climbing very steeply. On and on and on and on it goes, relentlessly upward, through thick forest, so I can't see the shape of the land around me. Eventually, I emerge at the visitor centre, near the summit of Whinlatter Pass. This can, in season, be a great place to watch the webcam of nesting ospreys near the foot of the pass, but I am about five kilometres south and two kilometres east of where I should be. My battery has, unsurprisingly, plummeted to well below half charge. I won't be able to reach my digs at Gilgarran without a full recharge. And then I'll miss the dinner my landlady has kindly booked for me at the only pub for miles around.

So I do the unthinkable and arrange to be picked up at Embleton in two hours' time. The Beast speeds me and my guilty conscience down into Lorton Vale and on northwards towards Embleton. From there, my route climbs the hill, past the golf course and through a farmyard, where I am joined by a small procession of one collie dog and one black cat, which I can see trailing me out of the corner of my eye. As the oddity of being followed on a bike by a black cat (not on a bike) sinks in, I trouble myself to stop and look round. It's not a black cat at all, but a small puppy of roughly sausage dog variety and wholly dissimilar to the collie I take to be its mum.

Elva Plain Stone Circle soon begins to emerge from the dank murk: it's not Premier League stuff. Its fifteen remaining stones are low or fallen and it seems at first glance to be no more than modest decoration applied to a sloping field. Clare comments that the vale to the south would most likely have been open water in Neolithic times: either a westward continuation of Bassenthwaite or a lake in its own right. I know from passing this way previously that the valley floor remains boggy today, even if I struggle to see far beyond the first hedge. Other than this observation, Clare struggles to find much justification for the specific situation of this modest circle, though he does observe that there's a crag to the north-west, where the summer sun would have set, while a line from the centre of the circle through an outlying stone passes through the aforementioned Wythop Woods and on through Castlerigg to the summit of Dodd Fell. That would be in a southeasterly direction, or towards the rising sun at mid-winter. So make of that, dear reader, what you will.

As I leave Elva Plain, it's still raining steadily and The Beast tells me he's only got a few K in the tank: I freewheel most of the way back to Embleton, where Julian Carradice, my host for the night, awaits in an SUV with a bike rack. I toss my relief into the dish at one end of the scales and my guilt into the one at the other. Once I add a little gratitude to the relief, the scales tip firmly in the former direction and I choose to dwell no more on my foolish route-finding, nor on the few kilometres of wet road and track I no longer have to navigate.

* * *

I can't move on from the Bassenthwaite area without at least a mention of the Lakes Distillery. I am, after all, a founder member, which means you can find my name etched into the end of a sherry cask by the car park. It also means I get a collector's set of each new single malt as it's produced. I calculate that these have appreciated by between 50 and 100 per cent since I got them but the trouble is that whisky is for drinking and I'm not drinking mine; nor am I cashing in on my growing asset, so it's all a bit of a dilemma. My interest in this distillery started when Linda and I once went out of curiosity to have a look at the Victorian 'model farm' where it's now based. It was derelict at the time but was subsequently acquired by Nigel Mills, whom I knew from his time as the man at the top of the Entrepreneurs' Forum, in Newcastle, as the ideal place to establish a whisky distillery. Of all the growing number of whisky distilleries in England this is the most similar to what you would expect of a whisky distillery from what you've seen in Scotland or Ireland. This is thanks in part to the eminent suitability of those model farm buildings I recall seeing so many years ago. Nigel Mills has always set his sights high and said after acquiring new multi-million-pound investment finance during the COVID pandemic: 'Our vision is to create a global luxury single malt whisky brand. It's an ambitious goal and one which means quality is at the heart of everything we do.' I think I can be sure that our Neolithic ancestors would not have distilled spirit but that does not mean they would not have stumbled across the 'joys' of alcohol. Indeed, in the Middle Ages, ale was a safer alternative to drinking water. That is likely to have also been the case in far earlier times, for the avoidance of waterborne parasites and infections. It most likely began when crab apples or cultivated barley were inadvertently left to ferment and so it is surely as old as farming itself.

* * *

In the car on the way back to Gilgarran, I chat with Julian who, like so many around here, works freelance for the nuclear plant at Sellafield. He is also a bit of an expert on Cumbrian mine workings and a former member of the Wasdale Mountain

Rescue Team, which is based close to Sellafield. He tells me he slightly fell out with his colleagues there as they had adopted, he suggested, a nuclear industry safety-first approach to health and safety for mountain rescue missions. Julian's view is that if a mountain rescue team sets out to avoid risk, it may as well stay under the duvet.

Although he's moved from what we might call eight o'clock to ten o'clock on the Lake District clock face, he's still a Wasdale lad through and through and knows all the near-mythical characters of the special dale, like Jos Naylor, the legendary fell-runner and those who would tell tall stories at the Santon Bridge Inn. Of this, more later.

Julian and his partner, Sheena, turn out to be keen cyclists and The Beast is happy to share digs with Sheena's more modest electric model for the night. They are also the proud owners of a newish camper van and have managed to get in ahead of the camper van mania that's poised to sweep post-lockdown Britain. Linda and I spent ages looking for a camper van before COVID was even a softly whispered secret. We couldn't quite agree on a spec: I wanted to convert a Citröen van, which would be modest enough to navigate just about any road; Linda fancied space all around the bed, no need to remake same each night... and a sauna (well, perhaps not this last). My main concern with such enhanced spec is the dramatic overhang at the back and the incompatibility of the same with a hump-backed bridge. And now, sadly, camper vans have become the 'new caravan' in the catalogue of vehicles other road-users despise. I'd still quite fancy one, though, for all that!

Sheena is new to Airbnb so I'm happy to offer a few 'top tips' from our own hosting experiences, but there's nothing I could ever find fault with in their house in the tiny village of Gilgarran. This begins with their generosity in rescuing me today and following on via drying all my sodden clothing and footwear, permitting me a long soak in a hot bath, lending me a smart Rab jacket for the evening, and then running me up to the pub in nearby Dean for my evening meal.

Aware that Gilgarran is blessed with neither pub nor chippy, nor much else beyond peace and quiet, I had tried unsuccessfully to book a meal at The Royal Yew – a fairly common occurrence in these emerging-from-COVID days, but Sheena had sorted it all for me and The Royal Yew turns out to be a fantastic country pub, belying the small size of the community it serves. The menu is so appealing to a slowly-drying weary cyclist that I succumb to the temptation of both a starter and mains. This proves a mistake, as the black pudding starter on its own would have sufficed. 'You're in West Cumbria now,' Julian says later. 'They don't do small here.'

A word or few about the yew: it's a large yew and might even date back more than the few hundred years since the pub was built, or even the thousand or so years of the village's history. Many of our yew trees could be as many as 4,000 or more years old and so those same trees that are around now would have been familiar to Neolithic and Bronze Age people. They may even have shot deer with bows fashioned from yew. The yew is, if you like, our olive, in terms of its longevity.

In his fascinating book, *The Immortal Yew*, Tony Hall comments: 'Some yew trees are so old that they predate many of our Christian churches, whose churchyards tend to be strongholds for these ancient wonders.' Noting that yews were venerated by pre-Christian religions, they were often planted in groves to create places for meeting and worship. '[They] are today surrounded in myths and mystery.'

Whether those same yews were actually around so long ago is, however, not very relevant, for the tree as a species has been around for millions of years. According to Ken Mills, in his nice little work, *The Cumbrian Yew Book*, the yew at the Royal Yew is a female tree and a mere spring chicken at a sprightly 400 years old, so not quite as old as I'd hinted.

It's believed that yews were planted at sacred sites to keep grazing animals away, as most parts of the tree are poisonous to most (but not all) mammals. Paradoxically, it is also attributed with healing properties, including the ability to alleviate the symptoms of some cancers. *Palitaxel*, a natural compound found in the bark of the yew, is sold under the brand name Taxol and is used to block the growth of cancerous cells. A synthetic form of the drug was developed in the 1990s and remains, says Hall, one of the most effective treatments for cancer. Another anti-cancer drug, *docetaxel* (Taxotere) is derived from the needles of the tree.

The yew tree, *Yggdrasil*, is thought to be the mythological Norse tree of life in the ancient Icelandic sagas, the *Eddas*, but its symbolic importance almost certainly predates these times. Terms like 'Druid' and 'Celtic' tend to be rather vague, but I quote Hall again: 'Druids believed that wands of yew would banish evil spirits, bringing purity and peace. And yew staves carved with early medieval Ogham text were used to perform magical tasks.'

The yew, continues Hall, 'was a symbol of death and resurrection in Celtic culture, due to its ability to resprout and put on new growth after years of inactivity. This tree is also said to symbolise death and resurrection in Christianity.'

Returning to Paul Frodsham's writings on the appropriation by Christianity of the rites of far more ancient cultures, it's worth also noting: 'Yews marked the end of the year in the Celtic calendar, and the autumn festival of Samhain is one of the most important dates in the pagan calendar.' We now celebrate it as Halloween as it was believed to be a time when spirits could more easily cross from the Otherworld to ours. It falls between the autumn equinox and the winter solstice and so I find myself wondering if the yew might indeed have enjoyed a role in the world of what went on at the stone circles. Britain's oldest known yew tree still stands at Fortinghall, in Perthshire, and is thought to be as many as 5,000 years old. Close by are found the remains of a number of stone circles. Not proof absolute, but perhaps more than a mere interesting coincidence.

* * *

The village of Dean has other historic attractions that the lateness of the day and the continued inclement weather have denied me. Earthworks and mounds are marked on the map on the southwest edge of the village, while some reports reference a cup and ring marked boulder inside the church (noting Frodsham's caveat that such ornamentation is rare west of the Pennines). Clare mentions, in addition, a standing stone, the remains of a possible stone circle and the finding of an 'encrusted urn' at nearby Branthwaite. 'Further urns were found in cutting the railway at Ullock where, within "bowshot", there was reputed to have been a circle of large boulders. By 1876, however, the latter had been either removed or buried, although two large slabs in the field boundary may be related.'

I shall in the morning be visiting a modest stone circle at Studfoldgate. Clare notes that this enjoys views towards another likely former circle at Lamplugh, and, taking all this together, we begin to see a picture of what Clare calls 'considerable prehistoric activity'. The Ennerdale valley would have afforded an easy route on foot or by boat from the central Lakeland fells and the axe factory at Langdale, I find myself reflecting that this rather inauspicious undulating plain to the north-west may once have enjoyed a status not equal to, but perhaps parallel with, those at Shap and Long Meg. Ongoing early settlement is suggested by Branthwaite Hall, said to be one of the best-preserved early pele towers in the country.

Chapter 5

The coastal fringe

Where early farmers tamed the fell flanks

By the morning I'm happy to note that some of my clothes are almost dry! My shoes are not, but I fancy that the air rushing past my feet may do the trick. I feel well refreshed after yesterday's misery and share with Sheena the hot news that there's a Neolithic stone circle (Studfoldgate) within a kilometre or two of their house. I also discover from BBC *Look North* that a local lad, Gary McKee, will today run his 110th and final consecutive marathon.

He's already run 26.5 miles every day since February 1. When he's finally done, later today, his total mileage will fall not far short of three thousand, and he'll have raised tens of thousands of pounds for cancer charities in West Cumbria, in memory of his father, who died of the disease. That's another thing about West Cumbria: it's a place that just gets on with its own thing and no one seems that bothered if they don't make the national headlines they perhaps deserve.

Gary works at Sellafield too, when not running marathons, and his father and granddad were both miners. A lot of Irish people were drawn to West Cumbria by the prospect of employment and it's not uncommon to find traditional Cumbrian villages cheek-by-jowl with more recent settlements of modest terraced homes. Cleator and Cleator Moor are perhaps the archetypes of this phenomenon, the latter first settled by Irish migrants escaping the potato famine. Gary lives there now and, if his name were not enough of a clue, a story of his attending a Gaelic football final in Dublin shortly before his father's death suggests his antecedents.

* * *

I leave Gilgarran heavier by one hearty breakfast and promise Julian and Sheena a copy of *Ring of Stone Circles* when it comes out. In the meantime, I'll send Julian my novel, *The Episode*, and hope he enjoys the chapter set in Wasdale. I'm very soon at Studfoldgate, where I clamber over the gate and trudge through the swampy reeds to where one edge of a moderately sized collection of stones sits atop a low mound. I fancy a second mound lies a short distance to the southeast. It's not easy to spot all the extant stones as the vegetation is high and a stone wall dissects the ring, which has a diameter of about 33 metres. Indeed, only by looking at Google Earth later do I begin to appreciate the full extent of the monument. As Tom Clare notes, there is a fine view eastward towards Lamplugh, and to the ridge of High Park to the south. With a bit of tidying up of wayward vegetation and a better way through the bog, rather more might be made of this circle, though I appreciate that may be far from uppermost in the minds of the owners.

I continue to cross the post-industrial-cum-pastoral landscape, heading towards Ennerdale Bridge, at the foot of the aforementioned eponymous valley. As I make to join the railway footpath and cycleway at Winder Brow, a knot of people, young and old, is gathered excitedly at a bridge over the old line: I'm going to be just in time to witness the 110th marathon of Gary McKee. I cycle a kilometre along the line to Rowrah and stop to get my camera out and then, quick as a flash, it seems, Gary and his entourage are both come and gone. Bloody well done, Gary, I think. But what are you going to do now for the next 110 days?

The cycle path leaves the old railway and winds me through the fringes of former quarry workings beside a National Nature Reserve, called High Leys, designated for its traditional hay meadow flora. As I continue, a single monolith stands to the right of the track, inscribed with a poem in local dialect. A barrow-shaped mound is beyond, but I strongly suspect it to be just a quarry spoil heap. The monolith is covered in lichen and I can't read all the words of the poem, beyond a reference to 'auld Ned', a woman and some hogs, and nor can I find any reference online later.

I have some distance to cover today and so my intention is to give The Beast a booster at Ennerdale Bridge. Ennerdale is by some distance the loneliest Lakeland valley. Like Wasdale, it's a road cul-de-sac. Unlike Wasdale, the road barely begins to go up the valley. Beyond the road's end are Ennerdale Youth Hostel and the legendary Black Sail Youth Hostel. The latter is a long walk in, though the warden will take your supplies in by Land Rover. We often spend New Year with a group of friends at various Lakes hostels, most frequently latterly at Honister Pass.

But we did have a run at both Ennerdale and Black Sail, though the Black Sail fad came to a sticky end for the gang when all the pipes froze one winter.

Another winter, at either one or the other of the Ennerdale hostels, we walked down the lakeshore to Ennerdale Bridge on New Year's Day and headed for the community pub, the Fox and Hounds, only to be greeted by a tale of woe. Thieves (from Cleator Moor, it was reflexively suggested) had broken in and stolen the safe and all its New Year's Eve cash contents. It felt like this disaster could spell the end of the whole venture. We headed instead for The Shepherds Arms.

Today I'm relieved to find the Fox and Hounds' doors open and, even though bar service won't start for another 20 minutes, they're happy to ply me with coffee while The Beast sups his 240 volts. 'No, no, we're not a community pub anymore,' the barmaid tells me. 'I think they found it was a conflict of interest with The Gather.' On a subsequent visit, it turns out that The Gather is a community café and meeting place now run by the same bunch as first got going with the Fox and Hounds. It's a great space, with great cakes, and it's gratifying to find that a modest village will support all three, but in any normal year the place would be full of enthusiastic Dutch people and others embarked upon Wainwright's Coast to Coast Walk.

There's a large interpretation notice on the outside wall of The Gather, with a big bold headline, MUSSELS. This explains that the valley's River Ehen is an important habitat for the endangered freshwater mussel, whose numbers have declined by more than 90 per cent across Europe over the past century. The Ehen has now the only remaining breeding population of the species in England of the continent's 'most endangered species'. Its fate is intrinsically linked with that of the Atlantic salmon, which has also been going through pretty tough times of late. The Ehen has been made a Special Area of Conservation, with the aim of tackling any form of pollution that might compromise the continued existence of a species that has been on the planet for 200 million years, long before the arrival of the dinosaurs. Apparently, they can grow to 15cm long and live for more than one hundred years, which suggests to me that they may well have been a decent food source for the early inhabitants.

A scan of the OS map reveals that there are, indeed, 'settlements' marked on the map amid the acres of forest cover, though the extensive planting of Sitka spruce, to which the valley was subjected for a quarter of a century from 1925, may have obliterated any significant remains. A fascinating document from the Forestry Commission archive chronicles the history of this vast artificial landscape. Of course, in saying this, I am conveniently ignoring the fact that open sheep-grazed fells are no less artificial. Indeed, it was the Neolithic and Bronze Age peoples who almost certainly did most to clear the Lakeland fells of their natural tree cover, which might have comprised the full range of indigenous species, with oak, sycamore and other larger trees on the lower levels, dwindling to birch and dwarf hazel towards the tree line. 'Have axe shall fell trees' must have been the favoured maxim of these early farmers, once they'd mastered the art of adze-making, be it from stone or, later, bronze.

Interestingly, in his book *Lakeland Wild*, Jim Crumley describes his 'discovery' of a 'forest' of dwarf oak, growing horizontally, high on a fellside. It's not that trees can't grow, just that they won't grow if sheep eat their saplings. You can go way north of the Arctic Circle in Norway and still find deciduous trees thriving at far higher altitudes than they are normally found in this country.

That Forestry Commission archive states: 'Prior to afforestation the lands now forming part of Ennerdale Forest were almost entirely devoted to sheep farming. The principle acquisition, which was in the Ennerdale Valley, comprised 5,547 acres [2,245 hectares] purchased from Lord Lonsdale and Mr John Tyson and records show that this land supported a breeding flock of 1,619 Herdwick sheep or thereabouts. The main farming unit was that of Gillerthwaite Farm and here a number of excellent rams have been bred in addition to other good breeding stock.'

All such activity was swept aside in the name of trying to make the UK self-sufficient in timber. However, from this came, ultimately, opportunity, with the creation of Wild Ennerdale, a partnership between the main landowners in the valley (Forestry England, the National Trust and United Utilities) and Natural England. Wild Ennerdale is affiliated to the Rewilding Britain network, dedicated to reversing habitat and species loss, which has acquired new impetus in a post-COVID world also suffering the impact of climate change.

Wild Ennerdale's 'manifesto' states: 'Thick sitka spruce plantations dominated the landscape for the last century, and high levels of sheep grazing reduced the biodiversity and habitat structure across the valley. The Wild Ennerdale project aims to let natural processes shape the landscape and ecology and will always take decisions which favour this, ultimately leading towards a wilder, more diverse and resilient place over time.' Two decades on, and a 'minimalist approach' and cooperation by a range of partners and stakeholders has seen the return of wildlife in abundance, alongside 'more diverse habitat, greater structure, expanding woodland, a wilful [correct] river that can respond to high rainfall events'. Highlights include returning salmon in the restored river systems and thriving marsh fritillary butterfly populations.

The 'manifesto' continues: 'A reduction in sheep grazing was undertaken to allow for the introduction of low numbers of bigger herbivores.' So, Galloway cattle were introduced in 2006 and natural regeneration was encouraged and supplemented with native tree planting. More than 100,000 trees had been planted at the time

of writing, while rivers and mires had been restored and new wetlands created. Deer numbers continue to be controlled and spruce trees have been removed and replaced with native species, with juniper and aspen, in particular, encouraged. As previously noted, reintroduced lynx are not now part of the model for deer control…
Healthy juniper cover, though, may be important: tracts of native juniper brush in Teesdale have been assaulted over the past decade by *phytophthora austrocedri*, an aggressive fungal dieback disease that originated in Argentina. I believe the Lakes Distillery, of which you may recall I am a founder member, has longer-term aspirations to use locally sourced Ennerdale juniper berries for its gin and our friends at the Lussa gin distillery, on the Isle of Jura, have embarked on extensive planting of juniper there in the name of ultimate self-sufficiency, rather than importing from Europe.

The belted Galloway cattle mentioned can be seen living 'wild' when you walk the valley these days; the manner in which they turn the soil is said to be an important part of the overall rewilding process. Among future plans of Wild Ennerdale is the reintroduction of beavers and on a somewhat larger scale than has already taken place on enclosed land on the Lowther Estate. Beavers and their enthusiasm for slowing upland run-off by building dams are now considered a potentially valuable component in strategies to alleviate flooding.

A rare visitor to Ennerdale, among its diversifying range of fauna, is the lesser spotted future US President and First Lady: Bill Clinton says he first proposed to Hillary on her first visit to the UK on the shores of Ennerdale Water. I'm unsure which is hardest to explain: what precisely the couple were up to by this the loneliest lake in Cumbria, or how she could possibly have turned him down… on this occasion at least.

* * *

I leave Ennerdale Bridge behind, climbing the hill onto the low fells to the south-west, which fringe the vast expanse of the unpeopled open landscape of the treeless Copeland Forest (reminding us that 'forest' once meant a hunting ground). I am bound for the delightful Blakeley Raise, or Kinniside, Stone Circle. I call it the Morecambe and Wise circle: just as Eric Morecambe famously assured 'Andrew Preview' (André Previn) that he was playing all the right notes, but not necessarily in the right order, so I can reasonably assert that this circle most likely has all the right stones... but they may not necessarily all be precisely where they should be.

Although different accounts exist of what may or may not have gone at Blakeley Raise, the consensus seems to settle around the notion that there was always a circle on this spot but that this was destroyed by a farmer in the eighteenth century. Where accounts then differ is around both the original location and the date on which it was restored. If only because it is clear and concise, I err towards the *Megalithic Portal* variant, which asserts that all the post-holes were carefully measured and the stones gathered from walls and gateposts to be set in concrete at the present (and supposedly original) site. This event is said to have taken place around 1925 and the suggestion is that each stone is in its correct hole, though I find this more than a little far-fetched after the passage of 300 years. Others doubt the rigour of the Dr Quine, of Frizington, who led the restoration.

Whatever... as the lazy-tongued and disinterested might drawl. The reality is an elegant circle of eleven stones (some accounts say twelve, and I confess to not having counted) sitting on a prominent shoulder, with views down in the general direction of the Irish Sea. The tallest stone is about a metre. There's a slightly raised mound at the centre of the circle, suggesting a possible cairn. The Beast enjoys posing upon this.

* * *

A short distance to the west of Blakeley Raise is the small town of Egremont, which falls mostly into the aforementioned 'traditional Cumbrian' classification, albeit with plenty of newer build around its central high street. In the first of these personae it is home to a quite exceptional tradition that's also loosely linked, once again, with Cumbrian Norman gentry, this time Lord Egremont, whose heirs, these days, make their home in a private residence at Petworth House, the grand stately home and deer park in West Sussex. The Petworth mansion itself and its extensive and important art collection are now in the hands of the National Trust. The creation of the Egremont Peerage, however, post-dates the event for which Egremont is most famed...

It was towards the end of a sunny day in September 2019 that I posed the following question: 'So, are you a gurner, then?' It was an inquiry framed in all innocence: I had only uncertain preconceptions as to what I should expect to see at the World Gurning Championships, in which the challenge for competitors is to pull the most contorted face possible. To be more precise, the challenge is to deliver the greatest possible facial transformation – from normal to gruesome – while your head is stuck through a horse's collar; and to do so in front of a few hundred people.

I ask a young woman if she's planning to compete in the event – for no better reason than that I have just seen her in conversation with Kevin Brown, the organiser for the last few years of the championships, which are the finale to Egremont's annual Crab Fair.

Her response to me is one of shock, however. Indeed, she pulls such a face that I rather fear she'll be sorely missed in the event, which is to start in a couple of hours' time. It turns out, however, that Janina Götz is actually from the German TV station, *ProSiebenSat.1.*

'We saw the competition on the internet and thought it might make interesting TV,' she explains, as she and her cameraman later take up position behind the five elderly male judges at Egremont's Falcon Club venue. It's the first time that the contest has been staged here, having previously been at the market hall, on Market Street. The atmosphere in the hall is becoming increasingly tense: this is, after all, the 'big one', even though it is actually only the second world championship to take place at the Crab Fair today.

The first was the 11-stone class in the World Cumberland and Westmorland wrestling championships, and I am quickly coming to appreciate that the term 'world' is quite loosely applied in Egremont, in much the same way as Americans love to talk about World Series in baseball and what they insist on calling 'football'.

The excitement is mounting broadly in parallel with the approach of tonight's gurning event and with the cumulative effect of a long day's drinking by a decent proportion of those now present. Janina, however, appears increasingly impervious to the general prevailing good humour, her face seemingly scarred by an emerging scowl, though not a gurn.

My wife Linda is worried that the result of the German team's attendance might turn out to be a TV exposé on the quaint English practice of cruelty to children in the name of entertainment, for the gurning – when it eventually gets going quite late in the evening – begins with the children's class.

I confess I have actually toyed with entering the gurning competition myself, just to be able to write from the perspective of a full participant, but I now reflect that it wouldn't be dissimilar to lining up for England at Wembley: gurning, like football, demands skill, training and much practice.

Kevin has already given us a run-down of how the contest will evolve: 'If you are ugly, it doesn't necessarily mean you are going to win the gurning,' he says. I check and study his expression – I hope he isn't specifically directing his remark at me. He doesn't catch my look and continues: 'It's the biggest transformation of face, from normal to virtually unrecognisable.'

There is no clear consensus today as to precisely how the contest evolved over time, but one theory has it that it started with people pulling faces as they bit into the sour crab apples munificently donated to the townsfolk by the local laird to celebrate the conclusion of a successful harvest. Other theories include the idea that a horse's collar was placed around the neck of the 'village idiot', who would pull faces in exchange for a pint of ale; or that a drunken farmer returned home to find his unimpressed wife pulling faces, whereupon he cast a horse's collar over her head and told her to 'stop gurning, woman'. At which point, unsurprisingly, she began to pull even meaner faces.

The reason for this conspicuous lack of precise detail as to antecedents is down to the simple passage of time: a great deal of it. While some towns and villages in West Cumbria date back only to industrial times, others have a much more substantial lineage, and Egremont is among them. Indeed, the Crab Fair is one of the oldest such events in the country, perhaps even the oldest, having been first granted a Royal Charter in 1267. It has continued annually ever since, bar wartime (and, rather more recently, COVID-19) and has always featured a variety of traditional local events.

Besides gurning, these include, or have included, Cumberland and Westmorland wrestling, grass track cycle racing, competitive pipe-smoking, cuddy (pony) racing, cock-fighting, bull-baiting, dialect singing, and who can eat the most 'biskeys and treacle', which I guess might just have been associated with the rum and sugar trade, through nearby Whitehaven.

Earlier in the day, we'd arrived at the showground, on the edge of town, in time to catch a few rounds of wrestling. Or, more accurately, in the first instance, to watch while an ambulance removed one of the contestants in the direction of the A & E Department at Carlisle. Then we got chatting to a chap from Workington way, called Phillip Gate, who was, he said, quite passionate about West Cumbria and, specifically its lore and traditions. As we stood in a loose circle around the roped-off ring, I found myself imagining this historic contest of man-on-man taking place in a stone circle: Blakeley Raise would be a perfect fit.

Phillip told us the chap in the ambulance had taken an awkward fall on his head. Like all forms of wrestling, the Cumberland and Westmorland variety is not without risk, though serious injury is rare. The dangers are significant enough for the Government to require a degree of form-filling by the organisers. The same applies to Cornish wrestling but not, for some reason, to Greco-Roman wrestling. Wrestling of this kind – in which the object is to floor your opponent – has parallels with styles of wrestling from across Europe and the world. Even Japan's sumo wrestling has strong echoes.

What's most distinctive about the Cumberland and Westmorland form (which is also practised in Northumberland) is the wrestlers' traditional garb of white embroidered vest, 'long johns' and black or coloured shorts worn over these. The bout begins with each wrestler grasping the other, their chins on each other's right shoulder. Strong similarities with the Icelandic *glima* form suggest it may have arrived, like so many other traditions in Cumberland and Westmorland, with the Viking settlers – though similarities with the Cornish variety of wrestling also point to earlier Celtic origins. Who knows, something like it may genuinely have occurred in smaller 'local' stone circles. In the past decade, partly following the Icelandic lead, women and girls have also increasingly taken part.

Although the epicentre of the sport is at Grasmere, where it is a core fixture in the annual Sports, Phillip explained that the world titles in each weight class rotate around the major wrestling events. Today it was the turn of the Crab Fair to host the 11-stone class World Title bout. We saw it won by Andrew Carlile, from Carlisle. A wrestler for some thirty years – now thirty-nine and quite a star in the sport – he told me how he had been touring in Iceland earlier in the year.

The Crab Fair events – including wrestling and gurning – are deeply engrained in the psyche of what some casually describe as 'the most westerly town' in the country – even though both Workington and Whitehaven lie to the west, and that's without even considering Cornwall. But that's the DNA of local pride, I guess. Gurning's biggest character, says Kevin when we meet up in the evening, was a chap called Peter Jackman, who sadly died in 2018. 'He would do everything in Egremont Crab Fair.' Indeed, I see that tributes on his *Facebook* page still recall a man 'who had crab fair running through him like a stick of rock'.

In a similar vein, Kevin laments the passing of Anne Woods, aka 'Mystic Mug', who, having won the women's contest no fewer than twenty-eight times, campaigned long, hard – and ultimately successfully – to be recognised in the *Guinness Book of Records*.

Notwithstanding its title – and recurrent international interest in the event, on account of its 'English eccentricity' – the World Gurning Championship, like the rest of the Crab Fair, is fundamentally a local event, enjoyed by local people. But then, it is also a WORLD championship… 'We have people from America, New Zealand, Australia,' continues Kevin. Even he is slightly incredulous as to why anyone would fly over the Atlantic 'just to pull a face in front of 300 people'.

Indeed, why would you travel even a mile to participate in an ugly mug contest? Could it be for the brief moment of glory? For the money, perhaps? Well, on this last count, I shall learn that there are a few modest benefits that come with winning: the four times winner of the women's event tells me that although she has an agent, she doesn't seem to get many gigs.

Or the fame, perhaps? 'Michaela Strachan from *BBC Countryfile* was our most famous winner, in 2002,' says Kevin, who is keen to introduce me to some of this year's contestants, beginning with the reigning men's champion, who goes by the prosaic moniker of 'Adrian from Coventry', though it doesn't take too much research to discover his full name is Adrian Zivelonghi. Adrian, fifty-two, boasts a pretty long history of gurning and lifted the trophy in 2016 and 2018.

'I've only missed three times since 2000 and I'm the reigning champion,' he reminds me. 'I think I have got a unique ability to put my bottom set of teeth over my top set.' He also boasts a bit of an egg-shaped head, domed and bald, slightly pixie ears, and the honed skill of not just letting his bottom dentures go freelance but also puckering his lips above a wrinkly prune of a chin at the same time… while simultaneously crossing his eyes. I can see he's going to be hard to beat.

But it could be a tough call this time round, as gurner supreme, Tommy Mattinson, from Aspatria, is back in the frame after missing two contests through illness. 'Tommy Mattinson is my hero,' continues Adrian, who has been up here for a few days getting himself psyched up. When he's not pulling faces, he works on the Land Rover production line. 'He's a legend and I always want to be as good as him, but I never will.'

It was seeing a newspaper picture of a gurn that first attracted Adrian's attention, but it was learning that it was possible to be a world champion that persuaded him to perfect his own gurn and compete. 'I never thought I had a chance of being world champion in anything, but when you find out that a gurner can become a world champion… I thought "this is my sport"!'

Time to track down the legend then. And I soon find the man himself: Tommy Pattinson is back in town and up for a fight. 'I was poorly, as I was diagnosed with kidney cancer,' he tells me. 'I had to have microwave ablation.' He looks fit and well now and he's a good looking chap... when not competing. 'I started gurning because my dad and granddad did it,' Tommy tells me. 'I started when I was eleven or twelve in the junior competition – the first ever junior competition, in fact. I was a lot younger than all the entrants in men's event in '85 and '86: I was a young guy, so the transformation was bigger. Sixteen times, I've won now.

'I've been all over the world: Hollywood, Japan, Germany. I've been on Saturday night TV, breakfast TV; I've been with my agency for twenty-one years and I've a lot of international fame.' Well, that's a world champ for you... and he's already building his gurning legacy: 'My two kids are very good gurners,' he says.

Kevin may not have been born to gurn himself, but with an uncle and cousin on the committee, he was perhaps, born to organise gurning. 'I'm a bit passionate about it,' he says with some understatement, as he goes on to tell me how long it takes to pull the whole event together and ensure health and safety compliance.

I reflect that, surely, gurning can't be as dangerous as wrestling... But no sooner has young Summer Dawson, from Milnthorpe, taken the junior crown from reigning champ, Georgia Lister, than there's a commotion in the women's heats: a contestant attempting a cross-eyed gurn is struggling to get her eyes uncrossed again and has to 'retire hurt', stumbling back to her seat with tears streaming down her cheeks and the German TV crew in hot pursuit. Her injury leaves the way clear for five-times champ Claire Lister to retain her crown, with her trademark gurn – eyes crossed and gazing down at a mouth that reminds me of one of those big red tube worms that lurk around hydrothermal vents at the bottom of the deepest oceans. 'The first time I entered, it was my sister who put me in for it,' she tells me, adding that only pregnancy and motherhood have interrupted her reign.

Summer's mum, Tiree, a photographer in Kendal, tells me she surprised herself by earning second place in the previous year's contest, which she entered as a fortieth birthday 'treat'. She comes third this time, but says: 'I just always pull faces and you can get better at that as you get older.'

And then Tommy effortlessly regains his crown with his characteristically understated angry pouting gurn. If I was still in any doubt about the contest's world appeal, then German Otto Squire, a young London-based business development consultant and his Mexican girlfriend, architect Ana Sofia Narro, put me straight: 'It's amazing,' says Ana Sofia. 'It would be so funny to do this in Mexico!' Yes, I bet it would!

But I'm less sure of how gurning has gone down in Germany, having failed in successive attempts to get hold of Janina Götz. Indeed, she now appears to have left the TV station in March 2020, at the start of COVID. I can find no evidence that her planned piece on Egremont's big day ever aired. So Linda's fears for the national reputation were most likely unfounded and she can sleep easy again.

As I write this, the Crab Fair organisers, alarmed at rising COVID numbers, have just announced the cancellation of the event for a second successive year, leaving me thankful to have had the foresight to attend two years ago. However tenuous the connection may be, I reflect on the roundness of a Cumberland wrestling ring, whose size is just about that of a smaller cairn circle, and upon the indigenous nature of the crab apple. Might our Neolithic ancestors have pulled faces as they bit into the wild but plentiful fruit? Or might they, however improbable, have boiled it with honey and made some kind of jam or early non-citrus 'marmalade'?

* * *

On leaving Blakeley Raise, my planned route is to make a detour to the east, via a fell track across Tongue How, which passes a number of landscape features, including cairns and a settlement. However, more detailed inspection raises some doubt in my mind as to whether I'll be able to complete the loop: a section of the return route is marked only as a footpath and, while some of this right of way may be on a farm track, some of it may not. I am also conscious that I still have much ground to cover today, including an ascent on foot to the stone circles on Brat's Hill, above Eskdale. I had originally planned to reach these via the bridleway from Miterdale, cross the fell to the circles and then descend on the bridleway to Boot, in Eskdale. However, Denise, the linocut artist, has already visited the circles and has warned that the route is very steep and very rocky. Cycling it is not an option.

The Tongue How landscape is listed by Historic England for its archaeological significance and so I quote from this listing: 'As a result of archaeological surveys between 1980 and 1990 within the Lake District National Park, these fells have become one of the best recorded upland areas in England. On the open fells there is sufficient well preserved and understood evidence over extensive areas for human exploitation of these uplands from the Neolithic to the post-medieval period.

'On the enclosed land and within forestry the archaeological remains are fragmentary, but they survive sufficiently well to show that human activity extended beyond the confines of the open fells. Bronze Age activity accounts for the most extensive use of the area, and evidence for it includes some of the largest and best preserved field systems and cairn fields in England, as well as settlement sites, numerous burial monuments, stone circles and other ceremonial remains. Taken together, their remains can provide a detailed insight into life in the later prehistoric period. Of additional importance is the well-preserved and often visible relationship between the remains of earlier and later periods, since this provides an understanding of changes in land use through time.'

Eleanor Kingston, lead archaeologist at the Lake District National Park Authority, tells me with a degree of frustration: 'We have undertaken over the years quite a lot of field surveys, particularly in the south-west upland areas. We understand where sites are but from that we have had very little excavation or seismic investigation into these to tie down dates and further information.'

Such surveying work as has been done took place mostly between 1982 and 1989 and is recorded in a weighty volume entitled *Cairns, Fields and Cultivation: Archaeological Landscapes of the Lake District Uplands*, published by Lancaster Imprints, part of Oxford Archaeology North. Lest there be any doubt about the importance of the whole fellside area of the Lake District, I quote from the book's summary, which tells of 'some of the most remarkable field systems and settlements in England, mainly of later prehistoric date' and notes that 'the greatest concentration of prehistoric landscapes within the Lake District is on the marginal uplands of Western Cumbria, adjacent to the Cumbrian coastal plain, which has been shown, as a result of extensive field walking, to be an area of Mesolithic and Neolithic activity.' Crucially, as it underpins much of this overall narrative, the book notes that the majority of remains identified in the programme appear to date from the Bronze Age and may very likely reflect an expansion out from the coastal plain during a period of more benign climatic conditions.

In the Tongue How Western Fells area, the survey work was divided into four 'plots' – Town Bank, Stockdale Moor, Whin Garth and Burnmoor (the higher ground between Wasdale and Eskdale). The first of these is an area of unenclosed fell on the south-facing slopes of Lang Rigg, immediately to the north of bridleway I had hoped to take. The survey here was carried out in April and May 1986 and recorded no fewer than 893 monuments, clustered in fifteen 'site groups'. Each group is illustrated with a detailed plan of all the survey findings, as though a colossal pepper pot had shaken these liberally across the entire landscape.

The earliest remains are late Neolithic or early Bronze Age and comprise funerary cairns; these were superseded by large a round cairn, most probably not in simultaneous use. The hillside boasted 'relatively sophisticated field systems, extending in a linear spread along south-facing, well-drained, sloping areas, each being associated with either stern-founded roundhouses, or house platforms'. Further east, this order gave way to larger, more randomly shaped fields, with a lot of clearance cairns and banks of other unwanted stone, between which were cultivated strips of roughly equal width. 'The differences between the field systems probably reflect a change of emphasis from pastoral towards arable farming.' The survey identified a distinctive type of unenclosed farmstead, with a hollowed-out enclosure linked to a roundhouse. These hollows would have been damp and so must have been used for stock, rather than human habitation. The whole was seen to be quite distinct from the adjacent less well-developed Stockdale Moor site, with its more random organisation and evidence of possible pre-cultivation activity. The survey concludes: 'Town Bank is extraordinarily significant; not only does it display activity extending between the Neolithic and Medieval periods, but it demonstrates a complex development of Bronze/Iron Age settlements and field systems.'

* * *

As I descend the fell road towards Calder Bridge, the enormous monstrosity that is the Sellafield nuclear complex hoves into view.

West Cumbria has long been home to some of the least desirable industries in the UK and the legacy of this is the curious juxtaposition between a national park and World Heritage Site to the east of the main coast road, and Sellafield and other ugly intrusions along the coastline, to the west of it.

One of the reasons for this is that, in its relative isolation, West Cumbria has acquired the tag of being an economically and socially deprived area. But this isolation and consequent issues also made it a great spot after the last war for the Government to locate its 'factory' for building the UK's nuclear deterrent. Calder Hall, within the Windscale nuclear complex, was the reactor that produced the weapons-grade plutonium for the arming of the country's warheads. Back in 1957, a fire in one of the reactors was just the latest in a series of nuclear accidents, some of them serious. Largely hushed-up by the Government of the day, it turned out to be one of the worst nuclear accidents in the world ever, spreading radioactive fallout across the UK and Europe.

One of the methods employed in the effort to banish Windscale's legacy to the history books was the simple expedient of renaming the place Sellafield. Of course, such airbrushing cannot clean up the mess that Windscale left behind. An article in *The Observer* in 2009 stated: 'Building B30 is a large, stained, concrete edifice that stands at the centre of Sellafield... Surrounded by a three-metre-high fence that is topped with razor wire, encased in scaffolding and riddled with a maze of sagging pipes and cabling, it would never be a contender to win an architectural prize. Yet B30 has a powerful claim to fame, albeit a disturbing one. "It is the most hazardous industrial building in western Europe," according to George Beveridge, Sellafield's deputy managing director. Nor is it hard to understand why the building possesses such a fearsome reputation. Piles of old nuclear reactor parts and decaying fuel rods, much of them of unknown provenance and age, line the murky, radioactive waters of the cooling pond in the centre of B30. Down there, pieces of contaminated metal have dissolved into sludge that emits heavy and potentially lethal doses of radiation.[2]

It goes on to describe how Building B38 next door became a dumping ground for spent fuel and cladding during the Thatcher Years miners' strike when nuclear plants were driven so hard that they produced more waste than could be disposed of. With Sellafield as a neighbour, it seems hardly surprising that other polluting industries chose the area as a desirable Pollution Is Us location. And it's still going on: even as I write, only a public inquiry stands in the way of locally widely supported plans for the UK's first deep coal mine since deep coal mining was supposed to have ended in the UK, back in December 2015. How ironic that local MPs from the party that did for deep mining are now shouting up for it! Sellafield now remains a busy place, even though it no longer generates electricity: don't they get irony? It will be 100 years before the 10,000-strong army of people employed at Sellafield completes the task of cleaning up the mess, if they ever can. Remember: this is the 'cheap, clean solution' to the climate crisis... Hmmm.

To the north and east of the national park, there's a ripple effect of wealth spreading outwards: there's a spill-over of visitors unable to find accommodation within the national park. There's work for people who are able to commute into the park honeypots from these areas and property prices reflect these factors. But the existence of the big employers that were supposed to be the salvation of West Cumbria has not enriched the area to the west of the park; rather they've dragged it down. If eyesores like Sellafield did not exist, the dramatic Cumbrian coastline, with its endless unspoiled beaches, would be a destination in its own right and it and the Lake District would together exercise more touristic clout.

I take a deep breath and turn off down the unsigned bridleway that leads directly to the aforementioned razor-wire fence. After a couple of kilometres, I am directly outside the vast Lego and Meccano disaster that is Sellafield and I continue alongside the fence for a similar distance. I pass Seascale Hall, a Grade II listed building, and note that extensive repairs appear to be underway. Des Res with splendid views across the nuclear plant. A little bit of research reveals that the building is owned by NDA Properties Ltd, which let the contract for the complete renovation during 2020. I perhaps ought to mention that NDA Properties Ltd manages the 'non-nuclear property assets' owned by the Nuclear Decommissioning Agency. Well, I guess it has to be better than letting it fall down.

I soon find myself on the road leading to the southern gate of Sellafield. It's straight and fast and a few cars are racing both in and out: all good for a fast getaway if it all goes up, I suppose. I have to examine the map carefully to work out how to locate the Bronze Age stone circle of Grey Croft. Pictures of this circle generally show a modest circle, completely overshadowed by the cooling towers of nuclear reactors, and so I expect to see the circle tucked in close to the perimeter fence. However, the puzzling reality of the landscape is that there is quite a deep, wooded valley immediately to the south of the Sellafield boundary and then, to the south of this, cultivated fields, sloping gently upwards towards farm buildings, to the south again. A right of way leads into the area as far as the edge of the golf links, to the west of the stone circle, out of sight somewhere over the brow of the hill. A sign on the gate warns that armed police patrol the area. The Beast and I enter and head for a modest stone relic across a couple of fields. I tuck The Beast in behind this and prepare to walk the rest of the way to the circle, wherever it may be. An interpretation board tells me everything I might want to know about the former Seascale

Mill, the ruins of which are in the valley a short distance away. Greenlane Archaeology has at some time carried out excavations and the information is quite detailed, especially given that few will ever venture this way. I sense a bit more nuclear greenwashing. The board features pictures of a snipe, red squirrel and badger and mentions rare natterjack toads and roe deer. Right on cue, a roe deer bounds from nearby cover and heads for the valley.

The land between here and where I think the circle should be is planted with barley, its shoots just poking through the treacly topsoil. A tractor track skirts the fields and so I set off along this, anxious not to disrupt the crop. The soil is claggy and I soon have moon boots of clay attached to the end of each leg. This is proving a real challenge…

Eventually, having crossed into a second field, I see stones piercing the murky damp sky that passes for a horizon. When my several kilos of clay and I finally make it to the circle I am more than pleasantly surprised: this is not the no-hope circle in the shadow of a nuclear complex that all the reports have led me to expect. This first thing that is clear is that most of the pictures must have been taken with a long lens, deliberately to bring forward the nuclear plant and exaggerate its impact on what should, of course, be a serene and peaceful location.

Grey Croft Stone Circle may date from Neolithic times, although there may have been Bronze Age additions. It was actually only 'excavated' as recently as 1947 having been buried by a tenant farmer in 1820 (that golden age of circle destruction again). It was re-erected in 1949: how sad that it could enjoy only a decade or so in the fresh air before the arrival of its ugly neighbour. As Burl himself puts it: 'Two sources of power are juxtaposed here. One is the Bronze Age stone circle. Immediately to its north are the dominating towers of the Sellafield nuclear power station partly hidden behind two monstrous, ugly banks of waste. The stone circle is lovelier.' Burl puts the diameter of the circle at 27 metres and says that ten of the original twelve stones are of local volcanic lava and about 1.3 metres high, though none weighing more than four tonnes. He notes a central raised kerbed cairn, which was found to contain traces of charcoal, bone fragments, flint flakes, a scraper and an early Bronze Age jet or lignite pulley-ring, as well as a broken Langdale axe.

On leaving Grey Croft, I elect to make a short detour into the village of Seascale, where I nip into The Village Pantry to buy lunch, which I sit and eat in the little shelter overlooking the sea. To my left, a mismatched terrace of houses – some stone, some pebbledash, some whitewashed, ascends the road that climbs up to a large white house overlooking the beach from where someone might once have thought about building a castle. On the other side of the road is a low wall and fence and then a grassy bank, dotted with benches and picnic tables. The houses enjoy commanding views across the sea to the Isle of Man.

The place should be a tourist magnet, but like so many others on this coast, it has an air of sadness and a down-at-heel look about it. I return to my earlier point about the blight that is the Sellafield monstrosity: no one really wants to live or take a holiday in the shadow of a giant nuke.

It's thought that, in Neolithic times, some of the unworked stone from the Langdale axe factory would be transported down here, where it would be shaped into tools for onward shipment. Some of these finished axes would have left Seascale by boat, according to Mark Edmonds, to find their way to places as far away as Ireland and Orkney. This was perhaps the very beginning of Seascale's association with munitions: there was a big ordnance factory here during the war, and plutonium production at Sellafield for Polaris missiles merely continued the tradition.

Sadly, there are no clear indications that things are heading in the right aesthetic direction in West Cumbria: the threat of a long-term nuclear waste repository won't lie down, and I've already spoken about the local appetite, cheer-led by the so-called Red Wall new Tory MPs, for digging coal again. There is an attitude here that dirty jobs are better than no jobs, which might be fair enough were it not for the impossible-to-quantify good clean jobs that have never been created because of a lack of belief in either the beauty or the potential of a Cumbrian Gold Coast rather than the so-called Energy Coast that we've been given.

At one time, when the place was going full blast, there was real concern about the health dangers posed by Sellafield – Ireland, the Isle of Man and Norway (think Gulf Stream Drift) consistently called for the closure of Sellafield, which habitually discharged low-level radioactive material into the Irish Sea. Concerns centred around the accumulation of toxic material in seafood, while on land, there appeared to be an abnormally high instance of childhood leukaemia.

When I used to edit *NHS Magazine*, I interviewed an epidemiologist at Newcastle University, called Louise Parker, about work she was doing that used data collected after World War II for the so-called Thousand Families study, in Newcastle. Originally set up to identify reasons for a falling birth rate (the post-War baby boom soon put that back in its box) the study tracked the medical history of some 1,042 babies born in the city in May and June 1947. It was a ground-breaking public health initiative, reflecting the grim reality that poverty and illness blighted the often short lives of youngsters then. About fourteen per cent of homes were deemed unfit for habitation, even by 1947 standards: one in three was overcrowded, one in four shared a toilet with neighbours and forty per cent had no bath. The babies' medical records were marked with a red spot and this enabled the creation of what would become a valuable tool for future research.

These children became known as Red Spot babies and my sister was one of them. Her friend, the late Ruth Knopfler, sister of the musician, Mark Knopfler, was another, though she fell out of the loop when the family moved to Glasgow. The data collected over the years via the ongoing monitoring of the participants created a rich database and insight into environmental contributors to a huge spectrum of illnesses. Dr Parker's team rose to the challenge of tracking down the Red Spot adults as they neared fifty to give all of them a full health check, as well as collating data about those who had died. Although the absolute size of the study sample was small, the data it collected was rich. It showed 'the importance of establishing the environmental and social context as well as medical information'.

My sister went to a big reunion party for Red Spotters at Newcastle Civic Centre in 2007 and was struck by how old some of the women especially looked. She was a sprightly sixty: others looked old and haggard. It's a reminder that social inequality is synonymous with health inequality and that is as true in West Cumbria as it surely remains in much of North East England, even if things have improved beyond recognition in seven decades in Newcastle itself.

As I concluded my interview with Dr Parker, she mentioned that was quite excited by the outcome of research she and colleagues had been doing into those aforementioned childhood leukaemias in West Cumbria: the rather unexpected finding was that the increased incidence of these illnesses could not, in fact, be laid at the door of Sellafield. Nor could a similar illness cluster at Thurso, near the Dounreay reactor. Rather, they were down to the large numbers of people coming to work in West Cumbria: as an isolated community, local people had less well-developed immunity to diseases carried by urban populations. Leukaemia, it seems, was an unusual reaction to infection by an unidentified micro-organism carried by the migrant workers. Similar leukae-mia bubbles could be identified in other places in which rural populations mixed with a large migrant influx. The nuclear indus-try was not a common factor. I did hope to get in contact with Dr Parker again, but failed: she was last known to be working at a university in Halifax, Nova Scotia, but may well be retired now.

We know as little about the pathology of Neolithic people as we do about most the aspects of their lives but it is worth reflect-ing that once people began to live in tightly-packed communities, even if their total numbers remained small, there would have been a trade-off between the gains that flowed from organised society and collective activities, such as agriculture, and the consequent increase in infectious illnesses, some of which would for sure have been fatal. As Mark Edmonds put it to me as we chatted in Orkney: 'They live in a totally different world: life is incredibly hard, with infant mortality, malnutrition…' The fragility of life itself requires us to view Neolithic and Bronze Age society through a quite dif-ferent lens, and with that the societal practices, traditions, and rituals that will have been driven by the realities of life and death. And there must surely also be the possibility that when the Beaker people arrived they brought with them pathogens against which the native Neolithic people carried no immunity. It would cer-tainly help to explain the steady demise of the latter.

* * *

My onward route takes me inland, passing without time to pause, the celebrated Santon Bridge Inn. Celebrated, because this is the venue of the annual contest to find the World's Biggest Liar, rekin-dling memories of my few brief moments on national TV while taking part in this very event a few months previously. Invigorated by my experience, in Egremont, of major world events staged in

West Cumbria, I had managed to secure tickets to one of the area's most exclusive world tournaments just a few weeks later.

It was a perfect excuse to spend a couple of nights at one of my favourite spots – the Wasdale Head Inn, which sits beneath Scafell Pike and Great Gable, at the opposite end of Wastwater from the Santon Bridge Inn. Santon Bridge is a tiny settlement on the River Irt, on its meandering course from England's deepest lake to its confluence with the Esk and the Irish Sea, at the attractive historic village of Ravenglass, a port in Roman and early industrial times. I'm sure I have read that its slightly elliptical high street was thus shaped so as to enable livestock to be penned each night against Border Riever incursions.

The Santon Bridge Inn itself is, of course, fully booked by overnight visitors who are considerably better known than I am – the tallest porky imaginable wouldn't have secured me a bed there. But, it should also be remembered that it is the Wasdale Head Inn, and not the Santon Bridge, that is the true home of the Biggest Liar event. And that's God's Truth. In the nineteenth century, when it was the Huntsman's Inn, its landlord was one Will Ritson: you can see Ritson's picture in the bar that bears his name today at the Wasdale Head Inn. Ritson was a fellsman, tap room philosopher, a keen follower of the hunt (he kept his own hounds at Wasdale Head) and the archetypal storyteller. Many of his tales, which he'd share with his regulars to keep them rapt and buying beer at his bar, were rooted in local lore and some had the ring of truth. He would tell one tale of a local woman's 'corpse' being carried over the fells for burial at a time when there was no graveyard at the little church in Wasdale. But when the pallbearers caught a rowan tree with the coffin, it fell to the ground and burst open – only for its occupant to emerge very much alive. She walked home and lived on for some years. Apparently.

William and Dorothy Wordsworth would sometimes walk over the fells to Wasdale, perhaps accompanied by the likes of Coleridge and Southey, and join in the storytelling. Maybe. When Will Ritson ran out of 'true' stories to share, he began to make them up: besides its deepest lake, tallest mountain and smallest church, Wasdale was also home to the country's biggest turnips, which local people would 'quarry' for Sunday lunch, before feeding the remains to their Herdwick sheep. And so West Cumbria acquired its third (or is that its fourth?) world superlative: Biggest Liar.

There have been famous winners of the title over the years, among them the fell runner, Joss Naylor, arguably – with Ritson – Wasdale Head's equal most famous person of all time. I'll be up against his nephew, Mike, a more recent past winner, at Santon Bridge. Curiously, I'm unlikely to face female competition: women rarely enter and Sue Perkins, of former *Great British Bake-Off* fame, remains the only female winner. Her tale about how the melting of the icecaps left people to commute by camel earned her the ceremonial plaque and liar's tie back in 2006. She does wear a tie sometimes, so may have welcomed this part of her prize.

I'm hoping that basing myself at the very epicentre of Wasdale fibbery will bring me inspiration as I rehearse my tall story and trim it to the clearly stated time limit of five minutes.

Perhaps I should explain why I want to take my courage in my hands and tell fibs before an audience. After all, I could just sit quietly in a corner and watch the experts. My explanation may surprise: in 2010 I fell off my bicycle and suffered an injury to a delicate part of my anatomy, which – to be candid – restricted my ability to process my waste products. My blood progressively poisoned, my condition deteriorated and, after scarcely sleeping for a fortnight, I was admitted to hospital. Psychiatric hospital, to be exact: I had become delusional and was 'suffering from' what they call a manic episode. I say 'suffering' because it was actually quite a lot of fun: my delusional self thought my little marketing company had grown like topsy and had become a world-beater, with a huge charitable arm to boot, dedicated to doing good the world over. I kid you not.

All this fantasy is relevant to Wasdale because, in my deluded world, I'd retreated to Wasdale Head with my most trusted colleagues and friends to run this global operation. And so I decided to elaborate on the fictionalised account of my 'madness', which I told in the form of a novel (*The Episode*, aforementioned) in the 2019 contest. My lie would be a tall tale about a mad scientist breeding talking Herdwicks and other mutations in a submarine moored deep beneath the surface of Wastwater. The vaguely plausible element in my story would be that the submarine would draw power from the old cable on the lakebed, which mysteriously failed a few years ago.

We arrive at the Bridge Inn and prise ourselves onto a table in the crowded bar. Linda spots Eric Robson on a stool at the bar – the former host of the BBC's *Gardener's Question Time* lives in Nether Wasdale and is the chair of the judges tonight. Also present is a team from TV's *The One Show*, and presenter A J Odudu (who would go on to earn acclaim on TV's *Strictly Come Dancing*).

I'm apprehensive ahead of my lying debut and one response might have been to drink copiously. But I'm the driver tonight, which is perhaps just as well. When eventually the throngs process to the back room in which the lies shall be told, we find ourselves on a table with John Rooney, aka Spartacus, from Kendal. His wife, Christine, is the official event artist, or so we are told. She's very good! Spartacus says he came third last year. How would I know?

I talk to Charlie Mandling, the compère, who says he's been doing this for twenty-seven years. He's a part-time DJ and also runs a menswear shop in Whitehaven. Rightly or wrongly I think of West Cumbria as an essentially working-class part of the country, but the judges too seem to be drawn from the local business community. Charlie even makes passing reference to the support of the local Conservatives in his opening remarks. Trudy Harrison, the local MP, is indeed in the vanguard of a Tory incursion beyond Labour's so-called Red Wall. But she can't compete tonight as politicians are barred as they're just too good at lying. Never a truer word spoken in jest, you may think.

Then I spot a face I know: it's Phillip Gate, the fan of Cumberland wrestling and all things folkloric in West Cumbria whom we met at Egremont. He tells me he's been watching the event closely for a couple of years and thinks he might be ready now to give it a go himself. The first liar to take the stage, however, is the afore-mentioned Mike Naylor, who, having worn the liar's tie some six times, tells a shocked audience that he's hanging up his fibber's boots and retiring. 'I first entered in 2004 and I had a fairly good run. This last year's been fantastic: the world tour was fantastic. I launched a new nuclear high-speed catamaran.' In a flurry of further baseless assertions, he continues: 'We're making all the lakes into one big 'un. And launching the world's first electric airport…'

Of course, we should all have guessed that this potpourri of fibbing fragments would prove to be no more than Mike's hors d'oeuvre, if that's not mixing my metaphors too much. In the meantime, the upshot is that I am next to take the stage, without the benefit of having watched any other contestants weave elaborate shaggy dog tales that shall all eclipse the five-minute rule by a country day or two.

So, I deliver my heavily edited story about a radioactively enhanced sheep called Herdy, while sticking closely to just five minutes. My turn ends up with a degree of immortality, as some two seconds of it survive the cut to appear on the following day's *One Show*, my Herdy telling viewers he's a nuclear spy. It's still there in the BBC archive…

'At least that's over,' I say to myself as I return to my seat, to be followed by a succession of what, it now appears, are professional stand-ups. Spartacus, I think it is, tells an intriguing story of how he shared a cuppa with the Queen while the Royal Train was parked in a siding on the coast somewhere. And to round off the performance, Mike Naylor earns his stripes as the 'Monkey Liar' by taking the stage again and telling a tall tale about seagulls in Whitehaven being trained by Weightwatchers to steal chips from overweight visitors. But surely they do that without any training?

While we await the result, I ask Charlie Mandling whatever happened to the five-minute rule. He tells me: 'We didn't need to do that this year, with just six entrants. There can be up to 24 but three from Maryport didn't make it because their minibus broke down.'

I feel slightly cheated: seemingly I was the only one who hadn't been told this salient piece of information. But I also know who the rightful winner is: it's our friend Phillip, who has woven a wonderful tale about the mining of underground seams of sugar beneath West Cumbria. Now, those from hereabouts know that, traditionally, the worst thing a bloke from Whitehaven can call one from Workington is a 'jam-eater'. And vice versa. The insult is regularly traded on the terraces at Rugby League games and is said to date from the idea that Workington lads couldn't afford meat in their sarnies when they went down the pit. And t'other way round…

In Phillip's immensely tall tale, the rich seams of sugar are drawn up by the area's hedgerows, enabling local people to create every conceivable flavour of jam by cooking the hedgerow berries. Indeed, he tells us all, jam should be celebrated in Cumbria, and never deployed as a casual insult. He rounds his tale off with an elaborate description of how the subterranean sugar could occasionally come to be caramelised beneath smouldering slag heaps, enabling the more savvy miner to concoct a caramel latte.

I chat with him afterwards and he describes how carefully he has done his research: the trick, he says, is to know your competition: 'Do you pitch it straight? Or do you go for laughs? This year there were a lot of funny guys so that influenced my delivery.'

Phillip, who works as a data architect at Sellafield (or so he says), would probably bleed Cumbrian jam if you cut him and he reiterates how much he loves the place. 'West Cumbria is great,' he says. 'All of Cumbria is great. I genuinely don't know what it is about the place. But there are lots of stories, and it's always good to have a story... and maybe not to take yourself TOO seriously.'

Spartacus comes second and Mike Naylor third. I've no idea where I came, but Charlie says: 'We had some very, very good entries this year, a good audience, good contestants and on a par with previous years.'

The Guardian's Northern Editor, Helen Pidd, is also among witnesses to Phillip Gate's triumph and describes him as the 'living, breathing, lying embodiment of the media's new favourite stereotype: Workington Man'. I'm glad *The Guardian* hasn't forgotten its penchant for the odd off-beat tale. Helen, after all, is the latest in a long line of Northern Editors with a reputation for leaving big boots to fill.

I already mentioned Martin Wainwright, whose journalism and broadcasting helped to earn him an OBE and an honorary degree from Leeds University, and who occupied the seat for seventeen years until the end of 2012. He would organise occasional walks in the Lake District to celebrate the publication of his books, to which he would invite media friends, politicians and others. Besides that hike up Kidsty Pike to mark the launch of his biography of his namesake, Alfred Wainwright, there was another occasion when we walked from Grasmere to the Lion and Lamb crags with, among others, Denis MacShane, a former leading light in the National Union of Journalists and latterly MP for

Rotherham, who not long afterwards was jailed for six months for lying about his Parliamentary expenses. Well, as an MP, he'd have been barred from Santon Bridge anyway.

Those of us who are long enough in the tooth will also remember Mike Parkin, Martin's predecessor in the Manchester hot seat – the last vestige of the days when *The Guardian* was the only national newspaper in England not headquartered in London. I remember Mike best for the wonderful tales of yore he would tell at NUJ branch meetings in Leeds; tales of the days when the city had two fiercely competing evening newspapers: *The Yorkshire Evening Post* and *The News*.

In those days of hot-metal printing, these rivals would compete to be on sale early on the streets of the city, with a big splash headline on the front page. Mike recalled a reporter, on *The News*, I think, who wasn't the sharpest tool in the box, who'd gone out to a house fire. This was back in the days when reporters used to phone the control rooms of police, fire and ambulance services several times a day, ready to rush out and get the news as it happened. The reporter arrived at the scene to find a chip fan fire already extinguished and left muttering 'Not much of a bloody fire!'. Later that morning, the rival title appeared on the streets with a big black headline: *Parrot Saves Family In City House Blaze*. The rival's reporter had arrived a little later and probed more deeply, discovering that it had been the pet parrot's squawking that had alerted the occupants to the fire on the kitchen stove.

Mike chuckled and told us all (eager young reporters): 'They said that after that the lad would never leave the scene of a fire without asking "Have you got a parrot?"'. The *Evening News* breathed its last in the early '60s when the rot was even then beginning to set in for local paid-for newspapers. The *Yorkshire Evening Post*, stripped of so much of its editorial resource once acquired by the Johnston Group, these days can muster a circulation of barely 6,000, down from a near six-figure number when I lived there. Its deadlines are so far ahead of publication that the story of a parrot saving a family in the early hours would only reach readers two days later. Johnston cut costs so deeply at the titles it gathered all over the country that, come a cash squeeze in 2018, there was nothing left to cut and it was placed in Administration. The titles are now owned by the Phoenix company, JPI Media. Do they have a future? Probably not as you would know it. It is only the most parochial of local titles that seem capable of holding their own these days.

And so, back in West Cumbria, where the tale of a life-saving parrot might have been just too mainstream, we take the winding inky-black road back up the dale, only to arrive at the Inn and find the door firmly bolted. We have no key and have to 'break in' via the fire escape. It feels like a rather unglamorous ending, but I decide I shall return with a fanciful story about Lakeland stone circles springing to life. Unfortunately, a global pandemic cancels all non-political lies for two years. You couldn't make it up, could you?

* * *

Having resolved not to chance it on the very steep bridleway from Miterdale to reach the stone circle collections on Brat's Hill, I head instead directly to Eskdale. Remember: a bridleway is just that, somewhere you can ride a horse or, indeed, lead one by its bridle. Since 1968 you have also been permitted to ride a bicycle, this change predating by some distance the invention of the off-road bicycle and by even more the advent of electric machines of The Beast's genre. However, legally permitted does not mean 'safely able'.

I make swift progress to Eskdale Green and on up the valley to Boot, just beyond the terminus of L'aal Ratty, The Ravenglass and Eskdale narrow gauge railway, which I first rode when knee-high to miniature steam loco. Julian earlier suggested I leave The Beast at the post office, run by his pal. Finding this has closed at 4 pm (it's now about 20 past) I instead park up round the back of the pub, trusting my valuables to their fate.

The track – bridleway – crosses the unused final section of the railway, which was built in 1875 to serve the iron ore mines above Boot. It was originally built to a 3ft gauge, like its predecessor over the water on the Isle of Man, but was converted to 15 inches during the First World War, at the same time as the final short section to Boot was abandoned. It was the first passenger-carrying narrow-gauge railway in the UK and, with a few interruptions, it has carried passengers as well as freight throughout its life.

As the track leaves the previously mentioned old corpse road to Wasdale and takes a far steeper path straight up the fellside, I am forced to concur that, however desirable the idea may have been to take The Beast up and over the fell, this would have been a major folly. This track would have been my descent into Eskdale and riding it would have proved hazardous in the extreme: it is all large loose stones and is the place for hoof not tyre.

As I ascend, I pass the preserved remains of the old mines and a (very) small stone circle, seemingly built quite recently by a bit of a joker. After half an hour's energetic ascent I reach the plateau, at around 300 metres. There are mounds, tumuli and a collection of extraordinarily romantic stone circles. The largest of these is Brat's Hill, which is 30 metres across and contains five cairns within its circumference of forty-two irregular stones. However, I am quickly drawn to the twin circles at White Moss, a couple of hundred metres to the north-west. These are linked by a south-west orientated avenue, with views across the Irish Sea. A further two circles are at Low Longrigg, another 200 or so metres to the north. The entire fell top is littered with cairns and Clare notes the lack of a commonly agreed and coherent explanation for their location. Burl observes that some of these are most likely clearance cairns, leaving me to speculate that, perhaps as may have happened at The Cockpit, the early farmers may have cleared the forest. It takes me a few minutes to get my breath back: not so much because of the steepness of the climb, but because the location is both magnificent and unexpected. I'm on a broad shoulder of Eskdale Fell, with the summit of Whin Rigg, across Mitredale to my north-west, and Illgill Head due north. The land falls away to the south-west, revealing a broad sweep of the Irish Sea, with the Isle of Man silhouetted against the declining evening sun.

I observe what appears to be a north-east to south-west alignment through the circle pair, suggesting a sunrise at summer solstice and the sunset at midwinter. A collection of recent charred fragments tells me that some have come up here relatively recently and perhaps wild-camped at the circles. Burl notes that somewhat earlier charred fragments were found in an 1827 excavation, which also found stag antlers and other animal bones beneath cists in some of the circles. Intriguingly, Burl appears to hint that there may have been a bit of jiggery-pokery when these excavations were recorded, as the contemporary 'plan' of a 'parallelogram of stones' near an outlying cairn appears to all but match that of the internal structure at Castlerigg. Coincidence, accidental confusion, over-stretching? Who knows, but it has been a recurrent theme of my journey that anything that nineteenth-century archaeologists recorded has to be taken with a bit of a pinch of salt, as they had no established methodology to work to. The alleged parallelogram no longer exists... perhaps it never did.

When I later arrive at the Eskdale Youth Hostel, I find a surprisingly comprehensive interpretation panel on the wall, much of it devoted to the area's prehistory. This suggests that it was the Langdale axes that enabled people to move inland, fell forest and occupy new locations. This may be, but this high plateau is some order of magnitude less hospitable than the landscape at Tongue

How, something of a pussy cat at just 200 metres above sea level. I find myself speculating that this may have been more of a summer shieling than a permanent year-round settlement. That said, Clare does note that a marked deterioration in soil quality appears to have followed Neolithic times, even as the progressive arrival of bronze made settlement more practical. We do know that the climate in Neolithic times was warmer and very possibly drier.

Whatever the explanations for the presence of no fewer than five circles in close proximity, there are times when location alone trumps interpretation. Just climb up one summer's eve and take in the setting sun over the Irish Sea, the trill of the skylark in your ears.

The youth hostel was the only place in the valley that was offering a bed for the night once relaxed COVID restrictions were announced a few weeks before my trip. Approaching my goal, I hear a cuckoo quite close by: it is the first I have heard this spring. It shall also be the last. The unmistakable call was always synonymous with spring when I was not that much younger but numbers have declined sharply. You may not like the cuckoo's lifestyle, but you have to admire its ingenuity and its talismanic voice. Like some other migratory birds, it seems it may face problems at both ends of its route from Africa, though no one can agree on the dominant reasons for a 65 per cent decline since the early 1980s. I'm so glad I have been lucky enough to spot the elusive birds from time to time but would like to be confident that my daughters will share that privilege.

I check in at the hostel, waste some time trying to open the cycle shed on which the most, though not very, recent guests have apparently swapped the padlock for their own, before leaving with the key, and then grab an early shower, which has to be booked so as to observe social distancing rules. I then skedaddle down the road on foot to The Woolpack in Boot, where I've reserved a table, leaving The Beast to enjoy his unexpected digs inside the hostel itself.

Chapter 6

To Morecambe Bay

Tall monoliths, the secret circle
and sea views

I return to The Woolpack for breakfast, this time aboard The Beast. As I park up, a little robin lands on the gutter above the pub door, directly above my head. The robin was always the favourite bird of my late mother-in-law, so I'm reminded of her memory at every sighting and hate it if their boldness ever gets them into trouble with our cats if they're in a hunting mood, which (thankfully) is not so often, since we banned them from Cumbria.

On coming out of The Woolpack, I set about unlocking The Beast, donning my helmet and ensuring the right map is displayed on my handlebar bag. And then I am joined by an unexpected passenger: the friendly robin is sitting barely half a metre from me, perched upon my handlebars. 'Come on then, what are you waiting for?' he seems to say, before ultimately deciding that wings trump wheels every time.

Progress is swift as far as Eskdale Green, from where I turn south on the road that crosses the fells towards Broughton. The plan, however, is to leave the road at its first summit and strike off towards Devoke Water, beyond which a bridleway crosses the fell through the middle of an extensive collection of cairns and other remnants of settlement, which date from the Bronze Age (possibly earlier) and on through Iron Age and Roman times.

The road out of Eskdale is by some distance the steepest The Beast and I have tackled: steeper even than my wasted journey to the top of Whinlatter Forest. As I approach the steep climb, I resolve to slip The Beast into the lower gear ratio, rather than finding myself wrestling with a gear change when the chain is under tension. The front dérailleur, which switches between the two ratios, is still a little out of true, a legacy of my encounter with the tree stump some days ago now and, as I make the change, the chain slips off and I grind to a halt. Slipping a chain back on is normally a reasonably easy job and can usually be accomplished with the cycle still in the upright position. Not this time: the chain has slipped at both ends and is jammed between the rear gears and the forks. I have no choice but to remove my three panniers and plonk the machine upside down at the road's edge. Five minutes of occasionally not-too-gentle persuasion and I have the chain back on: even better, I have it on the lower gear ratio. In the event, The Beast fair cruises up the hill and I find myself musing as to whether or not it would ever be realistic to cycle up the likes of Hardknott Pass, the one-in-three challenge that is probably the toughest road in all the UK. That may be for another time.

Leaving the road for the track to Devoke Water I continue to make good progress: it is just about drivable by car. I make the lazy assumption that this shall remain the case once I have left the shores of the lake. Pedants may well note that I have referred to Devoke Water as a 'lake' and may well argue that it is in fact a tarn, partly on account of its size and partly because it is high up in the mountains, whereas lakes are in valley floors. Frankly, you can take your pick: it's either the largest tarn in the Lake District or, if you prefer, the smallest lake. Now just don't get me started on meres.

Whether lake, tarn, or even mere, Devoke Water, when I arrive on its shores, proves a truly beautiful stretch of water. Cupped beneath the relatively gentle slopes of the high fells, it twinkles blue beneath a clear spring sky, across which fluffy cumulus are drifting in a gentle wind off the Irish Sea. Its waters lap the gently sloping shoreline beside an old stone-built boathouse. What wouldn't I do to trade idyllic landscape for a passable cycle route at this moment… Devoke Water is fed by countless shallow becks, trickling down through layers of peat and sphagnum moss. My nicely surfaced track has given way to bog, punctuated by footprints in the peat. I reason that, once beyond the lake (tarn, whatever), the track shall resume its determined progress towards the main road down the west coast.

I'm unsure just how long my traverse of the sodden shoreline takes, but I do eventually reach the other end of the water and something akin to a track leads me up a gentle slope to a broad coll, where I encounter what shall prove to be just the first of many cairns. I pause, and The Beast poses for pictures and refreshment before we press on over the fell. It proves to be by some distance the densest area of cairns, burial mounds and, I suspect, hut foundations, I have thus far encountered. They extend in every direction and conjure up images of people living in groups of huts, perhaps plucking trout from the nearby waters.

Apparently, Devoke Water is a fairly passable wild trout fishery: however, it could be better... In 2018, the Wild Trout Trust carried out an advisory visit and concluded that a range of measures around the shoreline could improve water quality significantly by reducing the flow of sediment into the lake. These measures might include 'buffer fencing' to keep sheep out, the cutting of channels into the access track to reduce run-off and, music to my ears, improvements to the paths and the building of simple bridges. It states: 'If buffer fencing of the watercourses (and any other areas around the tarn) is undertaken, the greater diversity of vegetation and trees and shrubs that could be promoted would benefit a wide range of wildlife. Reinstatement of more, natural, high-quality organic input such as leaf litter to the system is likely to also benefit many species, particularly invertebrates.'[1]

It seems reasonable to presume that people lived on the fell here, either all year round or, possibly, just in summer. To be able to do so, they would have had to clear what may well have been a mixed deciduous forest. The arrival of bronze tools made this an easier task. Historic England cites the Barnscar settlement, a couple of kilometres to the west of Devoke Water, and the surrounding landscape as being of national importance.

The listing states: 'Barnscar prehistoric cairnfield, hut circle settlements, associated field systems and funerary cairns survive well and form part of a large area of well-preserved prehistoric landscape extending along the fellsides of south-west Cumbria. The monument contains a complex and diverse group of prehistoric monument classes and together these provide evidence of long-term management and exploitation of this area in prehistoric times. Overall the monument is a rare example of a landscape within which evidence of human exploitation is visible through a range of remarkably well-preserved monuments dating to the prehistoric, Romano-British and medieval periods.'

It references two prehistoric hut circle settlements, each with an associated field system, fifteen prehistoric funerary cairns, a Romano-British farmstead with an associated field system and trackway, and a medieval shieling. The interesting thing to note here is that settlement of the area continued through the Roman occupation and on into medieval times, presumably also including the Viking occupation. Given our ongoing struggle to draw linkages from Neolithic and Bronze Age times to a more modern era of written history, this feels hugely symbolic to me.

The listing continues: 'The prehistoric cairnfield ... includes about 600 clearance cairns and a few short lengths of stone banking. In the southern part of this cairnfield ... is a prehistoric hut circle settlement consisting of a three-sided stone-banked enclosure within which there is a relatively level area that would have provided a platform upon which a hut or huts would have stood and within which the occupants of the settlement would have lived. Surrounding the settlement is a complex associated field system consisting of numerous small fields or plots. These fields are bounded by stone banks or cairn alignments which are interpreted as representing the line of old field boundaries in which sporadic patches of stone clearance were piled against a fence or hedge. The fields are relatively stone-free, flat and well-drained, and are interpreted as prehistoric fields, which were deliberately cleared of stone in order to render the ground usable for agricultural cultivation or stock enclosure.

'In the north-western part of the cairnfield ... there is a second prehistoric hut circle settlement and associated field system. It consists of a single stone hut circle with six small fields or plots either adjacent or in the vicinity. Three other large irregularly-shaped fields with boundaries defined by cairn alignments, and each containing land virtually bereft of stone, exist within the cairnfield. Also within the cairnfield are fifteen cairns which have been subjected to limited investigation, either by Lord Muncaster in 1885, or by persons unknown at an earlier date. Lord Muncaster's investigations found cinerary urns, fragments of pottery and burnt bones consistent with Bronze Age funerary practices known from sites excavated elsewhere in Cumbria.' A map of the area, presumably drawn by Lord Muncaster's team, as it bears the date 1885, shows the precise location of all the features located during the survey.

The Historic England report notes that a Romano-British field system 'partly overlies the earlier prehistoric cairnfield and part of the more southerly of the two prehistoric field systems' and goes on to say: 'It represents a major reorganisation of the landscape during the Romano-British period (the first to early fifth centuries AD) as the small irregular fields of the prehistoric period were superseded by parallel field boundaries formed by stone walls and banks, which divided the land into a series of strips at right angles to the contours. The field system consists of a series of very long, well-defined stone walls or banks, orientated along the ridge in an ENE-WSW direction.'

A medieval shieling, or summer pasture, was then built on top of the earlier remains and the report turns to pollen sediments from Devoke Water to cast more light on how this agricultural settlement might have looked and changed over the centuries. 'Pollen cores taken from the sediments of nearby Devoke Water have revealed the changing vegetational history of this area over the last 5,000 years and show episodes of forest clearance and a development of grassland during the prehistoric period. During one of these episodes most trees were cut down and were soon replaced by extensive grassland. The clearance is associated with the Bronze Age on the basis of its similarity to a clearance episode from Seathwaite Tarn 9km to the east, which has been scientifically dated to around 1000 BC. The next phase of clearance has been dated to between 70–330 AD and is associated with cereal pollen, which would imply that upland cultivation was taking place at this time. The prehistoric remains at Barnscar represent either sporadic or transient occupation over a long period. Sporadic occupation is then attested by the Romano-British farmstead and the medieval shieling.'

The most recent detailed survey of the area appears to have taken place in the spring of 1982 and is cited in a paper by Roger Leech, Visiting Professor of Archaeology at the University of Southampton. It was carried out by the then Cumbria and Lancashire Archaeological Unit of the University of Lancaster and took place over two weeks along a 1km line, passing just to the north of Devoke Water. It recorded 520 monuments, including nine groups of cairns. But it's clear that quite a bit of digging did take place in the nineteenth century and that this uncovered fragments of funerary urns and bones. Two urns are now held by the Cambridge Museum of Archaeology and Anthropology.

So, what can we infer from all this? Well, firstly that the formerly forested fellside was cleared for pasture and small-scale subsistence farming, most likely in the Bronze Age but possibly earlier, and that it was capable of supporting a sizeable population, which may have been seasonal. We also know that the Devoke Water fishery could have provided a useful additional source of food and that the tarn may have been more productive then, as the surrounding woodland would have prevented silty run-off from the fells. The land remained worth farming right through Roman to Medieval times, thus giving us a genuine continuum all the way from prehistory. It is hard to imagine this land being farmed today: the soil is poor and acidic, and it is high up and exposed. Drainage is also poor. We do not know the extent to which the abandonment of the area may have been down to a worsening climate or to the deterioration of the soil, perhaps due to over-farming.

I climb atop one of the many cairns and cast my eyes in a full circle as I try to imagine how life might have been so long ago… forest clearance would not only have released new land for early agriculture: it would also have helped to contain the larger and more aggressive mammals that still roamed the rest – brown bear and, to a lesser extent, wolves, lynx and wild boar. I picture a Neolithic and Bronze Age lifestyle in which people, now able to synthesise lactose (and thus drink milk), keep small herds of goats, sheep or oxen; grow a bit of bere barley and other cereals; and supplement their limited harvests by hunting in the forest and gathering fruit and nuts, such as hazelnuts. The rather curious question, however, is Why? Why did they tire of hunter-gathering in favour of a far more labour-intensive lifestyle, involving forest clearance, wall-building, tilling and then the milling of the cereals produced? And, that, I'm afraid, is just another facet of the great Neolithic mystery.

* * *

As the route west from Devoke Water and Barnscar settlement is marked on the map as a bridleway I have high hopes it'll be an easy ride down. At some point, however, I manage to find myself on the 'footpath', just a wee bit to the north. This truth only becomes fully apparent as I am crossing an extensive area of bogland, comprising upstanding tussocks of heather, reeds and dwarf birch and alder. It is no place for The Beast, but he politely does not complain as I half push and half lift him through the mire. In the very middle of it all an upstanding post is marked simply, and decidedly unhelpfully, 'footpath'. It is, at this point, too late to backtrack. Eventually, I reach a field boundary, at which something loosely related to a path heads for the far corner of the field, where there is a gate. Once through this, I'm on an enclosed track, possibly the bridleway, but masquerading as a fast-flowing beck. After no more than 100 metres, the river bears left as the track bears right and I can, once more, mount The Beast.

My original intention today had been to head down to Waberthwaite, where a firm of family butchers makes the finest sausages in Cumbria. They are, however, not going to be open and, given the time I have just lost traversing bogs, I need to make up for this, and so I opt to stick to the fell-foot and head for Bootle, where there's a good café and recharging opportunity.

* * *

I return to Waberthwaite three months later to meet Alistair and Joyce Woodall, ninth generation sausage-makers. Their shopfront is traditional. Inside are the meat counter, Post Office and a few shelves of groceries. It's curing day and Alistair is busy, though spares me enough time to give me a potted history of sausage-making. My interest stems from the idea that, in Neolithic or Bronze Age times, waste of any part of a carcass would have been severely frowned upon. Stuffing intestines with offal and scrapings of meat from the bone would have been a practical way of getting the most from an animal. The resultant early sausages might then have been smoked or possibly cured (salted) for longevity. My food historian friend Ivan Day has a theory about the Cumberland sausage, which is that the unlinked sausage survived here only because Cumberland was isolated from the mainstream. Similarly, the haggis too might have been superseded in Scotland, but for Rabbie Burns having invested it with a lore all its own. For Ivan knows that haggis was once just as common in England as it was north of the border: it just became old-fashioned.

Alistair is content to buy into Ivan's Cumberland sausage theory and tells me the length of a sausage is limited only by the length of the intestine you are putting it in. 'You make it as long as the skin will let you: anything from two to five metres.' But, although the traditional unlinked Cumberland sausage boasts Protected Geographical Indication, there's an economic argument too: 'A linking machine is £30,000 and a lot of rural butchers would not be able to afford a machine like that.'

Alistair, though, is a step up from that craft industry level and does indeed own a linking machine, though I have to say I just love the way the longer sausages curl protectively around the shorter ones. 'Granddad started making traditional sausages again after the War,' says Alistair. In the War, you couldn't get the spices. They asked us to put preservative in but Granddad refused. Apart from the War, we've been going since 1828. We use quite a variety of different spices. It's a secret recipe and every butcher in the area has their own. We use Cumbrian pork, slaughtered at Wigton, and a small amount of rusk to bind it together.'

What I really like about the Waberthwaite sausage is that it is really meaty. And when you prick it, it spits, not water (as some sadly do) but hot fat. For me, it really is the best. I put it to Alistair that sausage-making might date back to some time well before 1828 and he agrees: 'Smoking would have been one way of keeping it, but also the spices you would put in as well. The salt preserves it, though we don't put in as much in nowadays.' The extra salt in the old days meant the meat could survive the fortnight it might take to distribute to outlets throughout the country. 'Cold smoking over oak puts another week on it,' says Alistair.

So, there's good evidence for the use of salt in prehistoric days and, though some herbs didn't cross to these shores till Roman or Medieval times, there were plenty of indigenous herbal plants, such as wild garlic, fennel, nettle, borage, corn mint, dandelion and ground elder, that curse of gardeners everywhere.

Duly stocked up with sausage and other meat, cured and otherwise, we head up onto the moorland behind Waberthwaite. In truth, I'm getting the picture that much of the entire western flank of the Lakeland fells has seen settlement since prehistoric times and I can't help but think that, in a better-resourced world, more archaeological investigation might have yielded a greater understanding as to what was driving settlement patterns here. We drive close to the farm at Grange, from where a bridleway heads off across the open fell towards Ulpha. We are, once again, on limestone, and there are as many random lumps of that rock masquerading as cairns and stone circles as there are the Real McCoy. We do, however, succeed in identifying the 20-metre-diameter circle of fifteen granite boulders, identified in the Historic England listing and, indeed, some of the other listed features, including a larger enclosure, with a shallow rampart around its perimeter, as well as two possible ring cairns. I imagine the Neolithic and Bronze Age inhabitants thinking this otherwise slightly random spot on the fellside would make a great location for their communal activities, as – once again – the views out to sea are inspiring.

* * *

Leaving Bootle, it would be possible to strike off eastward across Bootle Fell, along a minor road, which then becomes a Byway Open To All Traffic. This is the route I would have taken in the opposite direction had The Beast and I not got so bogged down by Devoke Water. After about 4km, the BOAT becomes a minor road and, another kilometre on, there's a bridleway to the right, which leads down to Sunkenkirk, or Swinside, Stone Circle. Sunkenkirk is no more than a touch over 3km east of the nearest cairns and field systems marked on the OS map. So it is very tempting to see Sunkenkirk – one of the finer stone circles of my tour – as slotting into a much wider farming and funerary landscape, which the passage of five or so millennia has erased. No doubt it would be interesting to see what a lidar or similar survey might reveal.

Today, however, I am continuing southward, initially on the busy A595. Resurfacing work soon brings me to a halt, with no safe means of passing the line of stationary traffic in front of me. Eventually, I'm able to exit left, taking a field path to join the bridleway that runs due south along the foot of a steep fellside, which ultimately rises to the summit of Black Combe. It's easy to imagine I'm far more remote from the A595 than I am, and the grassy track surface is probably The Beast's favourite. Disturbingly, I pass no fewer than three dead sheep. I intend to report these at the nearest farm, but I don't pass one until it seems I'm too far from the 'scene of the crime'. Farmers are obliged by law to remove dead stock and I hope that these hapless ewes will be found before too long. I'm left pondering as to why there should be three of them and conclude that a dog off the lead may be the most likely explanation, there having been much of this nonsense during the COVID months.

I also, unknowingly, sail past the Whisky Barn, at Whitbeck, which is a wonderfully restored collection of farm buildings now offering quality accommodation and, as the name suggests, a well-appointed bar. I rejoin the A595 for a short distance, before crossing beneath the railway and turning off a little south of Silecroft Station. I have vague memories of having possibly taken a family holiday at Silecroft when I was no more than a wee bairn, though my only certain visit was rather more recent, when we drove down to the beach a year or two ago to take a look at a 'tiny house' atop the dunes that fringe the endless sandy beach, which extends about 7km, all the way from Haverigg, just north of Millom, in the south, to just opposite Whitbeck, where it turns to stones and pebbles. This is a south-west facing beach of gently sloping sand, with views across the Irish Sea: what's not to like? Once again, I fear it's the proximity of Sellafield and its ilk that has rendered a prospective paradise an under-visited 'secret'.

Almost immediately beyond the railway, a track gives access to two enormous standing stones at the edge of the field. They're called the Giant's Grave and are, Long Meg herself apart, by some distance the tallest I have thus far encountered on my Lakeland travels. Tom Clare's book has an aerial photograph of the site, in which a ring of pits is visible around the two stones. These, presumably, might have been the foundations either of wooden posts or of more stones. Clare also cites previously recorded, though now disappeared, stone circles on the coastal strip to the north of here, one of which was a double circle similar to that at Oddendale, near Shap.

'Together with a ring ditch and collared urn, these monuments are evidence of intense prehistoric use of this narrow lowland strip; an intensity of land use confirmed by the paleo-environment evidence,' he says. To this, I would add only that the 'narrow lowland strip' was in all likelihood somewhat wider back then, when sea levels were lower. Indeed, it doesn't require too much imagination to think of the whole area as a fertile coastal plain – adorned at intervals with stone circles, cairns, standing stones, avenues and all the other paraphernalia of Neolithic and Bronze Age settlement – backed by a sloping south-west facing range of fellsides upon which some form of transhumance may have been practised. That is to say that these early farmers may have taken their beasts onto the fells for summer grazing.

My next port of call does not quite fit with either of the above ancient landscape types: I'm bound for the steeply sloping site of Lacra Bank, above the village of Kirksanton. After a bit of a struggle, I eventually locate the footpath, which runs from behind the main street, across the railway by a gated crossing, and straight up the hill to where as many as five stone circles and perhaps two stone avenues may once have stood. I park The Beast behind the little cottage by the railway line, which may once have belonged to a crossing-keeper, and leave a note saying I'll be back. It's a steep haul up the course of a stream and my decision to leave The Beast grazing in the pasture quickly moves from 50 per cent to 100 per cent justified when I arrive at a tall stile.

Two walkers are coming down the hill towards me and they confirm that I am indeed on the right track for at least one of the circles. When I arrive at Lacra A, I find myself looking at a fairly modest circle comprising the five stones that remain in situ. Its position, however, is outstanding, affording views all the way south to Walney Island, at Barrow-in-Furness. Lacra B, nearby, is 15 metres across and rather more complete, though the other circles and avenues are harder to pin down in a landscape of randomly strewn rocks. Lacra B once contained funerary remains at its centre, though these appear to have been dispersed by nineteenth-century ploughing. However, the sum of them all might just be, it would seem, rather greater than the parts: *The Megalithic Portal* suggests that the whole collection was part of a predictive calendar.

The man behind the research was a retired farmer, called Jack Morris-Eyton, who spent eighteen years unravelling the purpose of stone circles, or of some of them at least. His research centred on Sunkenkirk, Castlerigg and Stonehenge and was incomplete when he died in 2011. Some of it had, however, been published on *The Megalithic Portal* five years previously under the title *The Great Stone Circles: How They Work*, while the totality of his work and helpful contributions of others was collected, edited and published by David Smyth, under the less zippy title, *Jack Morris-Eyton's*

Research Into Shadows And Light Cast By Stone Circles In The UK, in 2017.[2] It is a fascinating piece of work now running to more than 300 pages and replete with numerous diagrams and other illustrations. I mention it now because Morris-Eyton suggests in his work that Lacra D was a 'prediction calendar'.

He wrote: 'At these ancient prediction sites, the system is arranged to cast two shadows down a row of target stones, working over several days. One of the shadows is normally created by the ground or crest and this gets longer at sunset. Daily as the sun gets lower in the sky and vice versa at the sunrise, this shadow gives the "horizontal cursor". On a given date it will always be the same length. When this ground shadow reaches the bottom of one of the target stones in the row, at the same time a shadow from the pointer stone swings over the row, providing the "vertical cursor". This covers the target stone of the day, in many cases leaving the top in sunlight, thus measuring the height of the sun on that day. Using this method the ancients would have been able to count the days to the solstice or other Festival in order to ensure their activities were carried out on the correct day, despite the cloud cover. The sensitivity of the prediction was often enhanced by utilising a slope.'

Now, perhaps you haven't quite followed that… the gist of it is contained in the penultimate sentence: the intersection of two shadows enabled an accurate prediction of the precise day of, for example, the winter or summer solstice. Morris-Eyton was not a professional archaeologist and nor am I, but I am tempted to be persuaded of the logic of the arguments derived from his extensive observations. For me, given his comments about 'utilising a slope' it may also just help to explain why so many of the stone circles in Cumbria are indeed sited not on level ground but on sloping hillsides.

I consult Paul Frodsham to see what he might make of Morris-Eyton's lifetime's research and his response, if not quite damning, is such that I should at least invest in a pot of Neolithically recovered salt. 'With regard to Morris-Eyton's work, I'm afraid you are going to have to draw your own conclusions. What I would say, and you can quote me on this if you like, is that in a circle of seventy or more stones (nobody knows how many Daughters Long Meg had), plus the "centre point" and the horizon, it should be possible to find alignments on just about anything!' he tells me, continuing: 'I don't believe these sites were built primarily as calendars or for anything we would class as "scientific", but by building in one or more significant alignments the people were binding everyday life here on Earth with the cosmos, and no doubt the ancestors, in a complex web that would be as real to them (arguably more so) than God or Jesus is to today's committed Christian.'

* * *

Back down at the foot of the escarpment, I call my host for the evening, Jane Rousseau, who runs a café and casual bed and breakfast on the square at Broughton-in-Furness. I know she has quite a lot on her plate with health and family issues at the moment, so I know I must pay attention when she asks me politely to arrive by a particular time. I reckon I have just about enough time to get to Sunkenkirk circle and then take a look at a couple of standing stones, and still get to Broughton on time – providing I stick to the quickest route, that is to say, the main road.

I always prefer to use the name Sunkenkirk for the stone circle that lies about 5km a little north of west of Broughton and a little over a kilometre up a rough track. Some people call it Swinside, after the farm on whose land it sits, but there is at least one other Swinside in the Lake District and Sunkenkirk links directly within this circle's now particular legend. The legend appears in various guises in different accounts, but I prefer the one that says that the local people wanted to build a church but the Devil would steal the stones under cover of darkness and use them in his circle. There's a similar legend attached to the Chapel o' Sink circle, in Aberdeenshire. There is no church nearby, so *quod erat demonstrandum*, or there you go! Then again, it's some distance from the nearest settlement of any size...

When I first visited Sunkenkirk it was back in about 2009, I think, when I was first getting interested specifically in the stone circles of Cumbria. I really hadn't expected to find what I did, for – legends apart – this is a truly exhilarating stone circle tucked into the hills on a piece of level ground above Peathouse Beck. It is the basis of the cover illustration of this book. Indeed, the only known limited investigation of the site, in about 1901, revealed that the site had been levelled manually prior to the building of the circle, which is thought to be of late Neolithic origin. The website, *Britain Express*, says of the place: 'Swinside stone circle is one of the most impressive, and at the same time, one of the least visited, stone circles in Britain.' Burl too is unequivocal: 'This well-preserved ring is one of the finest stone circles in western Europe.'

The circle comprises fifty-seven stones, some fallen, arranged in a circle of a little shy of twenty metres across. To the western and eastern sides, the stones are closely packed, creating something close to a palisade, with more spaced-out stones between these two arcs. To the south-east is an opening and Tom Clare notes that anyone standing at the centre of the circle at the winter solstice would have seen the sun rise over the summit of a hill, most likely Bank House Moor, just above and beyond the church at Kirkby-in-Furness. Equally, they would have seen the mid-summer sun setting over the summit of The Caw, to the north-west. Clare postulates, from the arrangement of both the south-eastern portal and the palisades, and similarities with other sites in Cumbria, that the stone circle may have originally comprised a timber post henge. The stones are of local slate and the one at the north of the circle is tall and slender, though weighing only about five tonnes, according to Burl.

Whatever its precise origins, the result is a circle to rival Castlerigg in terms of location, but which may be felt to have more than just an edge on the same circle in terms of its appearance, thanks to the tightly-packed nature of its monoliths. Clare mentions that the circle boasts another rather curious distinguishing feature: a carving of an Egyptian 'ankh', found on one of the stones in 1952. The *ankh* is an ancient hieroglyphic symbol, representing the 'key of life'. It looks a bit like a Christian cross but with the top bit replaced by a spoon shape. Inevitably, therein must lie a tale, and I am keen to discover what such tale might be. The answer is to be found in a 1972 volume of the Transactions of the Cumberland and Westmorland Antiquarian and Archaeological Society, in a paper written by an R G Plint. On the basis that an R.G. Plint would not have had a contemporary with identical initials in Cumbria, he seems to have been a pretty dynamic and interesting chap, having served in the First World War and then done a three-year stint in the late '50s as President of the Lake District Fell and Rock Climbing Club.

In his paper, written in 1972 when he would have been in his seventies, Mr Plint notes that another member of the society, the late Hon Marjorie Cross, had referred to the carving, noting that it had not been found when the circle was excavated in 1900. Nonetheless, it had been the opinion of those who examined it that it was most likely the handiwork of an 'antiquarian enthusiast' in the seventeenth or eighteenth century. Not unreasonably, Mr Plint begged to differ, and wrote to Marjorie Cross in January 1954, suggesting that the symbol was of far more recent origin.[3] He wrote: 'Many years ago I had read the two well-known novels by H. Rider Haggard, *She* and its sequel *Ayesha*.

'Readers will remember that the author in the introduction to the sequel mentions that Leo and Holly lived for a time in a house belonging to Holly on the Cumberland coast, behind which was a hill with a stone circle on its crest. I remembered examining a map at the time in search of the circle and came to the conclusion that he must have picked on Swinside but used an author's licence and transferred it from the Duddon estuary to the coast proper. (Subsequently I discovered he had used even more licence in erecting a cromlech or dolmen in the centre of the circle!).

'It will also be remembered that Ayesha carried a jewelled *ankh* or looped cross as a sceptre, and it seemed to me that someone else had come to the same conclusion as myself but had gone a little further and carved the symbol on a stone in order to give "colour" to the story.'

Miss Cross replied in turn: 'I got *Ayesha* from the library and have studied it, and think it looks very much as if Rider Haggard carved the *ankh* himself! Either he or one of his fans who had just read the book. The year of the excavation, when careful search was made for marks, was 1901 – *Ayesha* was published in 1905. There is a link between him and this neighbourhood, because his brother, Col Rider Haggard [author of *King Solomon's Mines* and other novels], was an old friend of the late Dr Fawcett of Broughton-in-Furness and used to stay with him. Quite possibly the novelist may have stayed with him, too. Dr Fawcett became a member of the Society in 1895, the year when the Society visited the circle, and he may have taken both brothers with him to the meeting and the novelist's imagination may have been fired by that or by his brother's account of it, though he didn't use the idea till he came to write *Ayesha* years afterwards. Certainly he seems to have been obsessed with the symbol for it runs right through the book though, usually, he confuses it with the Sistrum, which Ayesha used for her sceptre. Thank you very much for pointing me on this track.'

If you are now wondering what a 'sistrum' is, it is an ancient Egyptian percussion instrument 'shaped like an *ankh*' and like a tambourine with a handle. It was used in the worship of the goddesses Isis, Hathor and Bast so as to keep Typhon, the god of chaos, at bay.

My own little Swinside mystery shall come to light later today when I post pictures of the circle on Instagram and spot a hitherto unnoticed ceremonial avenue of stones leading off to the south-east. On closer inspection these 'stones' turn out to be three very precisely positioned sheep, grazing at equal intervals from the circle. No more than an amusing coincidence, of course (unless the sheep are grazing on spiritual hotspots), but I am drawn to the way that Sunkenkirk has inspired the imagination over the years, my own included. I once wrote of a hero and heroine who find a time capsule in the form of a Farrah's Original toffee tin, roughly buried at the foot of one of the monoliths – it's second nature for novelists, given that we have so little real understanding as to the original purpose of these places, to use them as the backdrop against which to set mysterious or supernatural events.

As I arrive today, a middle-aged couple from Shropshire are just leaving: they make a point of visiting circles they haven't seen before and are well impressed with Sunkenkirk. Criminally, today I have too little time to linger as long as I'd like: I'm on a deadline to arrive in Broughton and I'm curious about the possibility of there being the remains of another circle a couple of kilometres to the south-east, in Mount Wood, where the previously mentioned standing stones are marked on the OS map. Access may be possible via a public right of way, leading past Ash House. However, as I approach the house, there are children playing outside and it all feels just a bit too private for comfort and so I turn The Beast around and resume my route. On arrival at Jane Rousseau's The Square café, in Broughton, I mention this to her, as I have previously told her about the standing stones in an email. Now it turns out that she's already beaten me to it and visited the stones because the occupants of Ash House are actually friends of hers. She shows me pictures, taken in the pouring rain, of two substantial boulders on a level clearing in the woodland.

Clare notes that Marjorie Cross (yes, the same) and a colleague from the antiquarian society visited and described the site and concluded that it was the same one alluded to by the eighteenth-century Cumbrian historian W Hutchinson, and described by the nineteenth-century guidebook author J Housman, who wrote about a 'second circle not far from' Sunkenkirk and situated on rising ground that appeared to have been levelled for the purpose. 'An opening towards the south-west affords views of Duddon Sands,' wrote Housman. 'This though on a more pleasing situation, appears to have had less attention paid to it; the stones are small and few in number, only twenty-two appearing above the surface.'[4] The same circle, now minus twenty stones? Or a completely different one, now minus any trace whatsoever? Who can really say? Given the enormous amount of evidence lost at circles and other remains across Cumbria, we can only be thankful that some circles and other relics do indeed remain substantial, even if, as Mark Edmonds casually suggested to me in one of our conversations, they were never really intended to last.

* * *

I'm very appreciative of Jane for having squeezed me in at The Square at a time when the café isn't open and nor, officially, is the B&B side of things. I'm here, having found no room at the inn, as they say. I'm not the only one, however, there'll be some overspill wedding guests from a ceremony in town arriving later. I'm especially grateful for the opportunity to have a good soak in the bath, after my adventures by Devoke Water. I set it running, noting that the water could not be said to be exactly gushing forth from the tap. I leave it to do its own thing at its own pace and retire to my bedroom to catch up on my notes and messages.

Imagine my horror when I return to the bathroom to find that a contributory cause of the modest flow rate has been a shower attachment, casually slung over the side of the bath. Water has gathered in pools across the bathroom. I raid the airing cupboard and do my best to mop it all up with towels, which I then have to wring out and hang to dry anywhere I can find. So much for a nice restful preparation for dining over the road at the Black Cock Inn.

This is not my first visit to the old market town of Broughton, but it is my first overnight stay. I've always been fond of the place, with its fine Georgian architecture and enclosed central square that echoes to the sound of happy voices. Close your eyes and scrunch your ears a bit and you could almost think you were in France or Spain. It also boasts local shops, like a butcher's and baker's. But not everyone knows that this is thanks in no small measure to the philanthropy of one Richard Parsons, founder and owner of CGP (Coordination Group Publications). He's a local lad who used to teach at Furness College but got fed up with the standard of teaching guides available and began, in 1995, to write and publish his own. The company's success since then has been quite extraordinary – it's the market leader in GCSE, A-level and other study guides and these sell by the million, generating turnover in excess of £30 million. Profits before tax in 2019 were close to £14 million. Not a bad return.

Parsons does not believe in squirrelling these profits away and has bought threatened local businesses, like the butcher's, the baker's and a pub, and re-employed the staff on favourable terms to ensure the maintenance of local services. There are economists who justify the entire capitalist system on the basis of the example set by Mr Parsons and others like him. Sadly such enlightened philanthropy is not as universal as these commentators would like to think, but CGP undoubtedly brings both wealth and sustainability to a tiny market town in a corner of Cumbria. What's not to like? you may ask… Sadly, Mr Parsons is not everybody's cup of tea and for reasons unknown he and his staff have been victims of verbal assault, trolling, slander and libel, to the point at which he was, at the time of writing, on the verge of commencing legal action for defamation. I for one am in his corner.

Keeping local businesses running has a real multiplier effect too: Broughton is predominantly a town of full-time residents who shop and socialise locally and properties have a well-cared for appearance. Little wonder that the town was chosen as an urban location for the BBC series, *The A Word*, which is mostly set further north, at Honister and Newlands Valley.

The Black Cock is a traditional pub with a bit of a bistro offer: it's all black oak beams and cosy firesides to the front, and a newer, starker dining area to the rear. I enjoy wild boar meatballs on a fluffy flatbread. My short stay in Broughton pleases me so much that Linda and I return later in summer and revisit the Black Cock, where the staff absolutely excel with their friendliness and initiative. Overhearing my complaints about having been bitten by red ants, Hayley, the manager, appears with a little bottle of a Chinese solution called White Flower and applies it to the scene of the ant crime, and to my wife's own midgie bites. The relief is instant and dramatic. 'You can use it for almost anything,' says Hayley, 'if you're feeling a bit snuffly, just put some on the radiator when you go to bed.'

But back to my earlier stay: Jane is happy to welcome me in part because the purpose of my trip appeals to her and she tells me about a rather special book that was given to The Square Café by the author. The story is told in the café's visitor book – three local women were sitting chatting over lunch when the author of the book, Father John Musther, overhead their conversation from his own table. He clearly liked what he heard and showed them a copy of his book, *Sacred North*, subtitled *Walking in the Footsteps of the Earliest Christian Missionaries to Cumbria, Northumberland, Scotland and Beyond*. Fr Musther and his photographer, Phil Cope, visited close to 250 sacred sites on a camper van journey in 2016 and 2017 and the result is this rather fine volume, which sells on Amazon for just a penny shy of £150, though (unusually) it is available elsewhere for a fraction of that sum. I think Jane sees parallels between Fr Musther's journey and my own; by the same token, I think Fr Musther liked what he saw in Broughton, just as I do, for he left a signed copy of the book, which now resides in the café as a community resource.

* * *

Before I leave the following morning, much fortified by Jane's fine breakfast, she tells me about a woman called Penni Harvey-Piper, who owns a place called Stephenson Ground, in the fells above Broughton Mills, in the valley of the River Lickle. We know, of course, that Langdale stone axes were transported overland in various directions and by water in others, and that stone circles and other monuments were erected where such routes intersected. It has equally been noted that there seems to be a bit of gap to the south-east of Langdale, where Stephenson Ground is, in which there appear to be fewer monuments.

It seems worth mentioning in this context that just because remains cannot be seen today, that need not necessarily mean that they never existed in any given place. Penni Harvey-Piper wrote: 'When, in 1983, I came across an obviously important grave just sitting in the middle of the fell, it was frustrating that, although various people in the neighbourhood knew it was there, nobody had the slightest idea why, where, or for how long, it had been there.' Satisfying her own curiosity led to a decade and a half of research and some significant finds. The Duddon Valley Local History Group brought in volunteers under the banner R2R – ring cairns to reservoirs – and earlier excavations were revisited. A project report reads: 'Beneath the northernmost of three cairns and extending over a large area to its west, a substantial spread of Bronze Age material was found. This included fragments of pottery as well as flint tools. Evidence of flint waste shows that flint was collected as pebbles on the coast and brought up into the valley where tools were fashioned as required. Large amounts of charcoal and other clear signs of occupation were found.'[5]

It also cites the following comment, attributed to Peter Ball, who wrote a guide to the archaeology of Stephenson Ground: 'It is worth reflecting at this point just how ephemeral Bronze Age upland archaeology tends to be. There was absolutely no visible trace of this site above ground when the project started in 1986. It was therefore a pleasant surprise to discover the site, but it also demonstrates how the picture of Bronze Age settlement in the area will always be haphazard and related to chance discovery.' I find this both encouraging and discouraging. I'm encouraged because the inference to be drawn is that perhaps even my putative stone circle at Casterton may actually be… a stone circle. On the other hand, I'm discouraged because I'm realistic enough to know that such putative sites are unlikely ever to be investigated because the resource just isn't there.

With these thoughts in mind, I freewheel down towards the main road and the station, at Foxfield, where a short, sharp hale-storm forces me to don waterproofs and gloves. I exchange a wave with the level-crossing keeper, whose workplace is a converted shipping container: ah, the romance of the railways.

My route continues across the flat estuarine lands of Furness, the Duddon estuary to my right. As with Morecambe Bay, just the other side of the peninsula, the map of the sands here is criss-crossed with assertive green hatched lines, indicating bridleways. They are straight and purposeful and seem to imply that any fool might take his or her horse and stride out for the opposite shore, at Millom. Unlike any other such marked pathways on a map, these are not intended to be a precise indication as to where a route lies: they are merely indicative of the fact that such right exists. Woe betide anyone venturing to cross the sands without expert guid-ance, for the topography shifts with every tide and what may have been a viable route yesterday may just as easily be under water today or, worse, quicksand.

Morecambe Bay itself is, at low tide, a huge expanse of treacherous sands and unexpected channels. Few will not recall the Morecambe Bay cockling tragedy of 2004, when at least twenty-one Chinese cockle-pickers, under the control of ruthless gangmasters, drowned beneath the advancing tide. A moving account of the disaster can be found in Karen Lloyd's book, *The Gathering Tide* (2016). There is, for those seeking to venture onto or across the sands legally, a guide to help you, and he's appointed by the Queen, no less. I was once lucky enough to make the crossing, from Arnside to Kents Bank, under the stewardship of the late Cedric Robinson MBE, Queen's Guide to the Sands from 1963 until his retirement in 2019. The post brought with it the prodigious salary of £15 a year – plus a rent-free home in the Grade II Listed fourteenth-century Guide's House, provided by the Duchy of Lancaster. Originally it was the monks of Cartmel Abbey who guided travellers across the treacherous sands: the first Royal Guide was appointed nearly 500 years ago but few if any of the twenty-three who followed will have reached Cedric's age of eighty-six at retirement. He was succeeded by Michael Wilson, then forty-six and, like Cedric, a fisherman from Flookburgh.

Customarily, Cedric would survey his route before guiding a group across, often marking it with withies stuck into the gooey sand. What lingers in my memory is the extraordinary feeling of being seemingly out to sea, gazing back towards the Lakeland fells, framing the sparkling roofs of Arnside and the railway viaduct at the head of the Bay. I shan't forget that day.

It's recollections like this that persuade me, falsely, to somehow imagine the whole of the Furness Peninsula as some kind of rolling sandbank. It is not – far from it. A spine of craggy limestone divides the coastal plains to east and west and these are laced in places with intrusions of hematite, an iron ore. It was this that first brought heavy industry to the Cumberland coast and to this annex of the county of Lancashire. It may be long gone now, yet its legacy, as previously noted, endures in the shape of other heavy and intrusive industries, including nuclear.

And so, it comes as something of a rude shock when I find myself cycling up one of the steepest ascents of my trip thus far, to climb over the spine of Furness, behind the village of Kirkby. As I begin my gentler descent down towards Birkrigg Common, skirting the edge of Ulverston, I notice several police cars pulled up on a verge at the side of the road. A uniformed officer is walking up the steeply sloping hillside, just the other side of the fence by the road. She is talking into a radio. I notice that one of the parked cars is not a police vehicle, but an SUV: it has a bicycle rack on the back... but no bicycle. My imagination starts to run riot... 'He said he was just popping out for a short ride on the common,' the distraught woman sobs. 'It's just not like him – he always gives me a call to say he's arrived, but this time, nothing... I'm so worried.'

Later I'll try Googling things like 'missing cyclist, Ulverston', but draw a blank. I then remind myself that I too should, perhaps, keep in more regular contact. What if I'd landed on my head, instead of my chest, that day in the forest?

The OS map shows numerous tumuli, cairns, settlements, burial chambers and standing stones between my final stone circle and Dalton-in-Furness, the town to the west from where I shall be catching my train home later today. It had been my intention to take a BOAT, towards Urswick Tarn, passing a (presumably Iron Age) fort and a tumulus. Like many rights of way post-lockdown, it turns out that this one has become somewhat overgrown and, I judge, not possible to cycle. Bronze axes have been found on the site of the fort. I continue along the attractive by-road to the limestone escarpment marking the edge of Birkrigg Common. This is Appleby Hill, where old records indicate there was once a small stone circle. The circle had at some point been covered by the construction of a larger cairn or barrow, in which investigations uncovered a skeleton with an awl, or tool for leather working. A little to the north, more cairns yielded three urns.

I now have Morecambe Bay, in all its enchanting splendour, filling my field of view. The great hulk of the old nuke at Heysham seems deeply incongruous. It's clearly visible to the south, while just off the coast in front of me is Chapel Island, which once provided sanctuary for those caught out by the tide while crossing the Levens Estuary branch of Morecambe Bay, from Cartmel. To my left, the scrubby limestone shelves are covered in bracken, not yet tall enough to obscure things too much.

Birkrigg Stone Circle, also known as Sunbrick or Druid's Circle (again!), is at the confluence of several tracks that crisscross the area. It is a double 'circle' of modest size, comprising ten stones in the inner circle and a slightly haphazard external crescent of about thirteen fallen (or never erected) ones. Burl is unexpectedly mute on Birkrigg but Clare refers to an investigation by North Lonsdale Field Club, which found that the inner circle had once been cobbled and that, beneath the cobbles, were various remains including a collared urn, burnt earth and bones and a sharpened sandstone disc. Today there is a small bunch of old flowers at the centre of the circle. They carry no dedication, but the person who placed them here may have felt a feeling of peace that so many speak of; perhaps they hoped somehow to connect with a lost loved one. But it is its setting that makes Birkrigg special: I savour the view in the milky sunshine and feel a growing sense of sadness at the approaching end of my journey welling up from the pit of my stomach. This book's illustrator, who has visited the circle a few days before me, was particularly taken by it and was curious about an apparent alignment of two stones with the spire of the church in nearby Bardsea and wondered if the church might perhaps have been built upon a site of earlier significance. We may never know, but should perhaps note previous comments by Paul Frodsham on the subject of illusory alignments.

When I first had the idea of a 'pilgrimage' around Cumbria's stone circles, the plan had been to walk and, under that plan, I would have stayed at the Ship Inn, at nearby Bardsea, and perhaps raised a glass or two with anyone who cared to join me. I'm pleased today that I have just enough time to toast the near completion of my journey and delighted with the fulsome welcome I receive at the inn: this guy is what every landlord should be. I return the compliment by ordering a waffle with bananas and blueberries and a half of ale. Well, one doesn't drink champagne alone, does one? I earwig the conversation of the people on the next table: it's all about the *Eurovision Song Contest* and the fact that, last night, the UK surpassed all previous failures by scoring *nul points*! I don't know if the song deserved better (I doubt it), but I'd have bet a rare Bronze Age artefact on that zero score, the Government having worked hard ever since the notorious Brexit vote to ensure that 'nobody likes us, everybody hates us'. The moral of the story may perhaps be that if you behave like a spoiled brat, then you shouldn't be too surprised if people treat you like one.

I leave the pub, which stands high enough above the sea to prompt speculation about its nautical name, resolving to return one day. I do indeed return very briefly to Bardsea and Birkrigg later in summer and enjoy an excellent snack at the little shack by the sea, just south of the village. Today, however, I point The Beast inland, towards Dalton-in-Furness. On arrival at the station, a notice tells me that the Tourist Information is on the eastbound platform. This turns out to be no more than a large, illustrated board, with pictures of attractions in the area, most of them not in Dalton. (On the aforementioned return to the area, I do get to see more of the town and it is indeed an attractive one and very possibly another worthy place from which to explore the extensive Bronze landscape of its surrounds.) The first Northern Rail train on my circuitous return home, via Leeds, is quite a posh one, bound for Manchester Airport. I work out that, rather than go all the way into Lancaster and back again, I can actually change sooner, at Carnforth, and here I have a surprise treat: the Brief Encounter tea-room may not yet have reopened but the little Brief Encounter Museum is indeed open.

Those of a certain age will know that *Brief Encounter* is the name of David Lean's end-of-war classic, starring Trevor Howard and Celia Johnson. It's one of those iconic films beloved of buffs the world over and renowned for what the lead characters do not say or do, rather than for what they do. The entire film is charged with the electricity of an anticipated affair that may or may not ever actually happen: that rare moment when two souls meet across a crowded room or, in this case, a café table. It's all subliminal nods and winks and a dialogue carefully framed in the terms of a war-clouded age in which people came to meet in circumstances in which they might not have expected to meet or in which the fragility of the time infused them with a sense of urgency which, in post-war years, might have receded into the background. It is such a period piece that it is close to impossible to imagine such a film ever being made in today's explicit times.

The outdoor scenes in *Brief Encounter* were shot at the station, though the dialogue was filmed in a studio recreation of the refreshment room. The whole station received a makeover at the turn of the twentieth century and the café was lovingly recreated in full 1940s splendour. Since then, it has enjoyed visits by many stars of star and screen, including the cast of *Coronation Street*, Michael Portillo, Sir John Major and Timothy West and Prunella Scales. For thirteen years to 2021, it was run by Andrew and Helen Coates, who even celebrated their marriage on the platform. Chef Liam Law and business partner Andrea Wren took over in autumn 2021 and now offer evening meals as well as daytime café service and a range of special events.

The curious thing about *Brief Encounter* is that all we know for sure is that the two married protagonists meet every Thursday and may go to the cinema or somewhere round about. There's no evidence to support the suggestion by some that the anticipated passionate affair ever actually goes beyond the occasional glancing touch or the rather abrupt final kiss. It's riddled with metaphor, suggestive of the imminent return to a safer, more comfortable and secure world, as symbolised by two rather dull marriages.

As I remind myself of the plot, I find myself thinking about that other mystery whose plot is alluded to but never entirely told. The flimsy traces of our Neolithic times sometimes seem to do little more than hint at the reality of the times without ever casting more than the faintest light upon them. My journey has truly enriched me and taught me far more than I ever knew about Neolithic and Bronze Age times. It has moved me deeply and nudged me a small way towards identifying links, however tenuous, with our own times. There remains, for me and for all of you, much to learn.

Chapter 7

Circles, circles everywhere!

Creating your own voyage of discovery

My journey around the best of Cumbria's stone and cairn circles grew out of a plan which evolved over time and spanned several months, two lockdowns and the progressive addition of more and more circles as I 'discovered' them from new sources. It's quite likely that, were I to do it all again, I'd come up with a different itinerary for getting around them all – visiting all those on Shap Fell and nearby, in particular, involved a certain amount of zig-zagging, punctuated by an overnight stop.

Anyone tempted to visit some or all the circles that I have may choose their own way of doing this, whether on two wheels, four, or on foot. My suggestion would be to consider first what I'll call the 'must-see' circles and the best-integrated landscapes, including those that comprise cairns, settlements and hut circles but, not necessarily any 'stone' or cairn circles. The following potpourri does not include any sites that required anything more sinful than the most minor trespass to visit.

Although this book's subtitle refers to 'Neolithic Cumbria', in reality there are no hard boundaries between the Neolithic and Bronze Ages. Nor between these and the transitional Chalcolithic Age. The focus is on the period when Cumbria's stone circles and cairn circles were built, that is from the early Neolithic, around 4000 or 3500 BC, when quarrying for axe-making began in Langdale and the first circles were created, up to around 2000 BC, or the early Bronze Age. This means that, if you visit any complex extended landscape you'll be 'arriving' not at a single point in time but an evolving slice of life across possibly hundreds of years.

The area of 'greater Shap', as I'll call it, is just such an evolving landscape and it should keep you occupied for one very full day, or two gentler ones, it being possible to devise a walking route that will cover all the circles and the remains of the ceremonial avenue, including the Goggleby Stone and the Thunder Stones. Most of the remains are on, or at least close to, rights of way, though the best stone circle, Gunnerkeld, is on private farmland. The owners, however, are usually happy for you to visit if you ask at the farmhouse first. It would be possible to extend this 'collection' to include the rediscovered circle at Shapbeck and the elusive stone-on-limestone circle at Knipe Scar, though a hike up to Four Stones Hill, overlooking Haweswater, might be more rewarding. Heading south-eastward from Shap will take you across the same fells as may have been crossed by early traders carrying Langdale axes, with the extraordinary rich cairned limestone landscape of Asby Scar to your left, as you arrive at the easily accessed Gamelands circle, near the lovely village of Orton.

Long Meg is, of course, an iconic circle and merits a decent length of visit, which can also be combined with the decorated stone at Little Meg, and the excavated cairn circle of Glassonby (though both the latter necessitate modest trespass). All these can be combined with the hugely impressive Mayburgh Henge and the associated King Arthur's Round Table, a few miles south-west.

Castlerigg merits a visit in its own right, though don't expect quiet contemplation: this must be among the busiest circles in the entire country. Sunkenkirk, or Swinside, matches or betters Castlerigg in terms of both the visible remains and its setting. It is also likely that you'll find yourself alone – to fully enjoy Sunkenkirk really demands time, and you'll also need a good 15 or 20 minutes to walk in both directions. The circle at Birkrigg is not huge but is worth visiting for its dramatic position, gazing across Morecambe Bay towards Heysham, and for the surrounding complex landscape of cairns and other remains.

Of the upland sites, Bratts Hill, above Boot, in Eskdale, features modest but elegant stone circles and fabulous views out to sea and of the surrounding peaks. It's truly worth the steep climb, which will take 45 minutes or so. Think about watching the sun go down on a warm midsummer's evening. On the other side of Eskdale, a walk through the ancient settlements by Devoke Water is really not to be missed, while a wander along the old drove roads that pass through settlements and farmsteads on the flanks of Lang Rigg, a little to the north, combines neatly with a visit to the small but perfectly formed Blakeley Raise circle. My final top circle tip is the Cockpit and other features of what was once a significant and extensive landscape, which most likely included a ceremonial avenue. All are easily reached from Askham, Helton or Pooley Bridge.

Finally, here's one for the sure of foot and hearty of lung: a visit to the axe factory, in Langdale, which is accessed from the coll at the top of a scree gulley (consisting mostly of axe offcuts from centuries of working), on Pike o' Stickle, high above Great Langdale. Take a look at your Vibram-soled boots and then imagine making the climb in, say, leather sandals; once up there sift through the extensive discarded shards; or clamber down from the coll to the Neolithic cave, big enough for two to shelter. The Langdale Boulders, at Copt Howe, near Chapel Stile, feature rare Cumbrian examples of rock art, which were only discovered as recently as 1999.

* * *

I began this book by stating that Cumbria was rich in stone and cairn circles in a way that the land east of the Pennines is very much less so. Conversely, Cumbria has few examples of cup and ring decorations. The wisdom, of course, is that the fashion for building stone circles originated in Orkney and spread south from there, culminating with the creation of the huge monument of Stonehenge, with its enormous lintels. People most probably did not make a single journey from the north of Scotland and then create a stone circle at their destination. On the balance of probability, most of those who made journeys at all most likely made shorter ones but might then have met up with others travelling in other directions and exchanged goods and ideas. We believe they travelled in seaworthy boats and the concentration of stone circles towards the west of Britain suggests the west coast, punctuated by islands, was the preferred route. Once people became established at a given location, overland travel was most likely for preference by dug-out or other types of canoe via lakes and rivers. However, we can also infer the existence of important foot trails, from which forest cover would most likely have been cleared.

All this means that there is no shortage of circles and other features to visit in areas neighbouring Cumbria. As in Cumbria, these most likely served a variety of purposes, from simple meeting places, to 'crossroad' sites at which goods were exchanged to grander purposes, such as burial sites, sometimes incorporating key astronomical alignments. As already stated, Northumberland and County Durham are not circle-rich, though if cup and ring marks are your bag, head for Roughting Linn, in the broad valley to the west of the Kyloe Hills, and in turn west of Holy Island (NT984367). The remains of a henge can be seen just north of Milfield, but Northumberland's crowning circular glory is Duddo Five Stones, also known as The Singing Stones, The Seven Turnip Pickers and The Women, which are found roughly halfway between Berwick-upon-Tweed and Coldstream. The small circle comprises, these days, five stones (as the name suggests) of local sandstone, heavily fluted by thousands of years of rain, which has given them the look of having been clawed by some giant beast. They can be seen up close by using a permissive footpath created for the purpose.

Yorkshire is a rich hunting ground and boasts magnificent henges, half-decent stone circles, standing stones and cup and ring marked boulders. The three Thornborough henges, near Masham, are vast earthworks, which have been dubbed 'Yorkshire's Stonehenge'. Historic England places the henges and wider landscape alongside Avebury, Stonehenge and Neolithic Orkney in terms of its ceremonial importance. These henges, or earthworks, date to the late Neolithic and early Bronze Age. Each of the three interconnected henges is about 240 metres across and the gap between each is about 550 metres, meaning that the whole assemblage is close to two kilometres long.

I began my own visit at the northernmost of the three: you have to be sure of your precise location by close map reading or using a location device. There is no formal entry point, but a number of pathways lead directly from the minor road into the henge itself. This is heavily wooded, to the extent that it is not possible to gain an overall impression of the size and scale of the henge, which is surrounded by a three metre deep ditch and three-metre tall embankment. It takes about fifteen minutes to walk its circumference which has two gaps in it, as does each of the other two henges.

I also visited the central henge, which is in open countryside and therefore somewhat more impressive: you can climb on top and gaze over towards the southernmost henge. There are also traces of an earlier cursus, or double-banked ditch, running north-east to south-west beneath the central henge, which is thought to have served an earlier ceremonial purpose. Thornborough's very contemporary problem is that the land is owned by Tarmac Ltd, which has extensive gravel workings in the area and wants to quarry right up to the edge of the protected landscape. The company does permit Druids to celebrate the May Day festival of Beltane, roughly halfway between the spring equinox and the summer solstice. Burl suggests that precious artefacts, such as Langdale axes, would have been exchanged when people met at Thornborough.

The henges at Thornborough are, in turn, just one element of a vast Neolithic ceremonial landscape extending about eighty kilometres north to south in the Vale of York. At the northern extent of this are henge remains at Catterick, alongside the airfield and racecourse, while there are several other henge remains, including Nunwick, near Ripon, and Ferrybridge, at the southern end of the Vale. Many of these remains are only slightly visible nowadays, some appearing only as crop marks, but that cannot be said of the Devil's Arrows, on the edge of Boroughbridge. These are three huge monoliths, aligned north-west to south-east and in turn about ten miles south-east of Thornborough. The tallest of the three, at 6.85 metres, is higher than Stonehenge and the second tallest standing stone in Britain after the Rudston Monolith, in East Yorkshire, which stands at 7.6 metres.

At one time there were certainly four, possibly five and maybe even seven stones and, though these may not be a stone circle, they most certainly deserve a visit, though it's best to avoid spring and summer when the field in which the two most northerly stones stand is under crop. One stone is at the field's edge, so you can get up close by walking carefully around the perimeter of the field. The tallest stone is maybe ten metres in from the field's edge and so should be visited up close only when the land is lying fallow. I did this on a day of heavy showers, meaning I ended the visit once again with moon boots of clay, bringing back happy memories of the day I went to Grey Croft, near Sellafield. The precise function of the arrows can only be speculated upon, but people went to a lot of trouble to erect the stones, which would have had to be dragged some nine miles from Plumpton quarry, near Knaresborough. This would have been quite some task, demanding a considerable workforce. The stones are also quite deeply founded when compared with some other monoliths, each being submerged to a depth of 1.4 to 1.8 metres and thus clearly intended to last. The tallest stone is the most southerly, on private land on the other side of the road from the other two. All are millstone grit and have become heavily fluted by millennia of rainfall, giving them a sculpted quality, not unlike the Duddo Stones in Northumberland.

The Devil's Arrows are so called because legend has it that the Devil, angered at some perceived snub by the people of Aldborough (the site of the Roman fort at Boroughbridge), tossed the stones from somewhere near Fountains Abbey. However, they fell short and became embedded in their present location. If I had to speculate on their raison-d'être, I'd say they were a prominent direction marker for those bound for Thornborough. If we can presume that the landscape had by then been cleared of forest, they would have been visible for miles around.

Further south, if you venture onto Ilkley Moor (with or without your 'at!), you'll find yourself in an extraordinarily rich landscape, which is likely to have provided hunting, farming and grazing land in warmer Neolithic and Bronze Age periods. The legacy of these times is some hundreds of monuments, including numerous cup and ring marked boulders. The location is more correctly known as Rombald's Moor, Ilkley Moor being just that part of the wider upland immediately above the spa town of that name. My own experience of this landscape goes back to when I took my first steps towards being a freelance rather than a staff journalist. My photographer friend Barry Wilkinson and I used to work as a team, pitching offbeat feature ideas to the broadsheet nationals. Barry, who lived in Ilkley, had been talking to the local archaeological group who were systematically surveying all the cup and ring marked boulders on the moor. I believe their extensive research ended up in a book called *The Carved Rocks on Rombald's Moor*, since reprinted as *Prehistoric Rock Art of the West Riding*. This was 1983, which was relatively early in the period during which cup and ring marks were starting to rise nearer the top of the in-tray marked 'Neolithic remains'.

I recall having to do my interview 'on the run' as the amateurs moved from rock to rock, recording what they saw and found, and looking for hitherto unseen markings that might have been covered over sometime in the intervening millennia. Barry too had to fight to get them to pose long enough for 'action shots' for his pictures. It was back in the days of celluloid, when every photographer's worst nightmare was a film that stuck or, now and again, forgetting to put a film in at all... As we walked back off the moor, Barry realised that was precisely what had happened:

we stumbled back through the heather and almost pleaded with the archaeologists for a second chance. By one of those quirks, the sun was now lower and the natural light cast the budding archaeologists in sharper relief. The pictures looked great and I worked really hard to craft words to do them justice. In those days you relied on the Royal Mail or Red Star parcels on British Rail to get your features submitted. But at least people answered the phone back then: they rarely do these days.

Both pictures and words looked good and we submitted the story to *The Times*'s feature editor, who liked it and offered me £500 for the words. It was my first big feature in a national newspaper and a payment of this size was up towards my wildest dreams: it's equivalent to about £1,500 now. Nowadays, you'd feel you were doing well to earn a fifth of that for a feature. I share this because I was of that generation that was able to make a half-decent living freelancing for national and regional papers. You have to be pretty special to achieve that these days. I have searched high and low for my cutting of that pioneering feature from the Abbott archive but to no avail: it seems not to have enjoyed the longevity of the cups and rings that were its subject.

If you follow the right of way more or less due south from above Ilkley Crags you will, after about a kilometre and a half, arrive at the Twelve Apostles Stone Circle, which is the pick of about four stone and cairn circles that can be found on the Moor. Unusually, given the usual discrepancy between circle names and what can be found on the ground, there are indeed twelve millstone grit monoliths, if that term can still be applied when the stone is but a metre and a half tall. All these circles – others include Great Skirtful of Stones, Grubstones and Backstone Circle – have an undoubted charm and, being close to Leeds and Bradford, attract visitors who may watch the sunset or, indeed, check out some of the supposed celestial alignments.

Lancashire is somewhat less well endowed with Neolithic and Bronze Age remains than the county of the White Rose, though this may not always have been the case. Indeed, the Pennine moors all the way down to the fringe of Greater Manchester, are dotted with a variety of remains, though not all have stood the tests of either time or deliberate destruction. Cheetham Close stone circle, near Ramsbottom, is a case in point, it having apparently been attacked with a sledgehammer by a local farmer in the nineteenth century. It's said to still attract local interest despite its diminished condition and it is surrounded by other remains, including cairns. It is not easy to find, so here is the map reference – SD716159. Other circles around the edge of Greater Manchester include the remains of a circle at Thirteen Stone Hill, on Oswaldwhistle Moor, and – just a little bit exciting – the remains of a significant circle at Hamer Hill, near Rochdale. Found as recently as 2010 by archaeologist Stuart Mendelsohn and dubbed 'Rochdale's Stonehenge' by local media, it's a 30-metre, early Bronze Age circle, probably the remnants of a burial site. Another ten-metre cairn was found nearby, as well as around twenty boulders of up to 1.5 metres across.

Further north, at Garstang, on the edge of the Forest of Bowland, are the remains of a Bronze Age urnfield, called Bleasdale Circle. Excavation at the site uncovered the remains of a wooden palisade, which now survives as an earthwork, with a causeway leading to the central mound, where three cremation vessels were found. Eleven concrete posts now mark the location of the wooden posts originally found. The circle sits in a tranquil location in the middle of a copse on the fellside and can be accessed on foot from the nearby minor road. There's an interpretation panel at Ribchester Roman bath-house museum, east of Preston.

Venturing further south, into the Peak District, and there are, once again, pretty rich Neolithic pickings, with half a dozen stone circles of significance within the Peak National Park boundary. I decided to take a trip to one of the larger, but less often trumpeted, circles, on Eyam Moor. It's reasonably easy to both reach and find and sits on the northern slopes of the moor, looking out towards the Hope Valley railway. It can be found within a complex pattern of funerary and clearance cairns, From the 'plague village' of Eyam, you take Edge Road, which, once it's climbed the escarpment, heads more or less due north until it joins Sir William Hill Road at a T-junction, with a BOAT to the left and minor road to the right. You can park here and cross the road, where two marked paths lead to Stanage and Abney (to the north-west) and towards Leam (to the north-east). An unmarked path precisely halfway between the two strikes off directly across the moor. You need not be deterred by its occasional meanderings, as it will eventually take you directly to the circle, which comprises a bank about 30 metres in diameter, atop which are ten or so remaining standing stones. The remains of well ravaged funerary cairns are more or less adjacent, one of them being Eyam Moor Barrow, next to which is a large green post-War Ministry of Works sign, which reads in block capitals: 'Notice is hereby given that under the provisions of the Ancient Monuments Acts… any person injuring or defacing the same will be liable to prosecution according to law.' Well, I'm hardly going to argue with that, but perhaps a little bit of rather more enticing 'interpretation' might not go amiss in this the twenty-first century.

Other Peak District circles include Arbor Low, an elliptical circle of thirty white weathered limestone blocks, in a barrow-rich landscape on the road from Ashbourne to Buxton. Nine Ladies is one of a complex of millstone grit circles at an English Heritage site on Stanton Moor and is popular at summer solstice. Nine Stones Close (also known as The Grey Ladies) comprises just four stones on Harthill Moor, near Stanton, another three stones having 'gone missing' since first recorded in the nineteenth century – the remaining stones are now set in concrete, which should at least stop them going walkabout. Barbrook circles I-III are small and located in a cairn and field settlement landscape, easily accessed from the A621 on Big Moor; Hordron Seven Stones, as the name doesn't suggest, is an embanked ring of about twenty stones on Moscar Moor, off the A576, near Ladybower reservoir. The circle at Doll Tor is a small but perfectly formed probable cairn circle in woodland, near Birchover – it has been restored to its original layout after a misinformed 'reconstruction' in the 1990s.

Another circle not too far from our North of England sphere, which I enjoyed visiting, is Mitchell's Fold, which stands near the edge of a gentle plateau over 300 metres high on the south-west flank of Stapeley Hill, in the Shropshire Hills Area of Outstanding Natural Beauty. A kink in the border means it's just a long stone's throw north of the Welsh border and within a few miles of the late-Neolithic picrite (an igneous rock) stone axe 'factory' of Cwm-Mawr. Its surviving doleritic stones measure up to a little shy of two metres. Burl says the tallest stone, at the south-east end of its main north-west to south-east axis, lies close to the 'line of the major southern moonrise'. Burl does not give a detailed explanation of what precisely this means and it is, for sure, complicated, being concerned with the 'lunar standstill' which is to do with the Moon's 'range of declination' and occurs every 18.6 years, when the moon will appear almost to hover over the southern horizon. The twenty-five to twenty-seven metre slight ellipse is not in the best of conditions but it is from its location and its legends that the monument derives its appeal. Elaine Gregory, an artist and Druid from the Order of Bards, who runs a centre for Druidic and other 'mystical' groups in Shropshire, told me: 'It's really special because of the expanse – you can see for miles!'

I rather like the legend attached to Mitchell Fold, which is one of a group of at least three circles in the vicinity. To quote Burl again: 'Legend says that the circle was used by a giant whose cow gave unceasing milk until tricked by a witch who used a sieve to drain the animal dry.' Apparently the cow legged it all the way to Warwickshire and became The Dun Cow, while the witch, as is customary, was turned to stone and then entrapped by the other stones of the circle. Apparently, there's a carving of the legend at the top of a column in the church at Middleton-in-Chirbury, a mile to the west. What intrigues me about all these stone circle tales is precisely when they originate from... the most likely answer is that they emerged as Christianity assimilated earlier legends. But what if they were first created back in the days when the circles were in active use? Who knows!

* * *

Some of our Cumbrian circles, unsurprisingly, share characteristics with circles in southern Scotland, according to Aubrey Burl and others. The Twelve Apostles stand between Holywood and Newbridge, at Locharbriggs, a couple of miles north-west of Dumfries, and merit mention because, at 79–87 metres in diameter, this slight oval is the largest stone 'circle' on the Scottish mainland. It is also the seventh-largest in Great Britain. Much meddled with, especially in the dreaded nineteenth century, only eleven of the original eighteen or so stones remain, and of these only five remain upright. Some of these are of non-local stone and would have been dragged from a couple of miles away. The largest are about two metres in length but one of these is fallen. The whole has a south-west alignment towards the midwinter setting sun.

Whiteholm Rigg, five miles east of Lockerbie and a similar distance north-north-east of Ecclefechan, 'has affinities with the great circles of south-west Scotland', according to Burl. The circle has seen better days, with only about seven or eight stones remaining from the original 20-metre circle. Once again, the Girdle Stanes, 11 miles east of Lockerbie and 6 miles north-east of Borland, sound powerful Cumbrian echoes. Burl states: 'The ring is similar to the rather smaller Swinside in the Lake District and the resemblance becomes closer when there appears to be an entrance at the south-east where two stones, 1.3 and 1.5 metres high, frame a 3.4-metre gap.' The circle also shares with Swinside (or Sunkenkirk) an alignment with the rising early November sun at the festival of Samhain. At some point in the last 5,000 or so years, the nearby River White Esk has shifted its course and taken with it about twenty of the original forty-plus stones. Before leaving southern Scotland, mention should be made of the huge glacial erratic, called the Lochmaben Stane, three-quarters of a mile south-west of Gretna Green, because carbon dating of charcoal from its shallow stoke hole confirms it was erected around 3275 BC, in accord, says Burl, 'with the postulated age of the great Cumbrian rings across the Solway Firth'. It stands at the end of the Sulwath, a muddy but still passable fording point on the Solway estuary and, until sometime in the first half of the nineteenth century, comprised a ring of stones measuring about 55 by 46 metres. The Lochmaben Stane is a 5.5-metre granite boulder of about 18 tonnes, which was perhaps more of a challenge for the circle-destroyers. Its residual importance appears to have endured until the late fourteenth century as this was where the English and Scottish representatives met in 1398 to negotiate a truce following the battle of Otterburn ten years previously.

Paul Frodsham notes in a paper contained in *New Light on the Neolithic of Northern England* that the Lochmaben Stane itself was radio-carbon dated to between 3500 and 2850 BC[1]. This was based on charcoal found in its socket prior to its re-erection in 1983 and suggests this was the only stone circle in the region of comparable date to Long Meg and he argues that, notwithstanding the broad date range, these circles may have predated those at Calanais and, indeed, even the Stones of Stenness. He notes the strategic positioning of Lochmaben close to routes across both land and water (via the River Esk, the Solway and Irish Sea).

* * *

Having permitted the mystique of the Cumbrian stone circle to percolate into your blood and then dipped a toe in the waters of other stone circles in northern England and southern Scotland, you may now feel ready to be inspired by the best these isles have to offer. While making the passing observation that there are places that can boast a density of circles to rival that of Cumbria – Cornwall, Wales and Aberdeenshire all spring to mind – the intention at this point is to nudge readers towards something different and special. At the top of the list has to be Neolithic Orkney, in its entirety, for – as extensively explained – this is really quite possibly where it all began and, in a very real sense, where it all continues to happen now. The process of excavation at the Ness of Brodgar is an ongoing one, interrupted only by COVID, so if you really fancy getting your hands dirty AND being on-site when the next extraordinary insight into Neolithic life manifests itself on the toe of someone's trowel, then it's wise to keep an eye on the Ness of Brodgar official website to know when and if volunteers are being recruited[2]. Ongoing excavation remains subject to the continued availability of the necessary funds from year to year.

The Western Isles have not been blessed by the same degree of investigative work as Orkney, but all the islands, from Lewis southward, are rich in Neolithic and later remains. The standing stones of Calanais (Callanish) are among the most iconic in Britain, their wind-scoured clustered forms towering nearly five metres above the endless heather and peat moorland. I recall on my first visit, when a savage gale was blowing off the Atlantic, cowering behind one of the stones, which are arranged in a cruciform extending from a central tight circle of thirteen monoliths. There are many other circles and other remains to be seen in the immediate area, where a ceremonial avenue extends through the village of Calanais itself. The main Calanais circle is thought to have been orientated in line with the lunar standstill, as loosely explained above. As with Orkney, there is much still to be discovered. In February 2020, The Calanais Virtual Reconstruction Project, led by the University of St Andrews with the archaeological charity, *Urras nan Tursachan*, and the University of Bradford, used a variety of survey techniques to probe what lay beneath the peat in the Calanais area and located some fifteen hitherto unknown circles in the surrounding landscape[3].

Perhaps even more intriguing in some respects are findings from field research by the universities of Reading and Southampton in 2016. *Submerged Neolithic of the Western Isles* describes survey work at three islets on lochs on Lewis, all of which were presumed to have originally been artificial constructions on which crannogs were located.[4] These round houses on islets have generally been presumed to be Iron Age in origin. More than 400 of them are recorded across Scotland, with between 100 and 150 in the Outdoor Hebrides, or Western Isles. Despite their number, crannogs, say the authors, have remained under-investigated and under-excavated. A key finding of their work was that many of these locations dated from well before the Iron Age, and were Neolithic in origin – 3800-2500 BC. Another crannog, Eilean Domhnuill, on North Uist, was earlier found by Ian Armit and his team from the University of York to also be Neolithic in origin and to have supported multiple phases of building between 3560 and 2600 BC. These dates suggest that Neolithic people were living in the Western Isles not just around the same time as they lived at Skara Brae, on Orkney, but possibly somewhat earlier.

And also that they lived in houses of a distinctly different form.

* * *

It has been stated more than once in this book that stone circles cannot be considered outside the context of their surrounding landscapes. Staying in Scotland, Kilmartin Glen might just be THE place to appreciate a complex multi-faceted early Neolithic and Bronze Age landscape. This landscape not only features profuse cup and ring markings but, taken at large, may well have been something of a celestial observatory, with both solar and lunar orientations possible at the various timber and stone circles at Temple Wood and a cursus with a potential lunar alignment. Once again, it's our friend the lunar standstill, with the southern section of this cursus aligning with the setting of the southern moon. In her paper *Contextualising Kilmartin: building a narrative for developments in western Scotland and beyond from the Early Neolithic to the Late Bronze Age*, Alison Sheridan says: 'While archaeo-astronomers will doubtless continue to discuss this matter, it does indeed appear likely that the Temple Wood circles were constructed with a view to marking significant celestial events.

'How the complex rock art on the outcrops of Mid Argyll fits within this scenario is another key question, especially since the tradition is not well represented in Orkney and probably did not originate there.'

The landscape is also 'diverse' in the way it reflects different prehistoric time periods and so a visit to Kilmartin Glen feels like a good way to get a feel for the manner in which lifestyles and 'fashions' established in Orkney may have spread from there, with Kilmartin a potential mixing pot and cultural gathering place. The redeveloped and expanded Kilmartin Museum was expected to reopen in 2023.

* * *

One could hardly write a book about Neolithic times without reference to the most iconic monument of all. Yes, Stonehenge: the huge edifice that may just be the ultimate crowning manifestation of a cult that originated hundreds of miles to the north and hundreds of years earlier. Given that, in its more recent manifestation, Stonehenge has been around for about 4,500 years, it sometimes seems it's scarcely been out of the news. In my lifetime, there's been concern that too many Druids at midsummer might destroy the fabric; about ongoing traffic issues and controversial solutions to this; and excitement at the recent 'hot news' that parts of the complex had been previously 'road-tested' at a stone circle in Wales.

Stonehenge is undoubtedly a very special stone circle, even if it may not be, technically, a henge at all. It is most likely the only Neolithic or Bronze Age circle to boast lintel stones, although there are a few other 'maybes' in this category (including the aforementioned Mitchell's Fold circle, though this is considered unlikely). It is also at the centre of a vast ceremonial landscape, and this is reflected in its World Heritage Site status and the inclusion in the WHS listing of other important locations, such as the vast stone circle at Avebury. The nature of the wider landscape is at the heart of one of the ongoing 'news stories' about the monument. Having finally, finally– after years of wrangling and prevarication – agreed to sink the A303 trunk road beneath the monument, the Government then opted for the shortest possible length of tunnelling. Archaeologists and others said the short tunnel would pose a major risk to the wider monumental and ceremonial landscape (and even the site's very WHS status) and demanded a longer tunnel. As things stand, their challenge has been upheld and all is back at Square One as I write this.

Then, besides all this, is the fact that – pretty much alone among all our stone circles – you can't actually get up close to the stones, let alone dare to touch them. Ten metres is about as close as you'll get these days, and that's having paid your hefty English Heritage entry fee. And then shuttle buses and glass-fronted visitor centres are about as far removed from Neolithic mysticism as you're ever likely to get. There is, apparently, a 'piratical' method of seeing Stonehenge, which I cannot personally vouch for, but it is there online. You pop Willoughby Road, Salisbury, into your sat-nav and park near the junction with Fargo Road and then walk along the track, which joins the public right of way that runs close to the stones and is outwith the control of English Heritage.

Although the 'stone' bit of Stonehenge arrived sometime after the building of the ritual landscape at the Ness of Brodgar, Salisbury Plain appears to have fulfilled an important ritualistic role way back in Mesolithic times. Some speculate that this arose because the thin soils of the chalk Downs did not support the dense woodland that would have prevailed elsewhere. That may or may not be the case, but the earliest known structures comprised tall pine poles and these were erected as early as 8500-7000 BC. Two enclosed cursuses and a number of long barrows followed around 3500 BC. Beyond this point, differences in interpretation begin to emerge: I have chosen to go with the dates cited by Aubrey Burl. So, at the monument site itself, the earliest structure was a circular banked ditch of about 100 metres in diameter and built around 3200 BC. This is the 'hengey' bit, though it may also have had stones mounted upon it, the so-called Aubrey stones, named after the seventeenth-century antiquarian, John Aubrey. More than sixty cremations have been found in this part of the monument. An unfinished ring of Welsh bluestones part-replaced the wooden monument around 2200 BC.

It was another 200 or so years before the 'real stones' arrived: the huge sarsens (each weighing between 25 and 50 tonnes) dragged 18 miles cross the Downs from Marlborough, possibly with the help of oxen, and erected to form a 'perfect' circle of just shy of 30 metres. Within this were more sarsens in a horseshoe shape and the Welsh bluestones were ultimately re-erected to form a circle between the two. It's interesting to note what Burl says about the construction of the monument: 'It was an astonishing achievement. There was no good building stone near Stonehenge nor was there any megalithic tomb within 17 miles. The natives of Salisbury Plain were woodworkers and they treated the sarsens as though they were timber, making bevels, chamfers, pegs, mortise-and-tenon joints, tongues-and-grooves. The carpentry techniques can still be seen. Even the inner faces of the rock-hard sarsens were smoothed like planed wood. Some of the scoured and battered tennis-ball to football-sized stone mauls used for the tedious shaping can be seen in Salisbury Museum.'

Burl suggests that the bluestones had 'more probably' been shifted to close to Stonehenge by glaciation but that idea was cast into severe doubt by the relatively recent location of a stone circle site close to the quarry in the Preseli Hills, in west Wales, from where the bluestones were hewn. News of the finding of this site broke as recently as February 2021. It seems that the 'stone holes' at this 'circle' at Waun Mawn pretty much matched those of the identically-sized original bluestone circle at Stonehenge and that the entire structure was quarried around 3300 BC (as evidenced by carbon-dated hazelnut shells) and then dismantled and moved to Stonehenge 400 years later. The stones were also a close match with the remaining face of the quarry site. The original circle at Waun Main would have been the third largest and among the oldest dated circles in the country, of similar age to Long Meg and Her Daughters, dating from around the same time as the remains at the Ness of Brodgar. The discovery was thanks in part to the fact that four stones were left behind at Waun Main, enabling the original stone holes to be found. It marked a crowning glory for Mike Parker Pearson, a professor of later British prehistory at University College London, who had spent twenty years dedicated to studying Stonehenge, the last five of them looking for the 'original site' of the bluestone monument.[5]

It now also seems most likely that the stones were then dragged overland to Stonehenge along a 'relatively easy' route, now preferred to a postulated sea route, which hugged the coast and would have required boats more sturdy than those argued about in the context of carrying cattle relatively short distances. In a paper published in *Antiquity* in February 2021, Parker Pearson and others discuss the idea that the movement of the bluestones overland to Stonehenge may have been accompanied by a wider migration of people: why did people from west Wales move with their animals and their sacred stones to Stonehenge?[6] They ask: 'If this was indeed the case, what were the drivers of such a migration? Were they climatic, economic, social or political, or a combination of these?' They ponder whether there may have been a social or political vacuum on Salisbury Plain that may have left its ceremonial complex ripe for take-over. 'Any such event need not preclude the possibility of both migration and unification,' they suggest.

They postulate 'a sacred *axis mundi* (world axis or world centre), where the sky and the earth were envisioned in cosmic harmony, and where people of different cultural and regional origins might gather for collective monument-building and feasting' in the context of a theoretical positioning of Stonehenge within a 'neutral zone' marked by 'a north–south line of henges, stone circles and cursuses ... from the Thames Valley to the south coast of England', which marked the boundary between different Neolithic traditions and an east-west genetic divide. Nothing in any of this actually makes it any easier to properly understand Stonehenge. Burl notes, for example, that the monument's lunar alignments mean that these must have been based on observations across three lunar cycles of 18.61 years, or two whole generations. He also notes that, around 2200 BC, users of Beaker pottery actually shifted the axis of the circle by four degrees, widening the north-east entrance and back-filling the ditch, to align it with the midsummer sunrise.

And then there's the legend: a legend more puzzling than those of Long Meg, Sunkenkirk, Mitchell Fold or any others, because it now, since 2021, has a tiny tinkle of truth about it. This ancient myth was first recorded 900 years ago by Geoffrey of Monmouth and tells how the magician Merlin assembled an army of 15,000 men to capture the magic Giants' Dance Stone Circle from the Irish and reassemble it at Stonehenge to commemorate Britons killed by Saxons during peace talks at Amesbury. The eagle-eyed will spot that the chronology of this doesn't fit recorded history... but western Wales was considered 'Irish' in Geoffrey's time and we should perhaps note that Merlin wanted the stones for their magical healing properties – and those who believe in the healing power of crystals will sit up at this point. The website *Crystal Age*, says of Preseli bluestone: '[It] has a strong connection with the electrical impulses produced by the human body, and has a par-ticularly strong connection with the heart. Bluestone clears the heart centre, and strengthens the electrical workings of the heart. It improves electrical communication throughout the body, which in turn serves to balance and strengthen the immune system. The electrical connection does not stop there, but helps us to link into the electromagnetic field of the Earth itself.'[7]

While most will consider this to be in the realms of pseudo-science, I find myself returning to the idea of ancient people, such as indigenous Australians, enjoying a far more fundamental connection to the Earth, just as traditional forms of Eastern medicine too demonstrate connections that fall outside normal scientific or medicinal explanation. I say no more.

So, Stonehenge is an extraordinary place and must surely be on the itinerary of anyone with serious interest in stone circles or the wider Neolithic and Bronze Ages. But if your interest is towards the more spiritual end of the Neolithic cultural continuum, then Stonehenge, with its seven-figure annual visitor numbers, may not be for you. My Druid friend Elaine Gregory says she tends to give it a wide berth, but adds: 'Someone said that Stonehenge does do a lot of good because it mitigates what the army does.' That's to say that those bluestones and their larger pals too, perhaps, do exert positive forces: positive enough to make up for the army driving tanks all around the area!

Elaine, though, would rather visit Avebury – more a 'people's place', with the village sitting within the circle itself. In her book, *Listening to the Stones*, Beatrice Walditch advocates that people learn to listen better while exploring Avebury and the wider Neolithic landscape: 'There are, of course, many other places to visit within the WHS area, though for its sheer impressive scale, Silbury Hill, which, as the English Heritage website puts it "compares in height and volume to the roughly contemporary Egyptian pyramids" should be near the top of the list. Not far behind Silbury Hill is the Marlborough Mound, which sits right in the middle of the school of that name. The difference between Silbury Hill and the Pyramids, of course, is that we seem to know far, far more about the latter.

Perhaps, then, we should begin by listening better, or as Beatrice Walditch puts it: 'If you are able to, visit Avebury regularly then get to know the henge and all the other prehistoric places which make up the entire World Heritage Site for a mile or more in each direction. If not, then explore and get to know special places in your own area. They may not be prehistoric henges, but England has plenty of places which were revered well into the Anglo-Saxon era. And outside England, or even the British Isles, the possibilities become even greater.'

Chapter 8

What do we really know; what can we guess?

Better understanding our past opens doors to our future

I was chatting with someone in Shap towards the end of this project when he casually mentioned that excavations for a home extension in the village had uncovered a 'stone circle'. The story went that these 'remains', which were probably just 'ordinary' stones, were unceremoniously reburied, but it all felt symbolically reminiscent of other events in and around the village that have been going on for at least two or three hundred years.

In researching this book, one of the stand-out messages that has come across again and again is that the loss of Cumbria's Neolithic and Bronze Age past is most keenly felt here, on the granite and limestone fells that connect the Lake District with the Westmorland and Yorkshire Dales. Once upon a time this now rather unprepossessing village on the Cumbrian fells stood at a major crossroads. Travellers carrying precious goods – prized axeheads from the Lakeland axe factories, jet from the east coast and pottery cast far away – would pass through its grand ceremonial avenue. The turn of the seasons would have been celebrated at the great stone circle of Kemp Howe, while more prosaic goods such as salt, preserved food and leather may have been bartered and traded here and near the numerous stone circles that dotted surrounding fells. Upon death, local leaders would have been buried with prized goods and sacrifices in cists and funereal cairns close to those circles and to the simple thatched huts of the early farmers.

The huge and carefully positioned boulders of the long ceremonial avenue were blown up in the eighteenth and nineteenth centuries and found their way into houses and garden walls. The enthusiastic railway promoters of the Victorian Age built what is now the West Coast Main Line right through Kemp Howe. Even as ongoing quarrying for granite and limestone has continued to nibble away at other Shap monuments for decades, just for good measure, the M6 was built just a few metres from the double stone circle of Gunnerkeld.

But for all this destruction, Shap might perhaps have shared with the Wiltshire landscapes of Stonehenge and Avebury the distinction of being a World Heritage Site. That is a measure of what has been lost. The idea that there's more to be found – be it out in the landscape or beneath someone's house – only hints at the true extent of what once was at this epicentre of the Neolithic North. Indeed one of three 'lost circles' at Shapbeck, a few kilometres north of the village, was only rediscovered during a field survey as recently as 1985.

Lost and undiscovered Neolithic and Bronze Age remains are by no means unique to Shap, however: the cup and ring marks at Copt Howe, Langdale, were discovered only in 1999. Dorothy Carrington's extraordinary book about Corsica, *Granite Island*, tells of her discovery in 1948 of Neolithic carved menhirs half-buried in an overgrown orchard. I await a more official verdict on my own chance 'discovery' of a hitherto unnoticed 'stone circle' near Casterton.

Extensive surveys by the Lake District National Park Authority in the 1980s and '90s opened a tempting door to the extraordinary potential treasure trove buried in extensive settlements on the westernmost Lake District fells in particular. Eleanor Kingston, the park authority's lead archaeologist, described to me the potential for further investigations to unearth secrets about how our early ancestors lived: 'There's a huge amount still to investigate and I would like to see a lot more work to answer some of the research questions we have got, but we need to attract someone to do that, whether universities, students or local archaeology groups. It's my job to support those coming forward and I am hoping in the future to develop a research strategy for the Lake District.' As ever, it is funding that is the stumbling block and universities, Historic England and others are all fighting for a slice of the same modest cake. Prehistory fights with Roman history, fights with medieval history, fights with industrial age history… and so on.

The archaeological consultant and author Paul Frodsham is rather more blunt and sees a clear North–South divide in the focus and funding of archaeological research. In response to this perceived imbalance, a conference was organised at Tullie House Museum, Carlisle, in 2016, in cooperation with the Prehistoric Society and the Cumberland and Westmorland Antiquarian and Archaeological Society. In their foreword to a collected edition of the papers presented, Paul Frodsham and Gill Hey, CEO of

Oxford Archaeology, wrote: 'Northern England barely features in accounts of the Neolithic in the British Isles or, if it does, it is as the source of stone or flint used and deposited in other parts of the country; its inhabitants are seldom actors in the grand narrative.' They bemoan the scarcity of university archaeology departments in the North and suggest that, underlying this is 'an institutional anti-North bias' that has led to lazy preconceptions about the Neolithic period in the North that 'have hampered research and have tended to lead to sites and discoveries being viewed through the prism of southern archaeology and not on their own terms'.

To make matters worse, in a move roundly condemned across the discipline, in the summer of 2021, Sheffield University announced the closure of its highly regarded Archaeology Department: universities can see the direction of travel of the Government, and that's towards subjects that will 'pay back' in the jobs market and thereby reduce the mountain of accumulated student debt attributable to the slow rate of repayment of student loans. Archaeology does not fit that money-orientated future. But in these days of glib throwaways like 'levelling up', if those of us who are interested share any ambitions, these should surely be to place northern archaeological research on a sounder platform through improved funding from whatever source; to establish better connections between all those in the field; and to enthuse volunteers eager to draw connections between our own times and the lives of people 5,000 years ago.

But why is ancient history important? Well, for the same reasons as our more recent history also matters. Penelope J Corfield is President of the International Society of Eighteenth-Century Studies and describes herself as an optimist. Her 'manifesto' about the importance of understanding our history is as relevant to prehistory as to eighteenth-century history: 'Understanding the linkages between past and present is absolutely basic for a good understanding of the condition of being human. That, in a nutshell, is why History matters. It is not just "useful", it is essential. The study of the past is essential for "rooting" people in time.'[1]

Why should *that* matter? She suggests that people who feel themselves to be rootless will go on to live rootless lives, perhaps causing damage to themselves and others in the process. 'In fact, all people have a full historical context. But some, generally for reasons that are no fault of their own, grow up with a weak or troubled sense of their own placing, whether within their families or within the wider world. They lack a sense of roots.'

A living example of learning from history is BBC Radio 4's *The Long View*, in which Jonathan Freedland compares historical events with current ones, as often as not demonstrating that today's leaders have not only not studied their history but – in the unlikely event that they have – have manifestly failed to learn from it. Melvyn Bragg similarly invites listeners to learn from our past in *In Our Time*. But neither of these worthy productions chooses to, and nor can it easily, enter the world that existed before, long before, the arrival on these shores of the written word.

Writing more specifically about why prehistory is important, Paul Astin, of the independent nature-focussed Manzanita School, at Topanga, California, writes: 'As an academic subject in schools, "history" has consistently omitted the lynchpin of a broad and encompassing framework for understanding human development; namely, the enduring legacy of our hunter-gatherer ancestry. The premise of most lessons in history is to "learn" from the past, to frame the present by examining the realities of people's past actions and behaviours. As G K Chesterton put it, "History is a hill from which alone men see the town in which they live or the age in which they are living". By ignoring prehistory however, a period that comprises 99 per cent of all human history, students focus narrowly on the deeds of post-agricultural peoples. This cannot help but give a distorted view of human development.'[2]

* * *

The difficulty with prehistory is that we struggle even to connect with it, let alone understand it. The people of Egypt, Greece and other modern countries with an early written history have less problem making this connection. I hesitate to assert that this consequently gives them a more powerful sense of either self or nationhood because I know of no research to back this idea up. But I strongly suspect this could be the case. Nor do peoples whose civilisations have remained unbroken since our own 'prehistoric times' and whose predominantly oral history is passed down through the generations share the same disjoint. I refer to traditionally-rooted hunter-gatherer people, such as the Inuit and other Artic peoples, American Indians, Amazonian peoples and, of course, the many different indigenous people of Australia, and many others besides.

In an attempt to find bridges across that gap, I have tried in this book to tease out possible links to the ancient world, focussing on those key human activities within which potential linkages may be most apparent.

The first and most obvious question to ask is whether we today share any genetic characteristics with those who first tilled our land – after all, Neanderthals, who predated Neolithic people by some considerable distance, gifted us a lasting legacy of between one and four per cent of the genome of non-Africans today... and they were actually a different species! Early non-Neanderthal hunter-gatherers living about 40,000 years ago are thought to have retained between six and nine per cent Neanderthal DNA.

However, to focus on this minor partner in the modern human genome is most likely a bit of a red herring, because the 'real event' we need to focus on is the apparent replacement of Neolithic DNA in Britain with the arrival of the Beaker culture, around 2500 BC. This genetic change is most fully documented in an article in the journal, *Nature*, published in 2018, and titled *The Beaker Phenomenon and the Genomic Transformation of Northwest Europe*, which states: 'The spread of the Beaker complex introduced high levels of steppe-related ancestry and was associated with the replacement of approximately 90 per cent of Britain's gene pool within a few hundred years, continuing the east-to-west expansion that had brought steppe-related ancestry into central and northern Europe over the previous centuries.'[3] The Neolithic farmers themselves had arrived in Britain from the North Sea coast of Europe, bringing with them early farming practices that originated in Anatolia (eastern Turkey) 3,500 years earlier.

The dramatic findings were based on the study of 400 ancient remains from across Europe and the authors infer a 'mass migration' from Europe by Beaker People. That is an interpretation that is not wholly undisputed, as others suggest a far more gradual process, taking place across several centuries. The disparities appear to arise from the gentle collision of two disciplines: archaeology and genetics. To take the latter first, Professor David Reich, lead author of the *Nature* paper talks of a 'highly unexpected' replacement of 90 per cent of the Neolithic gene pool, with the possibility that climate change, disease and ecological disaster may all have played a role.

So, out went the grand statements of the Neolithic: the Stonehenges, the Long Megs, the Silvery Hills, the Brodgars. In came more modest burial chambers in which the dead were buried with patterned bell-shaped beakers, copper daggers, arrowheads, stone wrist guards and distinctive buttons. Co-author, Dr Carles Lalueza-Fox, of the Institute of Evolutionary Biology in Barcelona suggests that the whole Beaker 'idea' probably began as a 'fashion' and spread north from Iberia, possibly by 'word of mouth' or as a modest movement of goods rather than people. Then a subsequent movement of people westward, which had originated on the steppes, far to the east from Ukraine to Kazakhstan, carried it to Britain and other parts of northern Europe. These people also brought with them the ability to work with metals – copper and its related alloy, bronze – thereby initiating the Chalcolithic and subsequent Bronze Ages. The suggestion is that the British Neolithic population had been suffering a period of decline ever since the building of the 'great monuments' and that this was only reversed by the 'Beaker genetic revolution' from about 2500 BC.

There are many possible reasons for the population decline, including periodic climate change, of which there is certain evidence[4]: when agriculture is a marginal activity, it may not take much of a shift toward climatic instability for crops to fail. I go so far as to speculate that the erection of enormous monuments that reflect the changing of the seasons, and thus when the sun will get higher and the days longer, may even indicate a societal reaction to changing climes and crop failure. To put it in a nutshell: did Neolithic peoples build stone circles as an antidote to climate change?

Another very clear reason for an acceleration in the decline of the Neolithic gene pool is a very simple one. It has been suggested that the Beaker arrivals brought with them the plague, to which the native population had no resistance. However, I venture to suggest that it may have been less dramatic: we already know of the potential impact of incomers on indigenous peoples, as reflected in the childhood leukaemia clusters in West Cumbria. And we know only too well how devastating were common European diseases for the peoples of Latin America, for example. So the Beakers may have brought with them pathogens far less deadly than the plague, but these may have wreaked a heavy toll on the Neolithic natives.

The broadcaster and author, Professor Alice Roberts, of the School of Biosciences at the University of Birmingham, has sought to reduce the tensions between archaeology and genetics. Writing in the *New Scientist* in May 2021, she cites the so-called *1000 Ancient Genomes* study, which has been using highly sensitive techniques to examine DNA from human and animal skeletons to find out more about crucial episodes in human evolution and prehistory. Referring to the *Nature* paper and its claim of a '90 per cent population turnover in the third century BC', she says: 'This information was met with consternation by some archaeologists. Did a mass of invaders sweep in and take over? Some headlines stoked that idea, suggesting that "Dutch hordes" had killed off the "Britons who started Stonehenge".[5] She stresses the importance of selecting appropriate terms. For example, "migration" means a deliberate and large-scale movement of people, such as an invasion or being forced to relocate, to archaeologists. However, for geneticists, the word covers people moving and settling somewhere different, perhaps over a number of generations. 'Differences in concepts and definitions can lead to misunderstanding. The lesson is that both fields must also heed their differences,' she continues. She quotes Tom Booth, of the *1000 Ancient Genomes* project: 'There has to be continuing dialogue. We may never agree on what terms to use, but we might at least understand each other's perspective.'

However, the whole genetics question can become even more nuanced. A late 2016 posting by the Colorado-based attorney, Andrew Oh-Willeke on his *Turtle Island* blog, named after a traditional native American name for the Earth or North America, references the arrival from the steppes of the 'proto-Beaker' people in the Basque Country of Iberia. He postulates that the highly paternal new culture gives Beaker men a major evolutionary advantage over local men, giving rise to a dominant Beaker DNA in the male line, whereas the mitochondrial (female line) DNA remains predominantly Neolithic or pre-Neolithic. I can offer no further source for what Oh-Willeke suggests, but would note that it is only in the last few decades that we have become fully aware of the distinct differences between male and female lines in certain relatively discreet cultures: the Viking male line and the Celtic female line in Iceland and the Faroe islands are a case in point.

These proto-Bell Beaker people, suggests Oh-Willeke, may have been responsible for the introduction of the lactose-tolerant gene to western Europe, which was crucial to the development of the dairy aspect of early farming. He goes on to suggest: 'From Iberia, the expansion of the newly formed Bell Beaker people is rapid because it is filling a vacuum caused by a first wave Neolithic slump that set back the first farmers and because of their superior technology. This expansion takes place up river basins, overland and by sea. It went to France, Sardinia, coastal northwest Africa, the Canary Islands, Belgium, the Netherlands, the British Isles, Ireland, Denmark and Iceland. There is a fair amount of trade and interaction within the Bell Beaker sphere. This expansion may have more men than women, but is not nearly so male dominated as proto-Bell Beaker.'[6]

* * *

Because we are all human and therefore survive by eating food derived from either plant or animal life or both, it is a bit easier to build bridges back to the Neolithic diet. Before Neolithic times, hunter-gatherer people did just that: they hunted for smaller prey and gathered fruit, nuts, leaves and roots, doubtless learning along the way which foods agreed best with their digestion or, indeed, which might kill them. Farming arrived from Anatolia and most likely via Iberia around 4000 BC and the new arrivals seem not to have mixed much with the hunter-gatherers. Indeed, just as the Beakers squeezed out the Neolithic people, so a similar process seems to have taken place with the arrival of farming. The hunter-gatherers bequeathed zero genetic legacy to the Neolithic arrivals. Just why these farmers decided it would be a good idea to leave Anatolia is a different question and is not one to which experts have rushed to give answers.

As these Anatolians trickled westward, they most likely adapted their agriculture to the changing conditions they encountered and, by the time they arrived in Britain, they were already 'tooled up', as Professor Mark Thomas, of University College London, puts it in a paper for the journal, *Nature Ecology and Evolution*. There is a broad consensus that these early farmers did pretty much what farmers were still doing hundreds and even thousands of years later.[7] They almost certainly were doing this on the western slopes of Lakeland. They used diverse strains of grain to grow wheat and barley, which they ground into flour, and domesticated goats, sheep and cattle. They almost certainly did not domesticate horses, though the use of oxen as beasts of burden is possible, and they most likely domesticated wild boar, retaining a tangential connection with the forest, which they so assiduously cleared. They may well have also grown peas and beans and some suggest they may have grown flax. Were this the case, then its fibres could have been used in the making of ropes and clothing. With farming would have come the idea of living in a fixed location and indeed, most likely living in larger social groups, with all the pluses and minuses that surely came with that.

We have to infer that, for all the hard labour it must have demanded, and for all the uncertainties around crop failure, farming offered a better way of life than hunter-gathering. For sure we can say it opened up opportunities to cover winter nutritional needs and it certainly reduced the risk of being attacked by wolves, lynx, bears and wild boar. Crucial to the success of farming must have been the ability to use milk, in both its 'raw' form and preserved as cheese and butter. In his unexpectedly fascinating book, *A Cheesemonger's History of the British Isles*, author Ned Palmer writes: 'The earliest direct evidence for cheese appears in what is now northern Turkey, in archaeological finds from 6500 BC, in the form of milk fat deposits on potsherds [pottery fragments]. That means that cheesemaking began soon after the domestication of animals, but *a thousand years before* adult humans developed the ability to digest milk.' This ability only came along in around 5500 BC in what is now Hungary, so Palmer suggests that cheese was originally just a clever way of enabling lactose-intolerant humans to consume milk. He then comes up with an imagined scene in which an Anatolian goatherd eight or nine thousand years ago, finds himself thirsty in the mountains and drinks some goat's milk which has started to 'turn'. 'The lactophilic bacteria hanging about in the vicinity have converted the lactose in the milk into lactic acid' and this coagulates the milk which, if drained, 'becomes a form of ur-cheese [cream cheese]'. So there you have it.

As for the grain, a variant of bere barley may have been the dominant cereal crop in Orkney, although it can only be dated with certainty to the arrival of the Vikings. This 'heritage crop' is still both grown and used today and is enjoying a notable renaissance in the brewing and distilling industries. Unlike 'modern barley', bere barley has adapted to its environment over a long period of time. My food historian friend Ivan Day also alerts me to the work of a chap called John Letts who has been working on the revival of hitherto 'extinct' wheats and marketing these pre-industrial varieties through his Heritage Harvest company.

We can't say for sure what the Neolithic Cumbrian farmers did with their flour but it is likely that they were able to use primitive 'earth ovens' as these are known to have existed in Europe from around 4500 BC. So barley or wheat bread may have been baked in covered pits or on hot stones. Just for amusement, I took some bere barley and started a fermentation with natural yoghurt then mixed this with more barley and yoghurt as you might a sourdough loaf. It wasn't the greatest culinary success: the lack of gluten meant it didn't bind too well, but I was able to make something a bit like a chapati.

Proof positive, if any were needed, of what the Cumbrian farmers were eating in Neolithic times arrived in 2015 during the excavation of quarry workings at Stainton, Furness. A large number of remains of carinated (etched) bowls was found in a limestone crevice and traces of dairy fats were found on the fragments. A paper states: 'This was consistent with previous larger studies but represents the first evidence that dairying was an important component of Early Neolithic subsistence strategies in Cumbria.' In addition, two deliberately broken polished stone axes, an Arran pitchstone core, a small number of flint tools and debitage [waste material], and a tuff flake were retrieved. The site also produced moderate amounts of charred grain, hazelnut shell, charcoal, and burnt bone. The paper continues: most of the charred grain came from an Early Neolithic pit and potentially comprises the largest assemblage of such material recovered from Cumbria to date. Radiocarbon dating indicated activity sometime during the 40th–35th centuries BC as well as an earlier presence during the 46th–45th centuries.'[8] Later activity during the Chalcolithic and the Early Bronze Age was also demonstrated.

What is less clear is the extent to which the Neolithic people maintained any hunter-gatherer habits. A 2002 excavation of a Mesolithic site (with later Bronze Age cist) at Howick, on the Northumberland coast, provided evidence of some of the earliest fixed settlements in Britain (around 7600 BC) and suggested that the site's coastal location provided an abundance of natural resources, including fish, seals, shellfish and seabirds and their eggs, as well as hazelnuts, whose charred remnants were found at the site. Another permanent Mesolithic settlement at Star Carr, Yorkshire, reinforces the idea of early permanent settlement and evidence there pointed to venison being the staple food.[9]

Given the earlier abundance of non-farmed food, it seems slightly surprising that evidence from Neolithic food remnants on pottery fragments from all over Europe seems to point towards the predominance of meat and dairy in the diet. Fish was eaten at the Ness of Brodgar, but it is clear this was supplementary. English Heritage has reported evidence suggesting that hazelnuts, sloes and crab apples were still being eaten around 2500 BC, derived from their excavation of a settlement at Durrington Walls, where the Stonehenge builders who moved from Wales are believed to have lived. I have previously speculated that people who settled near Devoke Water may have eaten trout from its waters and that those in Ennerdale may have enjoyed freshwater mussels, but it seems right to infer that, once people really got into farming, other food sources became simply that… 'other food sources'.[10]

If we accept this interpretation, then the idea of preserving and conserving food for winter use, or even for use next week, rather than this, acquires greater importance. Salt has long provided a means of extending the life of food, especially meat, and so its production and transport would surely have been central to even the earliest organised societies – indeed we know that salt was produced in Neolithic Britain and we also know that salters' tracks are among our earliest trader routes, reflecting the value of the commodity. Even in relatively recent times, salt's pivotal place in societal systems has been paramount: just think of Gandhi's salt march from Gujarat in protest against the Imperial British power's punitive taxation of the staple.

Sels et Salines de l'Europe Atlantique is an impressive and beautifully illustrated collection of papers, assembled by Loïc

Ménanteau and published in 2018 by the University of Rennes. The chapter on 'pre-historic' salt production freely admits its focus on the French Atlantic seaboard and Iberian peninsula during the third and fourth millennia BC and states that there has been no comparable depth of study in England, Wales, Scotland or Ireland on either sea-sourced or 'mined' salt. The diverse nature of salt and its various sources – water, soil, sand, plant, rock – meant that Neolithic peoples had to employ a wide range of different techniques to extract it. The focus of this collection is on the extraction of salt from seawater, either through evaporation or through artificial heating, to produce either granular salt or tablets of salt that would have been easy to transport across long distances.

It cites evidence of Neolithic 'camps' along ancient river banks and of the ceramic vessels that were employed in the evaporation and manufacturing process. It dates the start of the production of salt to around the start of the third millennium BC, in the area to the north of the Île de Ré. At the Neolithic site of Sandun, near the mouth of the Loire, interlinked evaporation and filtration ponds with vertical sides and slate linings point to larger-scale workings. The importance of marine salt production endured through the Middle Ages when the product was transported by sea from Portugal and France as far as England and Scotland and across the Baltic to Riga and St Petersburg.

In England, authors Roger Herbert and David Cranstone point to the origins of salt production as dating back at least to the Bronze Age, 3,000 years ago. Latterly, particularly in Cheshire, salt extraction became a highly industrialised process, requiring half a million tonnes of coal to produce a million tonnes of salt. The production of salt by means of evaporation on the Atlantic coast of Britain, however, did not enjoy a great deal of success, thanks to the more temperate climate than that of France or Iberia. It was, therefore, confined to a narrow band along the south coast.

However, in other locations, the construction of salt pans in shallow waters did at least enable the seawater to be concentrated by evaporation prior to boiling, and this technique is evidenced in Roman and medieval times the length of the Cumbrian and Solway coasts, from Morecambe Bay to Dumfries. And, as previously mentioned, recent archaeological discoveries on the Yorkshire Coast show that salt was being produced here much earlier - around the same time as semi-precious jet was first being mined just down the coast at Whitby.

Another means of preserving food is through the use of sugar, namely through cooking, to create jams or jellies. Today, our most common source of sugar is either home-grown sugar beet or imported cane sugar, from tropical climes. In pre-historic times, sugar would have had to come either from wild honey or from fruit and so would have been a scarce and valuable resource. The Durrington Walls excavation previously mentioned also revealed evidence that fruit and nuts were cooked, suggesting that there were indeed recipes for their preservation.

In warmer climates, the juice from high-sugar fruits could be rendered down into a concentrated syrup, but high-sugar fruit was not plentiful in northern England, especially in pre-Roman times. Grapes, for example, contain a lot of sugar when ripe, but not only do they not grow well in the moister climate west of the Pennines but it's unlikely they arrived here at all until the Romans brought them. So might the 'native' gooseberry have provided a substitute? Well, according to Sturtevant's *Edible Plants of the World*, the first mention of it is by J.M.W. Turner, in the sixteenth century, after it was most likely introduced from France, though De Candolle begs to differ, suggesting there is no reason to suppose that they were not growing wild here before that time. However – as Ivan Day will remind me later – this was in the days long before pollen analysis.[11]

Other fruits that we regard as 'native' might include plums, but these arrived from Syria and the Caucasus; damsons too only came here in the time of the Crusades. So native fruit was in all likelihood limited to crab apples, sloes and smaller berries like blackberries, currants, wild dwarf cherries and strawberries (possibly), rosehips, blaeberries and whortleberries. That's to say, generally requiring much labour and offering up little sugar in return. A more 'fruitful' source may have been the sap of the birch tree, which can be tapped, rather like a North American maple. Taken overall, however, we have to conclude that the scope for preserving fruit by boiling it in sugar would have been somewhat limited and, indeed, I have been unable to find any clear record of sugary residues having been found on pottery shards.

Alcohol and vinegar also enable food to be pickled and preserved and the evidence suggests that ale from barley and cider from crab apples were both produced on a domestic scale as long ago as 3000 BC. Stronger spirit did not come along until distillation was perfected thousands of years later, but the production of vinegar requires only the base ale or cider and a secondary fermentation of the dilute alcohol, which is converted to acetic acid when exposed to the air at room temperature. The first vinegar was most likely created by accident and the subsequent discovery of its preserving qualities was probably also accidental.

Britain's most recently surviving subsistence-based society lived on the St Kilda archipelago, 50 miles west of Harris, in the Outer Hebrides. There is evidence that the first settlers arrived on the main island of Hirta in Neolithic times, possibly as part of the 'journey of ideas' from Orkney down the west coast. I was fortunate to visit St Kilda in glorious sunshine, in which the sea sparkled on the volcanic cordillera so it looked more like Santorini than a bunch of rocks way out in the Atlantic. I climbed the steep hillside above the village, which is dotted with around 1,200 *cleits*, or stone larders. These loosely built structures would have permitted the wind to get in and dry the islanders' seabird harvest until the final evacuation of the remaining population in 1930. Hirta is home to the Neolithic Soay sheep, descended from the first domesticated Mediterranean breed and introduced from the nearby island of Soay following the evacuation. Other introduced populations exist on Lundy island, in the Bristol Channel and around Cheddar Gorge. Lundy is, to my knowledge, the only place that you can eat Soay sheep meat today.

Before leaving the island that day, I bumped into Jill Pilkington MBE, head of the Soay Sheep Project, which is a long-term study of the little feral sheep, in part to gain a better understanding of their modern domesticated descendants. Jill is the nearest St Kilda has to a permanent resident and has been studying her flock for thirty years now. Her 'second home' is in Hexham, Northumberland, where she has, she says, a husband. I reflect that hers must be an unusual kind of marriage. 'Yes,' she muses. 'If I've been on home leave for six weeks, my husband starts to ask "When are you going back to that island of yours?".' There was a certain amount of excitement a few years ago when evidence was found of Iron Age farming on the precipitous neighbouring island of Boreray on terraces etched into the guano-rich south-facing slopes. You would not have thought it conceivable to look at the terrifying verticality of the place, but it does perhaps raise the possibility of some form of farming in Neolithic times on the gentler slopes of Hirta.

The practice of wind-drying food is one that continues today in the higher latitudes – the cod-drying racks of Arctic and Subarctic Norway and Iceland remain a familiar sight, laden with cod from spring through the long summer days and then, traditionally, shipped to southern Europe. Basque mariners were heavily involved in this trade in the early days, which in a way reflects the idea of earlier connections between Atlantic northern Europe and the Basque Country when the Beaker migration first began.

Wind-drying in specially constructed wooden huts remains common practice today in the Faroe Islands which 'enjoy' a similar climate to that of St Kilda. The huts shelter drying fish and meat from the rain while allowing a steady circulation of air. It would be theoretically possible to replicate this form of preservation in Cumbria, whose climate, although very much more benign, is not wholly dissimilar to that of the Faroe Islands. As the technique is not practised in Norway, it seems possible that it may have been brought to the Faroe Islands by the enslaved women, captured by the Vikings and carried north. Might that technique have been learned in Ireland long ago in Neolithic times? As ever, we cannot know but only guess. Some Faroese sheep meat hung to dry in this way is also fermented – a process by which a mould forms on the surface of the carcass and begins to 'digest' the flesh. It's a technique that's been attracting increased attention these days because of growing interest in fermented food in general. Known as *skerpikjøt*, you may well encounter the fermented mutton, as I first did, if you participate in *heimablídni*, or home dining, whereby you share traditional dishes in Faroese homes. Its taste is strong but not unpleasant, despite the meat having hung for up to nine months – it lies somewhere between lamb and strong Cheddar cheese.

* * *

There was a movement of people in the seas to the west of the British Isles long before the Vikings arrived and captured Irish women, of course. We know that the first Neolithic settlers arrived in Orkney from the Scottish mainland, bringing with them farm animals and seeds from which to grow crops. As the Pentland Firth would have been too far for the animals to swim, we have to infer what the boats which carried them may have looked like, though they must surely have been sturdier than the flimsy craft recreated for the BBC series on Neolithic Orkney. Perhaps, as previously suggested, they were similar to the later 'Dover boat'. However, this was not the only movement: the genetics of the Orkney vole tell us that this animal can only have arrived on the islands via a single-voyage event: from either Iberia or western France sometime in the fourth millennium BC. And there were other, more regular movements, going on all the time: in her paper, *Neolithic connections along and across the Irish Sea*, Alison Sheridan references 'the now fairly substantial number' of Langdale axeheads found in Ireland – more than 100. And Irish porcellanite axeheads were making the same journey in the opposite direction. Peter Style too references 'island hopping' along the west coast, adding: 'Some journeys could be seen as special, particularly when they entailed the transportation of prestige goods representing power. While others may have been because people liked being mobile.'[12]

At the Ness of Brodgar complex, archaeologists have found precious and semi-precious goods brought from many parts of the British Isles. Conversely, two distinctive types of pottery were developed in Orkney and may have represented the emergence of elite strata of Neolithic society at different times. The earlier Unstan ware shallow bowls were found in large quantities when the Unstan Cairn was excavated in the nineteenth century, while the grooved ware, the shape of a flowerpot, came later and was found in Neolithic villages such as Skara Brae and Barnhouse. The latter in particular acquired status and fashionability and examples have been found as far south as the Thames Valley. So, Orkney was a factory of ideas and fashion and its large stone monuments predate the Stonehenge complex. Because the stone in stone circles cannot be carbon-dated, putting dates on specific stone circles relies on the finding of organic material in the stone-holes, for example. So it's very difficult to produce a league table of stone circles by age, though the idea that the stone circle fashion began in Orkney and spread out from there, possibly by means of word of mouth among traders and voyagers, may be an attractive one. Equally though, we cannot discount the possibility that it was actually in Cumbria that the first circles were built. Drawing upon recent evidence from Long Meg, Paul Frodsham puts it like this: 'Why shouldn't the earliest stone circles be Cumbrian, with the "idea" spreading out from here?'

Boats leave no footprint but feet do, and it's easier to infer the legacy of ancient trade routes overland in today's landscape than to prove who sailed where, and when. Note Style's earlier suggestion that the carriage of 'prestige goods' went hand in hand with the difficulty of the journey undertaken. The respect accorded to the person who was making the journey extends from journeys over water to journeys overland, and those carrying the prized Langdale axes would have therefore been 'accorded some respect'. He suggests a mythology would develop around the places at which these goods were exchanged, and so the stone avenue at Shap, for instance, would introduce a kind of formality around the described pathway by which the monument (Kemp Howe) should be approached. Mark Edmonds believes that local demand for axe-heads, along the coastal plain in Cumbria, ended up being supplied from an 'axe factory' on Scafell Pike, while Langdale met the 'export demand'. The routes followed from both locations have been speculated and there have been some suggestions they may even have been marked. 'In fine weather walking a ridge route heading north with a load of roughouts would have been a logical route, arriving at Castlerigg,' he says. 'Journeys south or east may have involved boats on Coniston, Windermere or Ullswater and down the navigable rivers, considerably easier with a load of roughouts.'

What is very clear, however, is that many Cumbrian stone circles do stand on logical routes through the fells and in places where journey by river canoe may have crossed overland routes. The Mayburgh henges, Long Meg, some of the Shap area circles, Elva Plain and Gamelands are all potential cases in point. At the same time, the recent discoveries at Long Meg appear to suggest that the circle locations may well have already been important long before anyone thought of erecting stones there.

* * *

Links between the language(s) spoken in the British Isles today and those that have died out or faded from common usage are fragile and tenuous: the Brittonic languages of Indo-European root that were spoken when the Romans arrived are as far back as we can go and still find any legacy at all in the speech of today. Indeed, as previously suggested, those Brittonic languages themselves appear to have had no links with the language or languages of the Neolithic farmers. In theory, there would have been a common 'proto-Brittonic language in the Bronze Age, spoken around 500 BC, though some sources place its origins as early as 1100 BC. It subsequently diverged into local variants, from Brittany in the south to Scotland in the North, although debate remains unresolved as to whether or not the Picts, in Scotland, spoke a local Brittonic variant or a language that did not belong to the Indo-European group at all. Interestingly, some suggest a Brittonic language was even spoken in Orkney before it was displaced by a Nordic language, which evolved into Norn. This, of course, then begs the question as to who brought the 'Neolithic language' here and where was it spoken.

I do find myself intrigued by the possibility that there may have been a pre-Indo-European language spoken on the Cumbrian fells back in the early days of farming. There are in Europe today languages that don't share the prevalent Indo-European root. These include the Finno-Ugric languages, mostly spoken in Finland, Estonia and the Sámi lands of northern Scandinavia. There is no absolute agreement as to where the Basque language, spoken in the Basque Country of north-west Spain and south-west France, comes from, though the consensus is that it predates the Indo-European languages. Could this, then, point to the possibility that when the Beaker People began to arrive in Britain in the third century BC, they may have brought with them a language that originated in Iberia, where the Beaker themselves originally set out from? As we moved into the Bronze Age, there began the large-scale 'DNA replacement' referenced earlier. I become vaguely excited at the theoretical possibility that one way or another our ancient people might have spoken a language wholly lost here, but which might just possibly have evolved elsewhere into a language that ultimately became Basque.

Dr Philip Shaw, Professor in English and Old English at the University of Leicester, urges caution: 'Possibly, yes, but there's not a lot of linguistic evidence for that. In fact there is none.' He reminds me that the various post-glacial periods triggered movements into the British Isles. 'You have the last glacial maximum about 14,000 years ago and at that point there probably wouldn't have been human beings in the British Isles,' he says. Subsequent repopulations would have come, inevitably, from warmer, ice-free, parts of Europe around 11,700 years ago and people very likely moved overland as Britain was still connected to Europe until 6100 BC. The Neolithic farmers probably arrived from the Mediterranean about 4000 BC and replaced the earlier hunter-gatherers. About 1,200 years after that, the Beaker culture made its entry. 'You have a more complicated population history in the British Isles, despite those who like to think it's very simple and clear cut,' says Phillip, who tells me how some have tried to hypothesise a 'proto-world language'. 'I don't think anyone very sensible has offered evidence of that.'

Before leaving languages altogether, I reflect on more words from the *Turtle Island* blog, in which Andrew Oh-Willeke speculates that the early male Beaker arrivals in the Basque Country may have adopted the Neolithic language of the area, which was spoken by the women who would in due course become their partners. Alternatively, the local Iberian population may have adopted the non-Indo-European proto-Bell Beaker language of the new arrivals. 'Either way, the end result of this ethnogenesis and language event is that post-ethnogenesis, the Bell Beaker people speak the non-Indo-European proto-Vasconic [proto-Basque or early Basque] language.'

* * *

One of the things that have consistently puzzled me is why the Neolithic and Bronze Ages seem to have been pretty much devoid of representational art. We know that people in Britain were carving deer, bison and other animals on cave walls at Creswell Crags, on the borders of Derbyshire and Nottinghamshire as long ago as 11000 BC. But, until the recent discovery of carvings of deer at a cairn in Kilmartin Glen, dating back to between 3000 and 2000 BC, there was as good as no figurative Neolithic or Bronze Age art to be found. Dr Tertia Barnett, Principal Investigator for Scotland's Rock Art Project at Historic Environment Scotland, said of that find: 'It was previously thought that prehistoric animal carvings of this date didn't exist in Scotland, although they are known in parts of Europe, so it is very exciting that they have now been discovered here for the first time in the historic Kilmartin Glen.'[13] Which brings us to the eternal question about the relationship between stone circles and the enigmatic cup and ring markings found on boulders across the North of England, including Cumbria, although they are less numerous here. Dr Tertia Barnett goes on to suggest: 'This also tells us that the local communities were carving animals as well as cup and ring motifs which is in keeping with what we know of other Neolithic and Bronze Age societies, particularly in Scandinavia and Iberia. Until now, we did not know of any area in Britain with both types of carvings, which poses questions about the relationship between them and their significance to the people that created them.'

The difficulty with cup and ring markings is that their 'true purpose' is probably even more enigmatic than that of stone circles, but they are every bit as much part of our visible Neolithic legacy as are circles, cairns, barrows, standing stones and all the other 'large scale' landscape furniture of those times. To have some understanding of their purpose would provide us with another linkage from modern to ancient times. We don't even know whether these marks were 'art' or if they may have served some more practical purpose, possibly as some kind of waymarking for travellers. In her 2015 paper referred to earlier in this book, Kate Sharpe, of Durham University, identified design commonalities between some of the thirty-five examples of cup and ring marked stones in Cumbria, many of which have come to light in the last twenty years or so.[14] At the same time, she says, the marked stones in the valleys of the central Lake District, are quite different from those found in the Eden Valley, to the east, which are more complex in design. The latter may have been associated with ritualistic activities, whereas the former, she suggests, are very possibly linked, once again, with the production of axes in Langdale and other places in the high fells. 'The distinctive situations selected and striking resemblance in style across the Lakeland panels appear to reflect common practices and shared ideologies, suggesting that the cup-marked locations held a similar significance for the various communities that created them,' she says.

The most spectacular example is at the Copt Howe boulders, at the entrance to Langdale, where, Sharpe notes: 'The vertical face of one large block is decorated with a striking array of complex motifs, including concentric rings, chevrons and parallel lines, the only example in the Cumbrian high fells region to have an elaborate design. From this (and only this) position in the valley the summer solstice sunset is spectacular, with the sun appearing to roll down the side of the highest of the five Langdale Pikes.' The other valley designs are generally near the head or the foot of lakes and suggest points at which those making challenging journeys to and from the quarries may have been swapping between travel over land and water, she says. They may have represented places where different groups might meet and may perhaps have enjoyed a spiritualistic ritualistic symbolism, with the alignment at Copt Howe plausibly introducing a seasonality into the entire process of 'harvesting' the rock for the prized Langdale axes.

To throw a spanner in the works, however, there are arguments to suggest that the Copt Howe 'art' may have been created hundreds of years after the main axe quarries were at their most productive.

* * *

Whatever grand ideas and designs may have been exported from Neolithic Orkney – from grooved and Unstan pottery to the very monumental stone circles themselves – housing was not one of them. The communities on Orkney may have lived in well-built stone homes fitted with hearths, beds and dressers, but the Cumbrian people did not. At best, Cumbrian Neolithic homes had a stone base and few courses of stonework, but the rest of the structure would have been of wood, perhaps a bit like a yurt or a wigwam, covered with animal skins or thatched with reeds or heather. However, the relatively recent discovery of the remains of a Neolithic house, near Grassington, in the Yorkshire Dales, may give a clearer impression of how people may have lived.[15] The remains were found in the course of excavations at the site of a henge and revealed a structure comprising large oak uprights and horizontal beams, with an infill of hazel, suggesting a wattle and daub construction. It appeared that the house had burned down and carbon-dating of the charcoal remains placed the structure early in the fourth century BC, which most likely puts it somewhat earlier than the settlements described in Cumbria in this book. Indeed, Mark Edmonds tells me: 'My understanding is that most of the settlements are late Bronze Age and early Iron Age. We have other kinds of monuments that show that people are around but we don't know where they are living.' However, the finding of a house as nearby as the Yorkshire Dales surely opens the possibility that the kind of further exploration on the Lake District National Park's wish list might just possibly unearth similar evidence in Cumbria. Indeed, the Dales report's authors echo that sentiment with a plea for more archaeological investigation there: now where have we heard that before?

* * *

So much for the smaller buildings... but what about the stone circles themselves? Over the years, people have gasped in awe at the mere contemplation of the movement of the huge rocks used in the construction of the circles. How, and indeed why, were the stones often moved such long distances? The BBC's Orkney series did demonstrate that, given enough people, moving the stones need not be too difficult, though all things are relative. The TV reconstruction deployed seaweed as a 'lubricant' beneath the stones, though what might be used instead at inland locations is an unanswered question. In his book, *Building the Great Stone Circles of the North*, Colin Richards offers a completely different take on the whole question as to the how and why. He takes us away from thinking about the creation of circles from within a twenty-first-century conceptualisation in which constructing a building is a process, which starts with a plan and then moves with maximum efficiency through various phases until it is ready to be unveiled in its finished state.

Richards, whose theories are supported by Paul Frodsham in respect of Long Meg, argues that in Neolithic times, the important element was the process of building and the more demanding this was, the better. He writes: 'It is the ability to gather the largest possible labour force that provides an index of the status of the organising or sponsoring social group. Yet again, uncritical contemporary ideas and assumptions appear to dictate the way materials and labour are understood in the context of building a stone circle.' He suggests that the 'making' of these monuments may in fact be more important than their actual end-use. 'Whilst it cannot be disputed that there is clearly an intended outcome, for instance, the erection of a monolith within a stone circle, the transportation of the stone may have constituted the primary social focus.' In support of this theory, Richards also cites the continued practice of the quarrying, dragging and erection of huge monoliths among 'primitive' people the world over.

This broader interpretation of the 'purpose' of stone circles also fits with Mark Edmond's notion that 'permanence' was not necessarily uppermost in the minds of their creators. But, as ever, this is not a universal truth: while many circles do indeed feature monoliths and boulders that have shallow foundations and have subsequently toppled, others have happily stood the test of time, as is by and large the case with Stonehenge. It is also the case with the Devil's Arrows, that avenue of tall monoliths in Yorkshire. These are rooted close to two metres deep and were probably close to that well-rooted even before the sands of time began to gather around their bases.

An interesting aspect of the Richards 'collective effort' theory of the 'why stone circles?' question is that it could reasonably be applied to circles of all sizes: after all, imitation is the sincerest form of flattery and one can imagine modest Neolithic communities thinking 'we really must have a stone circle like the one down the valley'. As Mark Edmonds reminds me, we find features of the great cathedrals copied in even the modest parish church.

But what did people do in these circles? Some clearly did have a ritualistic use, though this may not have been their sole purpose. So, at Castlerigg, for example, there is evidence of burial cairns within the circle, since flattened by ploughing, but these are almost certainly much later additions to this very early structure, implying that the possibly 'sacred' or 'magical' nature of the place endured long after the fall of the Neolithic people. Charcoal traces have been found in an older internal 'off-square' structure. But this need not necessarily mean that every stone circle has a mystical or 'religious' purpose. Some may have been more towards the 'meeting place' end of the religious spectrum and it is worth reminding ourselves that the idea of buildings devoted exclusively to the practice of worship is, in the greater scheme of things, relatively recent. There's good evidence, in the shape of Langdale axe finds, that precious goods were taken to or exchanged at sites where ancient land and water routes converged, such as Mayburgh Henge, and it doesn't seem unreasonable to imagine that there may have been more modest locations where people might have headed to exchange more prosaic goods – perhaps salted and dried food, earthenware pots and animal skins. So perhaps these smaller circles were more like a marketplace than a centre for ritual. Other 'stone circles', we know, were not really circles at all, but burial cairns whose subsequent erosion or excavation has revealed their circular stone supporting structure.

Which leads to the obvious question, 'why circles?'. Why not squares, triangles, hexagons? The answer to that question may lie within our very human psyche: it appears we are genetically predisposed to prefer circular forms over angular ones. Which begs the question, why have we, modern people, been building square and oblong buildings all this time? Is it for no better reason than that it's easier to fit desks and home furnishings into regular shapes with angles? A book by the data designer Manuela Lima in 2017, *The Book of Circles*, posed the question: 'Why do we Find Circles so Beautiful?' In its review of the book, the magazine *Science Focus* says: 'A preference for circular shapes is deeply ingrained in all of us from birth. A 2011 eye-tracking study found that at five months of age, before they utter a word or scribble a drawing, infants already show a clear visual preference for contoured lines over straight lines.'[16]

Lima explores both history and evolutionary science and argues that people have been fascinated by circles for at least 40,000 years, the date from which we see the emergence of the first circular petroglyphs or rock carvings. He writes: 'It's not clear what they were trying to achieve with them, but some of the oldest ones are concentric circles, spirals, and the wheel. You see that in different areas of the globe, in different areas of time. You can see there's some sort of fascination.' We should not be surprised: circles are everywhere in nature: the rings of a tree, the Sun, the Moon, the arc of a rainbow, the pattern a stone makes when thrown into the water, the human eye… And then there are the circular abstractions: the apparent circular movement around us of the sun and moon, again; the idea of plant matter coming from and returning to the earth; of the birth of people and their ritual return after death to the ground.

When we explore the purpose of the large circles two explanations repeatedly come to the fore: centres of ritual or astronomical calendars. Some circles undoubtedly have very clear astronomical alignments and knowing the day upon which the winter solstice passed and days began to lengthen would have been of critical importance to early farmers, as would the equinoxes. To create circles that reflected the reality of the earth's displaced axis would have demanded careful observations over time; to reflect the far longer cycles of the Moon in monuments of stone would have demanded cooperation across a wide span of time and the passing down of knowledge from one generation to the next. Some have also claimed to identify alignments with the 'quarter days' between the equinoxes and the solstices. And in particular, the festival of Samhain, marking the start of winter on November 1 and also associated with the 'day of the dead', which would become Halloween. The key alignments at Cumbrian circles and henges mark the mid-winter sunset, at Long Meg and Her Daughters; the rising of the sun at the equinoxes at Mayburgh Henge; the Low Longrigg rings, on Brat's Hill, above Eskdale, are on a northeast to south-west axis, reflecting the midsummer sunrise and the winter sunset; the mid-winter sunrise coincides with an alignment at Sunkenkirk.

There is persuasive evidence that Kilmartin Glen, in Scotland, may have represented a huge celestial calendar with many celestial and lunar alignments, but this seems to be exceptional rather than the rule; the theories explored and fleshed out by Jack Morris-Eyton across nearly two decades in support of his idea that circles, in general, were predictive agricultural calendars does not appear to have gained much traction in the serious archaeological community.

None of this has prevented the emergence of other ideas about why stone circles were built, some of them residing deep within the realms of pseudo-science. A theory that appeals to me is specifically connected with Stonehenge, which already stands apart because of sophisticated lunar alignments. Two highly respected archaeologists, Professor Timothy Darvill and the late Professor Geoff Wainwright, formerly the Chief Archaeologist at English Heritage, first suggested in 2006 that the monument was a kind of prehistoric 'Lourdes' – a place to which people went 'on pilgrimage' in the hope of being cured of illness.

The theory, published later, in 2011, explains why the monument's bluestones were dragged 250km from West Wales: there was a belief in the special healing qualities of the stones, which were originally quarried close to traditional healing springs. In support of their theory, the professors noted the presence of large numbers of bones from people who were either ill or injured, dug up in the vicinity of the monument. They postulated that people travelled to Stonehenge as a final throw of the dice in the hope of being cured. However, the large number of traumatised bones would seem to suggest that the metaphorical dice did not land on six for most of them... large numbers clearly never left the monument alive.

What is intriguing, though most will reject it as mumbo-jumbo, is what you will find if you conduct even the most basic research into the nature of Preseli bluestone itself. In the world of crystal healing, Preseli bluestone is an important gemstone whose healing properties are attuned to the solar plexus and will, if employed regularly, bolster your emotional, spiritual and physical health. I do confess to at least a passing interest in many of the traditional alternative 'medicinal theories'. I once knew a woman who could see people's auras and I've no reason to doubt that; and I can affirm that I have had my chakras rebalanced by a homeopath, following chemotherapy and surgery, and felt much better afterwards. But don't ask me to explain any of these ideas: if there's any scientific basis it has to lie in the realms of quantum something-or-other in territory as yet unreached by science.

I do however think it's worth reminding ourselves that some peoples do retain a connection with the Earth and the environment that has been completely lost in 'the West'. Michael Tellinger has researched and written about stone circles in South Africa and, specifically, a remote structure called Adam's Calendar. He claims it to be 'the oldest manmade structure in the world' and to have measured the vital bodily functions of a group of people staying at the location over a month. He asserts: 'The results were astounding. There is no doubt that exposure to the stone circles have a positive effect on the bodily functions which we measured over a 30-day period.'[17]

Well, you make of that what you will. What I will say, and have said throughout this book, is that, for whatever reason, people do feel a genuine sense of peace and calm when they pause at our own stone circles. How much of this is down to expectation rather than real experience we cannot know, but we do for sure know that people regarded these places with enough awe and respect that many of them survived for many centuries after those who knew what they were built for had gone. The Victorian years certainly brought a reversal in fortune, but times since then have seen if anything a revival in the sense of mysticism that many feel when they visit these places.

Some have sought to translate this fairly ephemeral observation into something more scientific and, as ever, this has to come with a government scepticism warning. On the other hand, before going any further, it is worth reminding people that water companies still employ people with divining rods to detect the presence of water underground. The basic proposal is that stone circles do indeed possess 'energy fields'. Whether the ancient peoples built the stone circles where they did because they felt (or possibly divined) the presence of energy fields, or if the stone circles themselves acquired energy over time, is an unanswered question, but there are many claims to the effect that magnetic fields at stone circles are large enough to be measured. An 'engineer' called Charles Brooker is claimed by the website invisibletemple.com to have measured a magnetic force at the Rollright Stone Circle, in Oxfordshire, and identified a spiral magnetic field pattern rather like water vanishing down a plughole. A biologist called Harry Oldfield placed shrimps in a blacked-out jar beside monoliths at the circle and found the creatures, which are said to be very sensitive to magnetism, gravitated towards the stones. Of this, and of whether ley lines genuinely exist, I say only that it may be best to maintain an open rather than a closed mind and to remember once again that the songlines and dreaming tracks of indigenous Australian people are interwoven with their relationship with the land and indeed their very raison d'être. But then again, perhaps we should also remember that stories of pyramids sharpening razor blades and of preventing food from rotting have not stood up to scientific scrutiny and nor, for that matter, has vaccine scepticism.

And then there are the Druids… at some point, the Druids emerged as a high-ranking class in early Celtic cultures and a strong linkage with the inherited stone circles of Neolithic and Bronze Age times evolved. It is a connection that endures today as a feature of what we might call Druidic revivalism, associated with the general growth in interest in mysticism. At least two of Cumbria's circles – Long Meg and Birkrigg – are 'officially' known as Druids' circles, which is to say that the road signage calls them thus. My Druid friend, Elaine Gregory, has even built her own stone circle called Seven Sisters. 'I feel it is marking my land and linking to the other Seven Sisters circles via the star, Sirius.' The

Seven Sisters are important in Greek mythology, as representing the daughters of Atlas, transformed into stars by Zeus to protect them from the hunter Orion. But the legend goes much further back, perhaps 100,000 years, to early Aboriginal folklore.

We have, of course, no oral or written record of what Neolithic and Bronze Age people believed – but the stone circles they left behind have gone on to stimulate rich written and oral legend ever since. I have described the legends associated with Cumbrian circles – Long Meg and her own petrification and that of her trainee witches; the devil and his conflict with church-builders at Sunkenkirk; and, in Yorkshire, the Devil and his attempt to throw giant arrows at Aldborough. There may well be others that have become lost in the mists of time. We are still telling stories about and set within stone circles because they continue to fire our imagination. We do this because we are, by our very nature, storytellers. Some of these stories are tall ones, lies even, as told each year at Santon Bridge. Some of the better and more engaging ones may in the fullness of time become legends themselves.

I like the idea of stories because, even if the stories themselves were not told by the people who built the circles, they nonetheless create a link between our present-day selves and the inheritance bequeathed by those builders. Paul Frodsham's book, *From Stonehenge to Santa Claus*, paints a picture of how some stories from Neolithic times actually have made the long journey through time and are still told today, albeit in an evolved and adapted form. This is the process of adoption and adaptation by subsequent cultures of the core rites and festivals of winter in ancient times. In his introduction to his *From Stonehenge to Santa Claus*, Frodsham says: 'Emphasis is placed throughout on continuity, demonstrating that while people occasionally introduced new elements into their festivities, many aspects of midwinter celebration have strived remarkably intact over thousands of years.'

I wrote in the introduction to this book of my aspiration to identify links between the people we are today and the people who farmed our land in the early days of fixed human settlement. My hope was and remains to build a stronger sense of ownership by us of our past in the way that Egyptians and Greeks feel a sense of pride and ownership, in large part because of both the sheer grandiosity of what remains and the written records of those times. In the process of my research, I have become increasingly persuaded that our connections are stronger than I may have supposed: by the very fact of their physical endurance, the stone circles – and indeed the many associated landscape and cultural features – do indeed offer us a direct link with our prehistory.

Through the evolution of their associated myths and legends, that link has been injected with renewed vigour at intervals through history. Things that we do today as matters of routine, like the conservation of food, the collection of treasured belongings and, less prosaically, our agonising about unanswerable questions like the afterlife more closely mirror early practice than I for one may have appreciated. I've had quite a lot to say about the desecration of ancient sites of symbolism and assembly by eighteenth- and nineteenth-century farmers, the gung-ho Victorian builders of railways, and the far more recent philistines in the Department for Roads and Motorways. I'd like to think that those days of destruction have passed, and yet stone circles that are ancient monuments are at risk across Cumbria. Burl describes the 'fascinating complex' of circles in Broomrigg Plantation, including an immense red sandstone circle 55 metres across. They are slowly being absorbed by a forest, casually planted all around them.

With the ownership of land upon which ancient monuments stand should surely come at least some responsibility for the privilege of owning such monuments. I am not necessarily demanding that landowners spend large sums of money consolidating

Neolithic and Bronze Age remains, but that they should at least be required not to endanger them, whether by permitting livestock to tumble them or planting trees all around them. I also believe that – in these days of agricultural diversification – there is no good reason not to support Geoff and Judith Robinson to create a modest tourist attraction at Gunnerkeld Stone Circle. As Paul Frodsham has suggested with good reason, Cumbria sits on the wrong side of a north-south archaeological divide by virtue of which our rich Neolithic and Bronze Age heritage has been treated by the powers that be as somehow less worthy of conservation and celebration than would be the case in the South. Regrettably, it is the 'powers that be' who set the budgets.

In the previous chapter, I outlined the scope for visiting groups of circles and other remains in discreet landscapes, such as Shap Fell. My hope would be that investment might be made to create a collective 'corporate' identity for stone circles and other remains that stand on or near land to which the public enjoys access – in Cumbria, and elsewhere. From this could easily be evolved simple trails connecting the different sites, encouraging increased interest among a broader public. This won't deliver answers of itself, but by developing public interest in this way, we can increase public demand for answers to the countless unanswered questions relating to our prehistory. And such demand may ultimately deliver the resource required to look harder and harder for those answers so we can take full ownership of our earliest origins.

Postscript

Have wheels, shall travel... but will he see?

The foregoing is the story of a journey through a landscape and through times past, illustrated with a little bit of the present here and there. Although it was the acquisition of an electric bicycle, or as I think I prefer to say, an *electrically assisted* cycle, that made the journey possible in a timescale squeezed at both ends by a pandemic, the story told is essentially about the Neolithic and Bronze Ages and how we relate today to these lost times.

So now – for those with a particular interest in the mode of travel – is perhaps the moment to reflect separately on the practicalities of making a six-day cycle journey, at times off-road, in extremely mixed weather, and what I would do differently if I were to do it again.

My first observation would be that The Beast, as I quickly dubbed my sparkly new machine, is no ordinary electric cycle and so I can offer no guarantees that other makes and models would perform in the same manner, especially when it comes to battery life and the degree of power assistance. I was hugely impressed with the performance of The Beast: I think, though I cannot be certain, that it would even get me up the notorious one-in-three Hardknott Pass without dismounting. The machine was also reliable, though it harboured an occasionally disconcerting ability to lose its final few kilometres of electric charge like a fading Will o' the Wisp. The lesson learned is that a 50km day, although technically doable on a single charge at 'Normal' power setting, really needs as close to a full recharge as you can reasonably get over a pub lunch. The alternative of taking a backup battery is both expensive and heavy. This requires a degree of pre-planning, including knowing where's going to be both open, and open to you plugging in, for lunch. It's useful to know that a full recharge will cost the owner of the electric socket a few pence at most - your custom will probably cover that!

My system of copied map segments was fine for so long as it didn't rain. I would probably laminate these next time or rely instead on digital maps and tracking – though then you have to think about your phone's exposure to flash floods, rather than that of your throwaway maps. I minimalised the clothes I took with me, but I wouldn't necessarily rule out spare shoes and extra socks if setting off into an ambiguous forecast. I did not minimalise my digital equipment and my laptop, though light (a MacAir), was scarcely used, by the time I had cleaned myself up and eaten each night. An iPad is high on my shopping list now.

This was actually my first ever trip on a bicycle laden with luggage and I followed advice to keep my centre of gravity low by not using a backpack. However, 'low' is not all that low, and a fully laden cycle still has a higher centre of gravity than an unloaded one, and this requires you to make some adjustments. Specifically, if you are unfortunate enough to snag your pedal on a tree stump, the bike will fall, and far faster than you might have expected. Also, you may be unable easily to mount the machine when pointing uphill. The Beast is a hybrid machine, so he has some off-road capability. However, steep downhills on rubble-strewn tracks are an absolute no-no.

Finally, with hindsight, I have had to reflect on the nature I spotted in the course of my journey. Now, when – a year previously – I completed a 90-something-mile walk, I had a lengthy catalogue of flora and fauna sightings to write about. That proved rather less the case on this journey, my sightings being largely limited to times at which I was stationary. Indeed, I would go so far as to suggest that the need to keep one's eyes glued to the road ahead is so acute when cycling that the chances of seeing interesting non-highway things are far reduced, even when compared with being in a car. This is a great shame and my only answer is to be less ambitious when calculating distances, so as to enable a more leisurely pace.

And, as recommended elsewhere in this book, to keep one's ears and mind wide open, as well as one's eyes.

Endnotes

Chapter 1

1 Card, Nick (*see* Bibliography).

2 'Early Trade Routes Through Shap', *A Way Through*, Yorkshire Dales blog, Karen Griffiths, May 2020, www.yorkshiredales.org.uk/category/westmorland-dales-landscape-partnership

3 *Cairns, Fields, and Cultivation: Archaeological Landscapes of Lake District Uplands*, Lancaster Imprints Vol. 10, Quartermaine, Jamie and Leech, Roger H, Lancaster Imprints, Oxford Archaeology North, 2012.

4 *North West Rapid Coastal Zone Assessment*, Archaeological Research Services Ltd, 2011. (see Bibliography)

5 *Polished axes, Petroglyphs and Pathways: A study of the mobility of Neolithic people in Cumbria*, undergraduate thesis, Peter Style, 1998

6 'Britain and Ireland in the Bronze Age: farmers in the landscape, or heroes on the high seas', Benjamin W Roberts in *The Oxford Handbook of the European Bronze Age*, Edited by Anthony Harding and Harry Fokkens, Oxford University Press, 2013.

7 'How significant is the Dover Bronze Age Boat?', *Heritage Daily*, www.heritagedaily.com/2011/05/how-significant-is-the-dover-bronze-age-boat/2135

8 *Archaeology: Theories, Methods, and Practice*, Eighth Edition, Colin Renfrew and Paul Bahn, Thames & Hudson, 2020.

9 'Seeing the Light: Aboriginal Law, Learning and Sustainable Living in Country', Ambelin Kwaymullina in I*ndigenous Law Bulletin* May/Volume 6, Issue 11, June 2005.

Chapter 2

1 'Early Neolithic salt production at Street House, Loftus, north-east England', Stephen J Sherlock in *Antiquity: A Review of World*

Archaeology, Cambridge University Press, March 2021.

2 *The Horse in Late Pleistocene and Holocene Britain*, Mollie Kaagan, Doctoral Thesis, University College London, 2000.

3 Closer inspection of the map reveals that, while the words "stone circle" are west of the A6, the circle remains are marked where they should be.

4 'Stone Circles & Avenue', *Shap Cumbria*, https://shapcumbria. wordpress.com/things-to-do/history/stone-circles-avenue/

Chapter 3

1 *W. Wordsworth: The Complete Poetical Works*, with introduction by Morley, John, Macmillan and Company, first published in 1826.

2 The Victoria and Albert Museum cites this couplet as being from *The Gentlemen's Magazine* of August 1791. Author unknown.

Chapter 4

1 'The spiral that vanished: the application of non-contact recording techniques to an elusive rock art motif at Castlerigg Stone Circle in Cumbria', Díaz-Andreu, M. and Brooke, C. and Rainsbury, M. and Rosser, N. in *Journal of archaeological science* 33 (11), 2006.

2 'A New Survey of the Carles Stone Circle, Castlerigg, Cumbria', Chapter 13, Al Oswald and Constance Durgea in *New Light on the Neolithic of Northern England*, Edited by Gill Hey and Paul Frodsham, Oxbow Books, 2021.

3 'Castlerigg Stone Circle', *Mysterious Britain and Ireland*, www.mysteriousbritain.co.uk/ancient-sites/castlerigg-stone-circle/

Chapter 5

1 'Wild Ennerdale', *Rewilding Britain*, www.rewildingbritain.org.uk/ rewilding-projects/wild-ennerdale

2 'Sellafield: the most hazardous place in Europe', *The Observer*, April 19, 2009, theguardian.com/environment/2009/apr/19/sellafield-nuclear-plant-cumbria-hazards

Chapter 6

1 Report of an Advisory visit to Devoke Water, The Wild Trout Trust, January 2018, https://www.wildtrout.org/avs

2 *Jack Morris-Eyton's Research into Shadows and Light Cast by Megalithics in the UK,* edited by David Smyth, 2017. The complete edited version is 326 pages long and can be downloaded at www.megalithic.co.uk/downloads/JackME_Final.pdf

3 'The carving of the "Ankh" on a stone in Swinside Circle.', R.G. Plint, *Transactions of the Cumberland and Westmorland Antiquarian and Archaeological Society,* Series: 2, Volume 72, 1972.

4 A descriptive tour and guide to the lakes, caves, mountains and other natural curiosities, *A Topographical Description of Cumberland, Westmoreland, Lancashire and a part of the West Riding of Yorkshire,* John Housman, first published 1800.

5 'Stephenson Ground Scale: a Gateway to the Past', *Ring Cairns to Reservoirs: Archaeological Discoveries in the Duddon Valley, Cumbria,* Duddon Valley Local History Group, 2009.

Chapter 7

1 'A "Most Noble Work" at the Heart of Neolithic Britain: Some Thoughts on the Long Meg Complex in the Light of Recent Fieldwork', Paul Frodsham in *New Light on the Neolithic of Northern England,* edited by Paul Frodsham and Gill Hey, 2021.

2 *The Ness of Brodgar Excavation,* www.nessofbrodgar.co.uk

3 'Ancient secret of stone circles revealed', *University of St. Andrews News,* December 2019, https://news.st-andrews.ac.uk/archive/ancient-secret-of-stone-circles-revealed/

4 *Submerged Neolithic of the Western Isles,* Interim Report, Duncan Garrow, Fraser Sturt and Mike Copper, March 2017.

5 'The original Stonehenge? A dismantled stone circle in the Preseli Hills of west Wales', *Antiquity: A Review of World Archaeology,* Mike Parker Pearson, Josh Pollard, Colin Richards, Kate Welham, Timothy Kinnaird, Dave Shaw, Ellen Simmons, Adam Stanford,

Richard Bevins, Rob Ixer, Cive Ruggles, Jim Rylatt and Kevin Edinborough, Cambridge University Press, February 2021.

6 Ibid.

7 'Preseli Blue Stone', *Crystal Age*, www.crystalage.com/online_store/stone_type/preseli-bluestone.cfm?iPageNumber=4

Chapter 8

1 'All people are living histories – which is why History matters', *Making History*, Penelope J Cornfield, https://archives.history.ac.uk/makinghistory/resources/articles/why_history_matters.html

2 'The Importance of Teaching Human Prehistory', Paul Astin, 2013.

3 'The Beaker phenomenon and the genomic transformation of northwest Europe' Reich, David et al in *Nature*, February 2018 www.nature.com/articles/s41559-019-0871-9

4 'Holocene fluctuations in human population demonstrate repeated links to food production and climate', Bevan et al in *PNAS*, Vol 114, No. 49, 2017, www.pnas.org/content/114/49/E10524

5 'Archaeogenetics will help us solve mysteries of past', Alice Roberts in *New Scientist*, May 2021. www.newscientist.com/article/mg25033360-100-alice-roberts-archaeogenetics-will-help-us-solve-mysteries-of-past/#ixzz7LXxS07fE

6 'A Bell Beaker-Basque Narrative', *Dispatches from Turtle Island*, 2016, http://dispatchesfromturtleisland.blogspot.com/2016/12/a-bell-beaker-basque-narrative.html

7 'Ancient genomes indicate population replacement in Early Neolithic Britain', Thomas, Mark, et al in *Nature Ecology and Evolution*, April 2019, www.nature.com/articles/s41559-019-0871-9

8 'Furness's first farmers: Evidence of early neolithic settlement and dairying in Cumbria', Gav Robinson, Matthew Town, Torben Bjarke Ballin, Ann Clarke, Julie Dunne, Richard P. Evershed,

Lynne F. Gardiner, Alex Gibson, Hannah Russ in *Proceedings of the Prehistoric Society*, Vol. 86, Cambridge University Press, 2020.

9 *Star Carr: archaeology project*, www.starcarr.com

10 'Food and Feasting at Stonehenge', *English Heritage*, www.english-heritage.org.uk/visit/places/stonehenge/history-and-stories/history/food-and-feasting-at-stonehenge/

11 Augustin Pyramus de Candolle, 18th-19th-century Swiss botanist whose work on plant classification was continued by his son and grandson.

12 *Polished axes, Petroglyphs and Pathways: A study of the mobility of Neolithic people in Cumbria*, undergraduate thesis, Peter Style, 1998.

13 'Amateur archaeologist uncovers earliest known animal carvings in Scotland', Harry Baker in *Live Science*, June 2021, https://www.livescience.com/earliest-animal-carvings-in-scotland.html

14 'Connecting the dots. Cupules and communication in the English Lake District' Sharpe, K.E. in *Expression*, 9, 2015.

15 'Excavation of a Neolithic House at Yarnbury, near Grassington, North Yorkshire', *Proceedings of the Prehistoric Society*, 83, The Prehistoric Society, 2017.

16 'Why do we find circles so beautiful?' Manuel Lima in *BBC Science Focus*, 2017, www.sciencefocus.com/science/why-do-we-find-circles-so-beautiful/

17 'The Healing Effects of the Properties of The Stone Circles of South Africa', Michael Tellinger, 2018, www.linkedin.com/pulse/healing-effects-properties-stone-circles-south-africa-tellinger/

Glossary

Built monuments

barrow – A generic term for a burial mound in much of England (the term 'cairn' being preferred in Scotland, Wales, Ireland and northernmost England). Built throughout Neolithic and later times and comprising a wooden or stone vault containing the dead and their burial goods, then covered in earth. Earlier Neolithic structures were long and contained several dead, usually related. By the Bronze Age, the dead were buried alone in round structures.

burial mound – An artificial hill (such as a cairn or barrow) made of earth and stones and with a burial chamber or vault at its heart.

cairn, cairnfield – More commonly used term for a barrow in Cumbria (see above). The term also applies to a collection of piled stones that have been cleared to enable agricultural land use. A cairnfield may comprise both funerary or clearance structures, or both.

causewayed enclosure – Early Neolithic structure comprising concentric ditches, breached by 'causeways', which may have served as meeting places in forest clearings, though human remains found in the outer ditches at some sites suggests a ritual component too. Relatively rare in northern England, though a probable one was discovered in Uldale, Cumbria, during routine aerial reconnaissance in 2000 and another was excavated at Houghton-le-Spring, Tyne & Wear, in 1980.

ceremonial avenue – A wide route (30 metres or so) marked at its edge by stones or timber and often leading to an important site, such as Stonehenge. The long ceremonial avenue at Shap led to the Kemp Howe circle and would have effectively 'funnelled' those arriving towards the circle. It is, tragically, largely destroyed, though some important features remain.

cursus – Early Neolithic structure comprising a long (up to 3kms), rectangular banked and ditched enclosure. There are examples in Yorkshire, including beneath the central henge at Thornborough. Their purpose is not fully understood.

cist – A burial chamber, usually of stone but also sometimes of timber and found within cairns or stone circles.

henge – A round or elliptical Neolithic enclosure defined by an earthen or stone bank, often topped with wooden or stone pillars. Mayburgh Henge, near Penrith is a particularly fine example. Generally preceded stone circles, though Stonehenge is an example of a henge site that evolved to become a stone circle.

hut circle – A circular depression surrounded by the remains of a wall indicating the location of a roundhouse, most likely from the late Neolithic or Bronze Age.

menhir – Standing stone (see below).

monolith – Standing stone (see below).

orthostat – Standing stone (see below).

ring cairn – A circular or near-circular embanked mound, with a hollowed centre, like a Polo. Probably not funerary in their original purpose, some acquired a central cist later, while standing stones were often added at the perimeter. Their construction may have coincided with that of the smaller stone circles. Deliberate excavation and erosion have often left us with what look, to all intents and purposes, like stone circles (such as Glassonby, in Cumbria).

standing stone. A single stone, or one of a pair or group of stones, erected in prehistoric times, often as part of a wider ceremonial landscape or stone circle.

stone circle – An umbrella term that often may include structures that are more properly defined as ring cairns or hut circles.
They were first built in Britain around 3000 BC and the practice
continued right on through the earlier Bronze Age. While not
necessarily built for the purpose, some certainly acquired ceremonial and funerary significance later in their evolving lives.
Although some contest this view, it appears that relatively few
were constructed as 'astronomical calendars', though there are
important alignments at larger circles, such as Long Meg and
Her Daughters. Later circles were sometimes concentric, as at
Birkrigg, Oddendale or Gunnerkeld, and may have had a cobbled centre, serving as a funerary area, as at Birkrigg and the
Cockpit. Most people imagine that stone circles are relatively
rare, but they number around 1,300 in the British Isles and
many more across Europe. Indeed, stone circles and variations
upon that theme appear ubiquitous in prehistory across all the
continents except Antarctica, which suggests a powerful shared
human investment in the concept of the circle as a shape. The
earliest stone circles in Britain are generally thought to be those
in Orkney and at Calanais, on the Isle of Lewis. Castlerigg, Long
Meg and Sunkenkirk are the earliest circles in Cumbria and
date from around 3000 BC. Some features at Long Meg are now
thought to predate those in Orkney. Stone circles in this book
comprise the full spectrum of circular and ovoid Neolithic and
Bronze Age structures.

   tumulus – See barrow and cairn.

Tools and artefacts

Beaker People – Beaker culture appears to have originated in
temperate European latitudes around 2500 BC and is so named
because these people produced distinctive bell-shaped beakers or pots, decorated with horizontal bands and fine-toothed

stamped patterns. It seems possible that they first arrived in Britain in an ongoing search for new sources of copper, tin, gold and other minerals. They brought with them the practice of burying their dead in single tombs with a Beaker pot, and one such grave was discovered relatively recently near Alston, in Cumbria. Beaker genes ultimately supplanted those of the indigenous Neolithic people.

Langdale axe – A type of stone axe blade sourced from the hard tuff rock of the Langdale Pikes and surrounding peaks, including Scafell Pike. These made up around a third of total stone axe production and were of such quality that they appear to have moved on to serve a primarily ceremonial purpose. The roughly hewn axeheads were carried from the quarry sites for grinding and polishing elsewhere, with the Cumbrian coast being one important location. The stone debris from the quarry can still be seen on Pike o' Stickle, where it now comprises a long scree run. Langdale axe rough-outs and finished axeheads have been found all over the British Isles and beyond.

grooved ware pottery – A Neolithic pottery style that most likely originated in Orkney. The pot was distinguished by its flat bottom, outward-sloping sides and grooved decoration at the top.

Geographical terms

Cumbria – The journey at the heart of this book takes place in Cumbria, a 'modern' county that was created by the radical 1974 reorganisation of local government in England. It comprises the 'old counties' of Cumberland, Westmorland, the Furness peninsula of Lancashire and part of the old West Riding of Yorkshire. Further changes are due in 2023, however!

Lake District, Lakeland –loose terms referring to the central part of Cumbria in which the 16 lakes and England's highest mountains are located. The Lake District National Park and World

Heritage Site encloses a slightly wider area, including parts of the coast and, to the east, parts of the Howgill Fells, up to the M6 motorway. The 'central massif' of the Lake District comprises three distinct geological areas: the Skiddaw group of sedimentary rocks to the north, the Borrowdale volcanic rocks in the centre, and the Windermere slates, to the south.

Cycling

electric bike – A cycle with an electric motor which assists the rider, generating more power as the rider inputs more effort. They are classed as cycles in the UK, so require no licensing or insurance. Their speed, however, is capped at 25kph when under power.

hybrid – A cycle with features from both the mountain or off-road cycle, and the touring cycle. It will have off-road tyre treads, but less chunky than those of the mountain bike and with a ridge in the centre to reduce friction while riding on the road. It will have plenty of gears, including a very low ratio for hill-climbing.

mountain bike – The idea of cycling off-road only dates back to the 1980s, in California, but it has gained hugely in popularity since then and now includes a variety of disciplines, including 'downhill', for the very brave. Even more specialist machines now include 'fat bikes', whose massively chunky tyres enable cycling over sand or snow.

touring or road bike – A 'regular' cycle for normal uses other than city or racing. They're designed for reliability rather than speed and won't usually have the drop-handlebars of the racer. They're tough enough to get you round most of the route in this book, though perhaps not all.

Bibliography

Books

Abbott, Stan L, *The Episode*, Sixth Element, 2019.

Abbott, Stan L, *Walking the Line: Exploring Settle & Carlisle Country*, Saraband, 2021.

Anon, *Old Tales of the Lakes*, Get Native, date unknown.

Bahn, Paul, *Archaeology: A Very Short Introduction*, Oxford, 1996.

Beckensall, Stan, *Life and Death in the Prehistoric North*, Butler Publishing, 1994.

Beckensall, Stan, *Prehistoric Northumberland*, Tempus, 2003.

Bradley, Richard, *The Prehistoric Settlement of Britain*, Routledge & Kegan Paul, 1978.

Burl, Aubrey, *A Guide to the Stone Circles of Britain, Ireland and Brittany*, Yale University Press, 1995, 2005.

Burl, Aubrey, *Prehistoric Henges*, Shire Archaeology, 1997.

Burnham, Andy (Ed), *The Old Stones*, Watkins, 2018.

Card, Nick, Edmonds, Mark and Mitchell, Anne (Eds), *The Ness of Brodgar as it Stands*, The Orcadian, 2020.

Chatwin, Bruce, *The Songlines*, Franklin Press, 1987.

Clare, Tom, *Prehistoric Monuments of the Lake District*, Tempus, 2007.

Clarke, Anne, *Does Size Matter: Stone Axes from Orkney: Their Style and Deposition*, Oxbow Books, 2014.

Cleaver, Alan and Park, Lesley, *Get Lost: In the Ancient Trackways of the Lake District and Cumbria*, Chitty Mouse Press, 2020.

Duddon Valley Local History Group, *Ring Cairns to Reservoirs*, Yorkshire Dales National Park, 2009.

Edmonds, Mark, *Arcadia: Land, Sea and Stone in Neolithic Orkney*, Head of Zeus, 2019.

Edmonds, Mark, *Stone Tools and Society: Working Tools in Neolithic and Bronze Age Britain*, B T Batsford Ltd, 1995.

Frodsham, Paul, *From Stonehenge to Santa Claus: The Evolution of Christmas,* The History Press, 2008.

Gere, Charlie, *I Hate the Lake District*, Goldsmiths Press, 2019.

Griffiths, Elly, *The Stone Circle*, Quercus, 2019.

Hall, Tony, *The Immortal Yew*, Kew Publishing, 2019.

Hey, Gill and Frodsham, Paul (Eds), *Introducing New Light on the Neolithic of Northern England*, Oxbow, 2021.

Kurlansky, Mark, *The Basque History of the World*, Penguin, 2000.

Lima, Manuel, *The Book of Circles*, Princeton Architectural Press, 2017.

Lloyd, Karen, *The Gathering Tide: A Journey Around the Edgelands of Morecambe Bay*, Saraband, 2016.

Martineau, John (ed), *Megalith: Studies in Stone*, Wooden Books, 2018.

Ménanteau, Loïc, *Sels et Salines de l'Europe Atlantique,* University of Rennes, 2019.

Miles, David, *The Tribes of Britain*, Phoenix, 2005.

Mills, Ken, *The Cumbrian Yew Book*, Yew Trees for the Millennium, Cumbria, 1999.

Palmer, Ned, *A Cheesemonger's History of the British Isles*, Profile Books, 2019.

Quartermaine, Jamie and Leech, Roger H, *Cairns, Fields, and Cultivation: Archaeological Landscapes of Lake District Uplands*, Lancaster Imprints, 2012.

Richards, Colin (Ed), *Building the Great Stone Circles of the North*, Windgather Press, 2013.

Roberts, Alice, Professor, *Ancestors: The Story of Britain in Seven Burials*, Simon and Schusler, 2021.

Schulting, R J, *A Tale of Two Processes of Neolithisation: Southeast Europe and Britain/Ireland,* Oxbow Books, 2017.

Sheridan, Alison, *Contextualising Kilmartin: Building a Narrative for Developments in Western Scotland and Beyond, from the Early Neolithic to the Late Bronze Age*, Oxbow Books, 2015.

Sheridan, Alison, *Neolithic Connections Along and Across the Irish Sea*, Oxbow Books, 2015.

Sullivan, Danny, *Ley Lines: The Greatest Landscape Mystery*, Green Magic, 2004.

Sturtevant, A H, Dr, *Sturtevant's Edible Plants of the World*, Dover Publications, 1972 (first pub 1919).

Walditch, Beatrice, *Listening to the Stones*, Heart of Albion, 2016.

Waterhouse, John, *The Stone Circles of Cumbria*, Waterhouse, 1985.

Watson, David, *A Guide to the Stone Circles of the Lake District*, Simple Guides, 2009.

Westwood, Jennifer and Simpson, Jacqueline, *The Lore of the Land: A Guide to England's Legends*, Penguin, 2005.

Winchester, Angus J L (Ed), *John Denton's History of Cumberland*, The Boydell Press, 2010.

Wright, Gordon, *Jura's Heritage*, D G B Wright, 1989, 1991, 1994.

A descriptive tour and guide to the lakes, caves, mountains and other natural curiosities in Cumberland, Westmoreland, Lancashire and a part of the West Riding of Yorkshire, by John Housman, first published 1800.

Journals and other papers

Allen, Michael J, Gardiner, Julie, Sheridan, Alison (Eds), *Is There a British Chalcolithic? People, Place and Polity and the later Third Millennium*, The Prehistoric Society, 2012.

Bates, C R , Bates , M , Gaffney , C , Gaffney , V and Raub , T D, *Geophysical Investigation of the Neolithic Calanais Landscape*, Remote Sensing, vol 11, no. 24, 2975, pub 2019.

Barrow, Duncan, Sturt, Fraser and Copper, Mike, *Submerged Neolithic of the Western Isles: Interim Report*, Universities of Southampton and Reading, 2017.

Barber, Martyn, *Bronze and Bronze Age: Metalwork and Society in Britain c2500 – 800 BC*, Tempus Publishing, 2003.

Beckensall, Stan and Gale et al, *The Excavation of Cairns at Blawearie, Old Bewick, Northumberland*, Prehistoric Society, 2014.

Bitfield, Sarah Jane, *Grooved Ware Pottery in the Upper Thames Valley: Context and Design*, University of Birmingham, 2012.

Bland, F, *A Link Between Two Westmorlands*, Cumberland and Westmorland Archaeological Society, 1881.

Brann, M L, *Two Flints from Askham Fell*, Cumberland and Westmorland Archaeological Society, 1983.

Trophy, Kenny and Sheridan, Alison (Eds), *Neolithic Scotland*, Scottish Archaeological Research Framework, 2012.

Butler, M, *Orkney to Somerset: The entrances to Stone Circles and Henges in Britain and Ireland*, Creative Commons, 2017.

Card, Nick et al, *To Cut a Long Story Short: Formal Chronological Modelling for the Late Neolithic Site of Ness of Brodgar, Orkney*, European Journal of Archaeology, 2017.

Carlin, Neil and Cooney, Gabriel, *Transforming our Understanding of Neolithic and Chalcolithic Society (4000-2200 BC) in Ireland*, Transport Infrastructure Ireland, 2017.

Clare, Tom, *Recent Work on the Shap 'Avenue'*, Cumberland and Westmorland Archaeological Society, 1978.

Council for British Archaeology, *Prehistoric Monuments in the A1 Corridor*, date unknown.

Dineley, Merryn, *Barley, Malt and Ale in the Neolithic*, University of Manchester, 2004.

Duddon Valley Local History Group, *Stephenson Ground Scale: a Gateway to the Past*, Duddon Valley Local History Group, 2000.

Edwards, Benjamin, *Pits and the Architecture of Deposition Narratives of Social Practice in the Neolithic of North-East England*, Durham University, 2009.

BIBLIOGRAPHY

Evans, Helen, *Prehistoric Landscapes of Cumbria*, University of Sheffield, 2005.

Ferguson, R S, *Stone Circle at Gamelands*, Cumberland and Westmorland Archaeological Society, 1883.

Frodsham, Paul, *Long Meg Excavation, Fieldwork Module 1c, Phase 2*, Altogether Archaeology, 2015.

Clare, Tom et al, *A Reinterpretation of the Levens Park Ring Cairn, Cumbria, Based on the Original Excavation Archives*, Liverpool John Moores University, 2021.

Craft, Alan W et al, *Cancer n Young People in the North of England, 1968-85: Analysis by Census Ward*, Journal of Epidemiology and Community Health, 1993.

Gibson, Alex, *Excavation of a Neolithic House at Yarnbury, near Grassington, North Yorkshire*, Prehistoric Society, 2017.

Hawes, Nean Michael, *Neolithic Living: Reconstructing the Lives of Ancient Orcadians*, Westminster College, 2017.

Inglesfield, Winifred M, *A Second Settlement Found at Kentmere*, Cumberland and Westmorland Archaeological Society, 1972.

Johnson, Ben, *North West Rapid Coastal Zone Assessment*, Archaeological Research Services Ltd, 2011.

Kaagan, Mollie, *The Horse in Late Pleistocene and Holocene Britain*, University College, London, 2000.

Leech, Roger, *Settlements and Groups of Small Cairns on Birkby and Birker Fells, Eskdale, Cumbria*, Cumberland and Westmorland Archaeological Society, 1983.

Oswald, Al, *Causewayed Enclosures*, Historic England, 2018.

Oxford Archaeology North, *Ennerdale Historic Landscape Survey*, National Trust and Forest Enterprise, 2003.

Phelps, Andy, *Clearance Cairns, Low Gilberthwaite, Ennerdale, Cumbria: Archeological Excavation Report*, Lake District National Park Authority, 2020.

Roberts, Benjamin, *Britain and Ireland in the Bronze Age: Farmers in the Landscape or Heroes on the High Seas?*, The Oxford Handbook of the European Bronze Age, 2013.

Robinson, Gav et al, *Furness's First Farmers: Evidence of Early Neolithic Settlement and Dairying in Cumbria*, Prehistoric Society, 2020.

Ross, A H H, *History of Ennerdale Forest*, Forestry Commission, 1952.

Sharpe, Kate, *Connecting the Dots: Cupules and Communication in the English Lake District*, Durham University, 2015.

Scottish Regional Group, *Discovery and Excavation*, Council for British Archaeology, 1961.

Sherlock, Stephen J, *Early Neolithic Salt Production at Street House, Loftus, North-East England*, Antiquity, 2021.

Simpson, Rev Canon, *Stone Circles near Shap*, Cumberland and Westmorland Archaeological Society, 1881.

Spiking, Penny, *Mesolithic Northern England: Environment, Population and Settlement*, Archaeolpress, Oxford, 2000.

Style, Peter, *Polished Axes, Petroglyphs and Pathways: A Study of the Mobility of Neolithic People in Cumbria*, University of Central Lancashire, 2009.

Timberlake, Simon and Marshall, Peter, *Copper Mining and Smelting in the British Bronze Age: New Evidence of Mine Sites Including Some Re-analysis of Dates and Ore Sources*, Eisenbrauns, 2018.

Turnbull, Percival and Walsh, Deborah, *A Prehistoric Ritual Sequence at Oddendale, near Shap*, Cumberland and Westmorland Archaeological Society, 2015.

Transactions of the Cumberland and Westmorland Antiquarian and Archaeological Society, 1972 volume. From a paper by R G Plint.

Online publications (not previously referenced in Notes)

Pearson, M P et al, *The Original Stonehenge? A Dismantled Stone Circle in the Preseli Hills of West Wales*, Cambridge University Press/Antiquity, Volume 95, Issue 379, pp. 85 - 103, Feb 2021. https://doi.org/10.15184/aqy.2020.239

Morris-Eyton, Jack, *Research into Shadows and Light Cast by Megaliths in the UK*, 2017. www.academia.edu/35098570/JackmeFinal.pdf

Maps

Ordnance Survey Explorer, sheet OL2, Yorkshire Dales, Southern and Western Areas; sheets OL4-7, The English Lakes, North-West, North-East, South-West and South-East; sheet OL19, Howgill Fells & Upper Eden Valley; sheet OL31, North Pennines.

Blogs and Websites

A Way Through, blog by Karen Griffiths. Early Trade Routes Through Shap, May 2020. https://www.yorkshiredales

Holtham Oakley, Catherine, 'How Significant is the Dover bronze Age Boat?' https://www.heritagedaily.com/2011/05/how-significant-is-the-dover-bronze-age-boat/2135

https://shapcumbria.wordpress.com/things-to-do/history/stone-circles-avenue/

BBC Science Focus, online magazine, 2017. www.sciencefocus.com/science/why-do-we-find-circles-so-beautiful/

The spiral that vanished : the application of non-contact recording techniques to an elusive rock art motif at Castlerigg Stone Circle in Cumbria. Durham Research Online, https://dro.dur.ac.uk/3682/

Acknowledgments

When I began writing this book, it was rather like stepping into the unknown, onto a distant planet whose true nature was theoretical rather than based on actual experience. While I might have visited more stone circles than most people, I was aware that my knowledge and understanding lacked depth. So I must sincerely thank the professional archaeologists and historians who were happy to help to bring me up to some kind of speed and permitted me to quote from their own work. In particular I thank Paul Frodsham, the Durham-based archaeological consultant, for giving me a broader understanding of the holistic nature of ancient landscapes and, having kindly read my first draft, for saving me from falling into any bear traps. I also thank Mark Edmonds for sharing his understanding of the magnificence of Neolithic Orkney with me.

Sharon Webb's assistance in pointing me in the right direction to understand more about the remarkable landscape that is Kilmartin Glen was most helpful. So too was that of Eleanor Kingston, at the Lake District National Park, who finds herself atop an archaeological goldmine: it deserves to attract the kind of resource that would enable its rich seems to be properly mined, and for our understanding of the ways of those who once farmed here to be more fully understood.

The food historian Ivan Day told me from the start that the Bronze Age (and by definition the Neolithic, too) was way before either his specialist period or his comfort zone. He nonetheless proved a veritable mine of information on finding the best sources – and on who knows whom in Westmorland and Cumberland.

ACKNOWLEDGMENTS

Philip Shaw, of Leicester University, was able to explain aspects of linguistic evolution to me in simple terms and left me to speculate on the mystery of how our Neolithic forebears may have sounded when exchanging stories round the hearth.

Andy Burnham and the enthusiastic followers of the Megalithic Portal website were constant companions and saved me from navigational ignominy on the first day of my travels, while learned authors Tom Clare and Aubrey Burl were always at my metaphorical side when a better understanding of what was in front of my eyes was required.

Jane Rousseau provided food and shelter in Broughton-in-Furness when there appeared to be 'no room at the inn' and gave an insider's perspective of this lovely little town. Likewise Sheena and Julian, at Gilgarran, proved the perfect Airbnb hosts and quite literally went the extra mile, before also drying out my sodden wardrobe.

The help of Kay Hyde, at Loganair, was invaluable in getting me to Orkney and back, and I thank the fickle weather gods for facilitating such beautiful weather there that the awfulness of that experienced on my circles cycle was all but compensated for.

Thanks to my wife Linda and to all friends and family who thought to share Neolithic snippets with me and to this book's artist, Denise Burden, a creative writing student of mine, for coming up with the idea of producing the delightful linocut illustrations that adorn the front cover and chapter headings of this book.

Finally, thanks to the Neolithic and Bronze Age settlers of Cumbria who created such an inspiring legacy – and an enduring mystery that we are nowhere near unravelling 5,000 years on.

Stan L Abbott is an award-winning writer on the outdoors, heritage and conservation. His career as a journalist began in Yorkshire, and he now lives in Durham and Cumbria. He has written extensively on travel and the outdoors, especially in the North of England, for national and regional newspapers and magazines. He has also worked in industry and tourism in the UK and Europe. He has written and edited books about local history, travel and walking, and published or edited several travel and conservation magazines. Currently chair of the Outdoor Writers & Photographers Guild, he is involved with railway restoration and writes regularly for the *New European* newspaper.

Illustrations are original linoprints by Denise Burden. See more on her Instagram: @deniseburdenart

The sites illustrated are:
Page 13: Ring of Brodgar, Orkney
Page 35: Kemp Howe
Page 75: Long Meg and Her Daughters
Page 105: Castlerigg Stone Circle (also on page ii)
Page 135: Brat's Hill, Eskdale
Page 173: Birkrigg Stone Circle
Page 205: The Devil's Arrows